1974

5

DRYDEN'S MIND AND ART

DRYDEN'S MIND AND ART

JOHN HEATH-STUBBS   D. W. JEFFERSON

ARTHUR W. HOFFMAN   BRUCE KING

ELIAS J. CHIASSON   A. D. HOPE

JAY ARNOLD LEVINE   T. W. HARRISON

BONAMY DOBRÉE   WILLIAM FROST

Essays edited by
BRUCE KING

BARNES & NOBLE, Inc.
NEW YORK
PUBLISHERS AND BOOKSELLERS SINCE 1873

First published in Great Britain, 1969
by Oliver and Boyd, Ltd
First published in the United States, 1970
by Barnes & Noble, Inc.

ISBN 0 389 03985 3

Printed in Great Britain by
Cox and Wyman Ltd., London, Fakenham and Reading

ACKNOWLEDGMENTS

For permission to quote W. B. Yeats, "Swift's Epitaph", acknowledgments are due to Mr. M. B. Yeats, Macmillan & Co. Ltd. and The Macmillan Company, New York.

Several of the essays in this collection have already been published elsewhere and for permission to reprint them here the following acknowledgments are also due: D. W. Jefferson, "Aspects of Dryden's Imagery", reprinted from *Essays in Criticism* (1954) by permission of the author and editor; Arthur W. Hoffman, "An Apprenticeship in Praise", reprinted from *John Dryden's Imagery* (1962) by permission of the author and the University of Florida Press; Elias J. Chiasson, "Dryden's Apparent Scepticism in *Religio Laici*", reprinted from *The Harvard Theological Review* (1961) by permission of the author and Harvard University Press; A. D. Hope, "Anne Killigrew: or the Art of Modulating", reprinted from *The Cave and the Spring* (1965) by permission of the author and Rigby Ltd., Adelaide; Jay Arnold Levine, "John Dryden's Epistle to John Driden", reprinted from *Journal of English and Germanic Philology* (1964) by permission of the author and the University of Illinois Press.

INTRODUCTION

Dryden is one of my favourite authors. Whether in the wit and imaginative patterns of his poetry, the ironic intelligence expressed in his plays, or the engaging personality exhibited in his prose, he has an infinite capacity for giving pleasure. There are greater writers in our language, but few who offer such civilised and sophisticated satisfactions. In bringing together this collection of essays I have tried to provide guidance towards an understanding of Dryden's achievement. Although the book is meant to serve as a modern introduction to Dryden for the university student, it will, I believe, prove stimulating, even challenging, to those with a specialised interest in Augustan literature.

As for the individual essays: The early stages of Dryden's poetic development are traced by A. W. Hoffman. John Heath-Stubbs' survey of Dryden's ambivalence towards heroicism discusses both the major poetry and the plays. D. W. Jefferson also examines the plays in his analysis of Dryden's imagery. *Absalom and Achitophel*, the *Anne Killigrew Ode* and *To My Honour'd Kinsman, John Driden* are examined in detail by Bruce King, A. D. Hope, and Jay Arnold Levine. Elias Chiasson places *Religio Laici* in its proper intellectual tradition and clears up misunderstandings about the nature of Dryden's scepticism. William Frost, T. W. Harrison, and Bonamy Dobrée have written studies of such neglected aspects of Dryden's work as the *Discourse on Satire*, the translation of *Aeneid* and the prose writings. While the essays treat primarily of Dryden's art, the book, taken as a whole, should give the reader a strong impression of Dryden's thought, temperament, and literary personality.

BRUCE KING

Lagos 1968

CONTENTS

Acknowledgments   v

Introduction   vii

I. GENERAL ESSAYS

John Heath-Stubbs   Dryden and the Heroic Ideal   3

D. W. Jefferson   Aspects of Dryden's Imagery   24

II. THE POETRY

Arthur W. Hoffman   An Apprenticeship in Praise   45

Bruce King   *Absalom and Achitophel:* A Revaluation   65

Elias J. Chiasson   Dryden's Apparent Scepticism in   84
                       Religio Laici

A. D. Hope   Anne Killigrew: or the Art of Modulating   99

Jay Arnold Levine   John Dryden's Epistle to John Driden   114

T. W. Harrison   Dryden's *Aeneid*   143

III. THE PROSE AND CRITICISM

Bonamy Dobrée   Dryden's Prose   171

William Frost   Dryden's Theory and Practice of Satire   189

                       Select Bibliography   206

                       Index   211

ix

I. GENERAL ESSAYS

John Heath-Stubbs

DRYDEN AND THE HEROIC IDEAL

To remark on the extraordinary range and variety of Dryden's work is only to repeat what has been said time and time again. His acknowledged greatness is as a satirist, but he wrote with success in pretty well every form current in his time – heroic tragedy, comedy of manners, ode, elegy and song, polemical didactic verse, and narrative. But the last named of these is represented only by *Annus Mirabilis*, rather early on in his career, and by the translation of the *Aeneid*, and the *Fables* (likewise translations or adaptations) at the end of it. This is a little surprising. For it is to the ideal of Epic or Heroic verse (in his age the two terms were synonymous) that, I think, all his work really points. One might suggest that it is haunted by the epic poem which he never got around to writing. That this poem existed in his mind we know. Its subject was to be King Arthur, or the Black Prince's expedition to Spain to reinstate Pedro the Cruel as King of Castile.

Dryden indeed did write an opera on the subject of King Arthur, which we remember only for its lyrics, and more especially for Purcell's settings of them. If Dryden had written his Arthurian epic, it would doubtless have made more lively reading than the two that were written on that theme by his younger contemporary, Sir Richard Blackmore (though Blackmore has his moments). We do not, I think, regret a lost masterpiece – something to set beside *Paradise Lost*. But it is worth enquiring both why Dryden wanted to write an epic and why he did not in fact do so. And such an enquiry may, I suggest, throw some light both on the strength and the weaknesses of the poems that he actually did write.

The occasional nature of the greater part of Dryden's work has led to his sometimes being termed a verse journalist. Now it is undeniable that there went towards the making of many of his poems, especially the satires, an impulse which today would find its most natural outlet in some form of journalism. But the flair of a journalist and technical virtuosity alone are not enough to make a great poet. And a great poet Dryden certainly was. The fact is that he is a transitional figure. He has not yet really attained the Augustan view of society as a field for the exploration of the moral nature of man. This was to be the vision of Pope and of the eighteenth-century moralists and novelists. But he still carries with him something of that renaissance view which saw human society, and specifically the monarchical nation state, as ideally exemplifying the earthly realisation of a transcendent and cosmic order. What had once been imperial ritual had in his age passed into state ceremony. For Spenser and his contemporaries it was not absurd to impute to Elizabeth all the attributes of a goddess. Her court was that of an earthly Cynthia, surrounded by chaste nymphs and by heroes. In his baroque panegyrics Dryden is attempting to do the same sort of thing for Charles II and James II. The gap between ideal and reality was probably not actually any greater, but it was more patent. Dryden's age attempted to project its ideals in the Heroic mode: but its sensibility had now been invaded by a new, ironic and sceptical intelligence. And the latter was inevitably destructive of the former.

Annus Mirabilis may be considered, I think, as Dryden's first mature work. He was a slow developer, and although he was thirty-six at the date of its publication, it has a certain youthful verve and baroque extravagance about it, which is sometimes a little absurd but which is also endearing. The baroque wit of *Annus Mirabilis* is in the tradition of Cowley and Cleveland. It depends, in the metaphysical manner, on extended rhetorical figures often involving a union between the transcendent and the extremely mundane. The notorious passage, in which the Almighty extinguishes the flames of the Fire of London with a crystal pyramid, like a householder snuffing a candle, is an example, and so is that in which the Angel with the Flaming Sword descends to protect the powder magazines.

Dryden never wholly abandoned this kind of wit. In his maturer work it is more often apparent in his Pindaric poems. His adoption of the heroic couplet, in the Augustan form which he developed from Waller and Denham, had in itself a restraining influence. The closed couplet does not very readily admit of the extended trope. Hence its fitness for clarity of exposition and argument. Dryden calls *Annus Mirabilis* an Historical Poem, but it is clearly to be considered as a preliminary exercise in the epic manner by a poet who has wider ambitions in that field. Its subject matter is contemporary, the events of the year 1666 – the naval victory over the Dutch, and the Great Fire of London. But clearly Dryden is doing more than writing a journalist's report on these; he is attempting to give them the wider and timeless context of epic poetry. In his prefatory letter to Sir Robert Howard he says:

> I have call'd my poem *Historical*, not *Epick*, though both the Actions and the Actors are as much Heroick, as any Poem can contain. But since the Action is not properly one, nor that accomplish'd in the last successes, I have judg'd it too bold a Title for a few *Stanza's*, which are little more in number then a single *Iliad*, or the longest of the *Æneids*. For this reason (I mean not of length, but broken action, ti'd too severely to the Laws of History) I am apt to agree with those who rank *Lucan* rather among Historians in Verse, then Epique Poets: in whose room, if I am not deceiv'd, *Silius Italicus*, though a worse Writer, may more justly be admitted.[1]

Annus Mirabilis then may be considered primarily as a Lucanian poem, though Dryden also acknowledges his debt to Virgil, especially in his epic similes. These latter, incidentally, are largely taken from animal life, and are often very lively; in them, Dryden writes as a naturalist and a member of the Royal Society. But the reference to Silius Italicus is also significant. He was the author of the *Punica*, an epic treatment of the Punic Wars. The point of the first part of *Annus Mirabilis* largely consists in an implicit identification of London with Rome, and of Holland with Carthage.[2] The poem is dedicated to the "Metropolis of Great Britain"

---

[1] Preface to *Annus Mirabilis*. *The Poems of John Dryden*, ed. James Kinsley, Oxford (Clarendon) 1958, Vol. I, p. 44.

[2] "Our second Punic War." The same comparison appears in Marvell's *Last Instructions to the Painter*.

and the City of London is in effect the hero and the unifying factor of the work. In the dedication it is addressed in quasi-religious terms: "You are now a Phoenix in her ashes, and, as far as humanity can approach, a great emblem of the suffering Deity." One of the best passages in *Annus Mirabilis* is that in which Dryden describes the repairing of the English fleet, after the first, apparently indecisive, encounter with the Dutch. Here the ship, the "London", is introduced with special emphasis. As the gift of the citizens to the King it typifies their loyalty, and by the recurrence of the phoenix image it becomes almost a symbol of the city itself, and prepares the way for the second part of the poem, dealing with the Great Fire:

> The goodly *London* in her gallant trim,
>   (The *Phœnix* daughter of the vanish'd old:)
> Like a rich Bride does to the Ocean swim,
>   And on her shadow rides in floating gold.
>
> Her Flag aloft spread ruffling to the wind,
>   And sanguine Streamers seem the floud to fire:
> The Weaver, charm'd with what his Loom design'd,
>   Goes on to Sea, and knows not to retire.
>
> With roomy decks, her Guns of mighty strength,
>   (Whose low-laid mouthes each mounting billow laves:)
> Deep in her draught, and warlike in her length,
>   She seems a Sea-wasp flying on the waves.
>
> This martial present, piously design'd,
>   The Loyal City give their best-lov'd King:
> And with a bounty ample as the wind,
>   Built, fitted and maintain'd to aid him bring.[3]

This passage is preceded by an extended simile in which the industry of the dockyard workers is compared to that of the bees. The bee image has a long tradition behind it, going back through the Middle Ages, and suggesting not only industry but also the ideally ordered commonwealth. But the introduction of the "London" leads on immediately to a remarkable passage in which Dryden treats of the evolution of the art of navigation from its

[3] *Annus Mirabilis*, 601–16. Kinsley, Vol. I, p. 79.

primitive beginnings, and prophesies the progress of modern
scientific discovery:

> By viewing Nature, Natures Hand-maid, Art,
>   Makes mighty things from small beginnings grow:
> Thus fishes first to shipping did impart
>   Their tail the Rudder, and their head the Prow.
>
> Some Log, perhaps, upon the waters swam
>   An useless drift, which, rudely cut within,
> And hollow'd, first a floating trough became,
>   And cross some Riv'let passage did begin.
>
> In shipping such as this, the *Irish Kern*,
>   And untaught *Indian*, on the stream did glide:
> Ere sharp-keel'd Boats to stem the floud did learn,
>   Or fin-like Oars did spread from either side.
>
> . . . .
>
> Of all who since have us'd the open Sea,
>   Then the bold *English* none more fame have won:
> Beyond the Year, and out of Heav'ns high-way,
>   They make discoveries where they see no Sun.
>
> But what so long in vain, and yet unknown,
>   By poor man-kinds benighted wit is sought,
> Shall in this Age to *Britain* first be shown,
>   And hence be to admiring Nations taught.
>
> The Ebbs of Tydes and their mysterious flow,
>   We, as Arts Elements, shall understand:
> And as by Line upon the Ocean go,
>   Whose paths shall be familiar as the Land.
>
> Instructed ships shall sail to quick Commerce;
>   By which remotest Regions are alli'd:
> Which makes one City of the Universe,
>   Where some may gain, and all may be suppli'd.
>
> Then, we upon our Globes last verge shall go,
>   And view the Ocean leaning on the sky:
> From thence our rolling Neighbours we shall know,
>   And on the Lunar world securely pry.[4]

[4] *Op. cit.*, 616–56, pp. 79–81.

B

Annus Mirabilis serves to remind us that Dryden has a foot in two worlds. One is the medieval-renaissance world, in which natural objects exist mainly to typify spiritual truths, and in which angelic intelligences intervene. The other is the modern scientific world in which objects are to be experimentally investigated, and subject to evolutionary change.[5]

Dryden had already some years before embarked on his career as a writer for the theatre. His numerous plays present something of a problem for the critic. Hardly any of them is wholly without interest or merit, but they are an acquired taste. The Heroic Tragedy is a curious phenomenon. Basically it is a resumption and extension, modified by neo-classical influence, of the type established before the civil war by Fletcher and Massinger. Its relationship to the French classical tragedy of Corneille and Racine is rather remote. A closer contemporary European analogy is to be sought in the post-Monteverdian baroque Italian opera, as in the work of Cavalli and Chesti. Dryden himself in the Essay prefixed to *The Conquest of Granada* traces the origin of the form to Davenant's *The Siege of Rhodes*. This was written as an opera under the Commonwealth, when dramatic entertainments were banned, and rehandled as a play after the Restoration.

Dryden wrote for the stage because that still represented the field in which a writer could most readily earn his living. His natural bent was not essentially dramatic: but if this be so, it is astonishing that his plays should exhibit so much genuine vitality. What he seems to have aimed at, in the period of his early career in the theatre, was to make a virtue of necessity by transferring his

---

[5] That evolutionary ideas were in the air in Dryden's time, much earlier than is often supposed, can be shown from a passage in *The Hind and the Panther*, in which the doctrine of the fixity of species is put in question. Speaking of the wolf he says:

> The *Fox* and he came shuffl'd in the Dark,
> If ever they were stow'd in *Noah's* Ark:
> Perhaps not made; for all their barking train
> The Dog (a common species) will contain.
> And some wild currs, who from their masters ran,
> Abhorring the supremacy of man,
> In woods and caves the rebel-race began. (190–6)

(*Dryden's Poems*, ed. Bonamy Dobrée, London [Dent] 1966, p. 176.)

epic aspirations to the dramatic form. It is clear from the rather euphoric prefatory essay to *The Conquest of Granada* that the acclaim of that play convinced him, if only temporarily, that he had succeeded:

> That an heroic play ought to be an imitation, in little, of an heroic poem and, consequently, that love and valour ought to be the subject of it.[6]

Speaking of the character of Almanzor he says:

> The first image I had of him was from the Achilles of Homer the next from Tasso's Rinaldo (who was a copy of the former), and the third from the Artaban of Monsieur Calprenède, who has imitated both.[7]

Dryden's definition of the epic, therefore, includes not only the classical exemplars and the Italian Romantic Epic of the Renaissance, but the contemporary French Heroic Romances, considered as a species of prose epic. These once popular and now more or less unreadable forerunners of the psychological novel, their plots hinging on high-flown conflicts of love, honour, and virtue, represent one side of the seventeenth century's image of itself. The obverse is represented by the realism and cynicism of Restoration Comedy.

The central theme of *The Conquest of Granada* seems to me to consist in the juxtaposition of natural virtue, represented by Almanzor, and the corrupt and faction-ridden state of Granada under its ineffectual king, Boabdelin. But in fact Almanzor is more convincing when temporarily in defeat and placed in a pathetic situation. This occurs at the end of the first part of the play. He is compelled to resign Almahide to the king, and she to dismiss him:

ALMAHIDE. Adieu, then, O my soul's far better part!
    Your image sticks so close,
    That the blood follows from my rending heart.
    A last farewell!

---

[6] "Of Heroic Plays". *John Dryden: Three Plays*, ed. George Saintsbury, New York, n.d., p. 8.

[7] *Op. cit.*, p. 11.

For, since the last must come, the rest are vain,
Like gasps in death, which but prolong our pain.
But, since the king is now a part of me,
Cease from henceforth to be his enemy.
Go now, for pity go! for, if you stay,
I fear I shall have something still to say.
Thus – I for ever shut you from my sight. *(Veils)*

ALMANZOR. Like one thrust out in a cold winter's night,
  Yet shivering underneath your gate I stay;
  One look – I cannot go before 'tis day. –
      (She beckons him to be gone)
  Not one – Farewell: Whate'er my sufferings be
  Within, I'll speak farewell as loud as she:
  I will not be outdone in constancy. –
      (She turns her back)
  Then like a dying conqueror I go;
  At least I have looked last upon my foe.
  I go – but if too heavily I move,
  I walk encumbered with a weight of love.
  Fain would I leave the thought of you behind,
  But still, the more I cast you from my mind,
  You dash, like water, back, when thrown against the wind.[8]
      (Exit)

There is even a certain pathos in Almanzor's relapsing into his
habitual bombast ("I'll speak farewell as loud as she") as if he
could not help it. This bombast of Almanzor is of course frequently absurd, and invited the burlesque of Drawcansir in *The
Rehearsal*. But surely Dryden did not intend it to be absurd. If
he had there would have been no point in the burlesque. But
there is also an intentional element of ironic humour – what
Saintsbury has called "purple comedy" – in Dryden's Heroic
plays. One should consider the scenes in which the scheming
coquette Lyndaraxa appears. She belongs essentially to the world
of Restoration Comedy, and is first cousin to Congreve's Mrs
Marwood and Vanbrugh's Lady Fancifull.

It is in relation to the scenes between the Emperor and the
Empress in *Aureng-Zebe* that Saintsbury used the phrase "purple

[8] *The Conquest of Granada*, Part I, v, ii. Saintsbury, p. 80.

comedy". This, the last of Dryden's rhymed Heroic plays, is more restrained, and mitigates the snip-snap of the heroic couplet by a freer use of enjambement. *Aureng-Zebe* seems to me to have a greater coherence of theme than any of its predecessors. The moral is the typically Drydenian one of the danger of faction and disorder in the state. The Emperor, in allowing this to come about, is guilty of a levity not unlike that of King Lear. Beside him is placed the sinister Empress Nourmahal. She stands for unregulated passion, which eventually issues in insanity. She has, of course, to run stark mad not only in white satin but also in regular heroic couplets. But the passage in which she does so is a not uninteresting example of the tendency of the baroque to spill over into the surrealistic:

> I burn, I more than burn; I am all fire.
> See how my mouth and nostrils flame expire!
> I'll not come near myself –
> Now I'm a burning lake, it rolls and flows;
> I'll rush, and pour it all upon my foes.
> Pull, pull, that reverend piece of timber near:
> Throw't on – 'tis dry – 'twill burn –
> Ha, ha! how my old husband crackles there!
> Keep him down, keep him down; turn him about:
> I know him, – he'll but whiz, and go straight out.
> Fan me, you winds: What, not one breath of air?
> I'll burn them all, and yet have flames to spare.
> Quench me: Pour on whole rivers. 'Tis in vain:
> Morat stands there to drive them back again:
> With those huge bellows in his hands, he blows
> New fire into my head: My brain-pan glows.
> See! see! there's Aureng-Zebe too takes his part;
> But he blows all his fire into my heart.[9]

Against these forces of disorder stands the heroic virtue of Aureng-Zebe himself, less flamboyant than that of Almanzor. It is contrasted again with the courage of Morat, in whom it is related to no moral principle but merely to that of self-seeking ambition. In this Morat is a kind of forerunner of Achitophel. One of the best scenes of the play is that in which Morat has got

[9] *Aureng-Zebe*, v. i. Saintsbury, p. 353.

the heroine Indamora into his power. She has nothing to rely upon except her honour: but here this abstraction which everybody in these plays is always talking about suddenly comes before us as a real, positive and effective quality:

> INDAMORA. How you confound desires of good and ill!
> For true renown is still with virtue joined;
> But lust of power lets loose the unbridled mind.
> Yours is a soul irregularly great,
> Which, wanting temper, yet abounds with heat,
> So strong, yet so unequal pulses beat;
> A sun, which does, through vapours, dimly shine;
> What pity 'tis, you are not all divine!
> New moulded, thorough lightened, and a breast
> So pure, to bear the last severest test;
> Fit to command an empire you should gain
> By virtue, and without a blush to reign.

> MORAT. You show me somewhat I ne'er learnt before;
> But 'tis the distant prospect of a shore,
> Doubtful in mists; which, like enchanted ground,
> Flies from my sight, before 'tis fully found.

> INDAMORA. Dare to be great, without a guilty crown;
> View it, and lay the bright temptation down:
> 'Tis base to seize on all, because you may;
> That's empire, that, which I can give away:
> There's joy when to wild will you laws prescribe,
> When you bid Fortune carry back her bribe:
> A joy, which none but greatest minds can taste;
> A fame, which will to endless ages last.

> MORAT. Renown, and fame, in vain, I courted long,
> And still pursued them, though directed wrong,
> In hazard, and in toils, I heard they lay;
> Sailed farther than the coast, but missed my way;
> Now you have given me virtue for my guide;
> And, with true honour, ballasted my pride.
> Unjust dominion I no more pursue;
> I quit all other claims, but those to you.[10]

[10] *Op. cit.*, pp. 337–8.

Dryden's characters have been called puppets. But, although Morat's conversion is rather sudden, we have here what is surely a convincing psychological picture of a man realising for the first time that the principle on which his life has hitherto been founded is wholly wrong.

After *Aureng-Zebe*, as everybody knows, Dryden grew "weary of his long-loved mistress, Rhyme" – that is, of course, as far as plays were concerned. With the abandonment of rhyme went to a large extent the abandonment of the idea of Heroic Drama, in the sense of a transference to the stage of the principles of the Epic. The best of the later plays are therefore more truly tragic in conception. *All for Love* is "written in imitation of Shakespeare's style". This phrase, I think, refers to the adoption of blank verse. For the play is really very un-Shakespearean in conception. It is perhaps the only English Tragedy which can seriously be compared with the work of Corneille and Racine. What Dryden gives us here is a kind of mathematical demonstration of the balance of abstract forces. The symmetrical patterning of cross-relationships of love, honour, jealousy, and friendship is characteristic of Restoration Drama in general, comedy as well as tragedy. They give to the whole a structure which, if we imagine it spatially, is analogous to the balanced mathematical construction of Baroque architecture. In *All for Love* this principle is carried to the point where the whole meaning of the play depends upon it. Antony and Cleopatra stand for the values of love; Ventidius and Octavia for Roman virtue, which is however the value of a world well lost. Unlike Dryden's earlier heroes, Antony in defeat has allowed his heroic virtue to be wholly eclipsed by his passion, so that the two are now no longer compatible. Ventidius represents stoic virtue untouched by passion. He succeeds in temporarily arousing Antony and attempts to wean him away from Cleopatra to Octavia. Perhaps the most striking scene in the play is that in which Octavia and Cleopatra confront each other. The Restoration dramatists were fond of this kind of scene, which undoubtedly offered an opportunity for virtuoso acting by the actresses. But the scene in *All for Love* has more power than the similar one in Lee's *The Rival Queens*, which is probably its model. It is more than a mere slanging match, because Octavia and Cleopatra represent the two main conflicting forces of the drama.

The third force is friendship, represented by Antony's relationship to Dolabella. By a tragic twist Antony is brought to believe that Dolabella is about to betray him with Cleopatra. In repudiating her, he is divided from the one value still remaining to him, and his final destruction is thus made inevitable. Dryden's Cleopatra, much less complex than Shakespeare's, is a pattern of faithful devotion, and thus has no way of winning Antony back once he has ceased to believe in her. The stratagem of bringing to Antony a false report of her death, which leads to the final catastrophe, is not of her devising, but the ruse of her servant Alexas. In Alexas is concentrated all the Egyptian deviousness which was an integral part of the character of Shakespeare's Cleopatra. Alexas is a eunuch who has never loved; his cunning is of the head and not of the heart, and hence can be of no real service to Cleopatra nor withstand the inevitable workings of Fate.

It is not so easy, however, to determine what kind of love Antony and Cleopatra stand for in this play. It seems to change its nature according to whether we look at it from the point of view of Octavia and Ventidius or that of Antony and Cleopatra themselves. The first two of these characters stand for Rome with its connotation of Law. From their point of view Cleopatra is a seductress; at best Antony's love for her is Romantic Love – but that Romantic Love which is never consonant with marriage. But Cleopatra herself, in the moment before her death, claims the high title of wife, and abrogates to herself the Roman values. Her suicide is in the end not so much a romantic one, as that extreme assertion of virtue which Roman stoic tradition justified. This seems to imply that Love embodies a higher value with its own transcendent law.

But in the Prologue, Antony is, apparently, no better than "every Keeping Tony of the pit". In that line the whole heroic structure of the play is abolished – and indeed this is often the case with Dryden's prologues and epilogues. Their values are those, presumably, of at least part of the audience – a part which was not prepared to take heroic tragedy seriously. They went to the Theatre, one must suppose, for a temporary escape, to see characters motivated by ideals of Love and Honour which they did not envisage as being really relatable to actual contemporary life. Actual contemporary life was the subject of comedy, a

school of manners. As a man of the world Dryden was probably
in agreement with them: but not, I think, entirely so as a poet.
It is precisely its ambiguity, or at least its double standard of values
which makes *All for Love* a true tragedy, in a sense that this word
does not really apply to the other Heroic Plays.

I have spoken of the element of ironic comedy in Dryden's
Heroic tragedies. In comedy, as such, he was, as he himself
admitted, less successful. *The Spanish Friar* and *Marriage à la Mode*
are generally accounted the best, and the second of these is
probably the more interesting to modern readers. As far as I can
remember, it is the only one of Dryden's plays to have been given
on the London stage in the last quarter of a century. There are
two very loosely connected plots, the one, heroical-pastoral, in
verse, and the other a typical piece of Restoration prose comedy.
It is perhaps idle to look for any unity in it, but part of the theme
of the verse plot is the contrast between pastoral innocence and
the sophistication of courts, while that of the prose plot is the
ironic discrepancy between the ideal of love or gallantry and the
social reality of marriage. Furthermore, there is perhaps some
parallelism between the way in which the characters of the verse
plot change places in relation to the throne, and the swapping
of partners in the prose plot, as in a dance set. A game of hide-
and-seek and a masked ball are also features that set the tone of
the play; for all the characters are in some sense victims of illusion
and deception. There is some rather beautiful pastoral verse in
the scene in which Leonidas and Palmyra remember their first
innocent falling in love when they were supposed peasants. We
may set against this idyll the cynicism of the song with which the
play opens:

> Why should a foolish marriage vow,
>   Which long ago was made,
> Oblige us to each other now,
>   When passion is decayed?
> We loved, and we loved, as long as we could,
>   'Till our love was loved out in us both;
> But our marriage is dead, when the pleasure is fled:
> 'Twas pleasure first made it an oath.[11]

[11] *Marriage à la Mode*, I, i. Saintsbury, p. 185.

But this purely pragmatic view of marriage is not, after all, what is finally accepted – here, or elsewhere in Restoration comedy. Rhodophil must eventually go back to his Doralice, having escaped being cuckolded (though only just). And Palamede, at the injunction of his father, woos and wins Melantha whom he does not love. The irony is that Rhodophil really does have in Doralice a witty and charming wife, yet he is infatuated with Melantha. Palamede, who is obliged to marry the latter, sees her for what she really is – an affected *bourgeoise*, who apes the manners of the court and second-hand French fashions. The last interview between Palamede and Doralice is touching:

PALAMEDE. Yet, if we had but once enjoyed one another! – but then once only is worse than not at all: It leaves a man with such a lingering after it.

DORALICE. For aught I know, 'tis better that we have not; we might upon trial have liked each other less, as many a man and woman, that have loved as desperately as we, and yet, when they came to possession, have sighed and cried to themselves, Is this all?

PALAMEDE. Well, madam, I am convinced, that 'tis best for us not to have enjoyed; but, gad, the strongest reason is, because I can't help it.

DORALICE. The only way to keep us new to one another, is never to enjoy, as they keep grapes, by hanging them upon a line; they must touch nothing, if you would preserve them fresh.

PALAMEDE. But then they wither, and grow dry in the very keeping.[12]

There is a great sadness underlying this. The ideal of romantic love is deeply felt, but felt to be unattainable.

When *Absalom and Achitophel* appeared in 1681 Dryden was fifty. This is certainly his most read and probably his finest and most characteristic work. The contemporary events which were

[12] *Op. cit.*, v. i., p. 255.

its occasion provided Dryden with a subject with which he was really concerned. Growing up as he did during the Civil War period Dryden had come to believe in the necessity of a strong central monarchical authority, accepted as of divine right, and to hold in abhorrence violent mob rule and private opinion. For him, the attempt of Shaftesbury and the Whigs, with Puritan backing, to capitalise on the alleged Popish Plot, and to settle the succession on Monmouth instead of the lawful heir, threatened an outbreak of chaos and anarchy which was satanic in its nature.

Absalom and Achitophel is not mock-heroic, but, as Mr Ian Jack correctly states, epic satire. Cowley's unfinished epic, *The Davideis*, had had as its subject-matter the career of King David. At a first glance, a hypothetical reader unacquainted with the events of the day might almost take *Absalom and Achitophel* to be another and better written book of Cowley's poem. Dryden had also read *Paradise Lost*. There are direct echoes of it in *Absalom and Achitophel*. The gap between the two poems is not so great as one might think (in spite of Dryden and Milton being on different political sides). Achitophel-Shaftesbury is a satanic figure; "Hell's dire agent". Like Morat (and like Milton's Satan) he is "irregularly great".[13] So, in a different way, is Zimri-Buckingham, the timeless type of the dangerously irresponsible intellectual, as Achitophel is of the unscrupulous power-driven politician. The characters of these are the best known passages in the poem. They are anthologisable and will stand on their own. It is quite legitimate to allow them to do so, for they belong to the widely practised seventeenth-century *genre* of character-writing. But they gain immensely in significance in the context of the narrative of the poem. The passage in which Achitophel wins over Absalom is one of Dryden's best dramatic scenes, and should be compared with the temptation scene in *Paradise Lost*. In a sense Absalom-Monmouth bears the same relationship to his father the king, who as the Lord's Anointed is God's representative, as Adam does to God. The temptation which Achitophel

[13] This phrase applied by Indamora to Morat has aesthetic and critical connotations. What might be said of a great but imperfect work of art is here used of a noble but morally faulty man. Nothing could illustrate better the way in which, in the neo-classical period, moral and aesthetic values were felt to be interdependent.

presents to him is essentially the same as that which Satan presents to Eve. In both cases it is Proper Pride that is appealed to, in order to break the principle of Degree.

Absalom and Achitophel, as epic satire, is *sui generis*: but, in *Mac Flecknoe*, Dryden practically invented, as far as English literature is concerned, the mock-heroic poem.[14] Dryden seems to have conceived of the mock-heroic or burlesque as a kind of anti-image of the true heroic, as the following remarks from the prefatory letter to *Annus Mirabilis* may show:

> Such descriptions or images, well wrought, which I promise not for mine, are, as I have said, the adequate delight of heroick Poesie, for they beget admiration, which is its proper object; as the images of the Burlesque, which is contrary to this, by the same reason beget laughter; for the one shows Nature beautified, as in the picture of a fair Woman, which we all admire; the other shows her deformed, . . . at which we cannot forbear to laugh, because it is a deviation from Nature.[15]

The realm of Non-sense over which Shadwell presides is thus antithetical to Nature, the imitation of which is the object of all good writing. Shadwell is not only king over the realm of Non-sense, but also its Messiah or rather Anti-Christ. Flecknoe is his Elijah or John the Baptist. The near blasphemy of the passage in which this is implied is thus not wholly frivolous:

> *Heywood* and *Shirley* were but Types of thee,
> Thou last great Prophet of Tautology:
> Even I, a dunce of more renown than they,
> Was sent before but to prepare thy way:
> And coarsely clad in *Norwich* Drugget came
> To teach the Nations in thy greater name.[16]

Mac Flecknoe provided the model for Pope's *Dunciad*. The latter has the scope of a full-scale anti-epic. In it the Goddess of

[14] Spenser's *Muiopotmos* and Drayton's *Nymphidia* are earlier examples: but they are purely and delightfully exercises of fancy, and do not have the satiric content of the classical mock-heroic.

[15] Preface to *Annus Mirabilis*, Kinsley, pp. 48–9.

[16] *Mac Flecknoe*, 29–34. Dobrée, p. 123.

Dullness, the daughter of Chaos and old Night, threatens to destroy the whole Augustan order of reason and good sense through her "uncreating word". The best parts of it are perhaps Pope at his most truly serious. For although in his age the true Epic still remained in theory the goal to which the poet must strive, the mock-heroic more truly represented its characteristic spirit. The relation of the mock-epic to the true epic is therefore somewhat like the relation of comedy to tragedy, though it does not seem quite to have been conceived in those terms. Indeed, the mock-epic could not exist without the values of the true epic continuing to be taken, at least in theory, seriously. The mock-heroic is not a criticism of the epic, but of life. By magnifying trivialities to heroic proportions it shows them to be the more trivial. This is very obviously the method of the *Rape of the Lock*, for instance. But in so far as the age became increasingly concerned with practical reason, rather than with ideas, the neo-classical mock-heroic is a vital form, whereas the serious epic, after Milton, is not. It continued its theoretical existence till the end of the eighteenth century, realising itself in such works as Glover's *Leonidas* and Wilkie's *Epigoniad*. When it finally expired, the mock-heroic died with it. The "comic epic poem in prose" of Fielding, with its Cervantean derivation, was also related to the mock-heroic. It started one main stream of the English novel. The other began when Richardson transmuted the values of the Heroic Romance into those of *bourgeois* realism, and produced in *Clarissa Harlow* the only true tragedy of the eighteenth century.

Immediately after the passage quoted above from the preface to *Annus Mirabilis*, in which Dryden treats of the burlesque, he says:

> The same images serve equally for the Epique Poesie, and for the Historique and Panegyrique, which are branches of it.[17]

As panegyric writing we may class the *Heroic Stanzas on the Death of the Lord Protector*, *Astraea Redux*, and the *Threnodia Augustalis*. But the finest example is surely the *Ode to the Memory of Mrs. Anne Killigrew*. It is of course nothing to the point that the accomplished lady was a very minor versifier. In this poem she is treated as a

[17] Preface to *Annus Mirabilis*, Kinsley, p. 49.

symbol of Poetry and the place it should occupy in the court, and
of virgin purity:

> Thou youngest Virgin-Daughter of the Skies,
>   Made in the last Promotion of the *Blest*;
> Whose Palms, new pluckt from Paradise,
> In spreading *Branches* more sublimely rise,
>   Rich with Immortal Green above the rest:
> Whether, adopted to some Neighbouring Star,
> Thou rol'st above us in thy wand'ring Race,
>   Or, in Procession fixt and regular,
> Mov'd with the Heavens Majestick pace;
>   Or, call'd to more Superiour *Bliss*,
> Thou tread'st, with Seraphims, the vast *Abyss*:
> Whatever happy region is thy place,
> Cease thy Celestial Song a little space;
> (Thou wilt have time enough for Hymns Divine,
> Since Heav'ns Eternal Year is thine.)[18]

This baroque heaven is on the model of the earthly court, and the
promotion of the blest a kind of celestial honours list. The
Deity Himself is a sort of *grand monarque*:

> And if no clust'ring Swarm of *Bees*
> On thy sweet Mouth distill'd their golden Dew,
> 'Twas that, such vulgar Miracles
> Heav'n had not Leasure to renew.[19]

The reference is to the legend that bees swarmed upon the cradle
of Pindar, appropriate because this is a Pindaric poem. With all
these images implying the relationship of poetry to an ideal
order, Dryden poignantly contrasts the uses to which poetry has
actually been put:

> O Gracious God! How far have we
> Prophan'd thy Heav'nly Gift of Poesy!
> Made prostitute and profligate the Muse,
> Debas'd to each obscene and impious use,
> Whose Harmony was first ordain'd *Above*,
> For Tongues of *Angels* and for *Hymns* of *Love*!

[18] *Ode to the Memory of Mrs Anne Killigrew*, 1–15. Dobrée, pp. 32–3.
[19] *Op. cit.*, 50–3, p. 34.

Oh wretched We! why were we hurry'd down
　　This lubrique and adult'rate age,
　(Nay, added fat Pollutions of our own)
　　　T'increase the steaming Ordures of the Stage?
What can we say t' excuse our *Second Fall*?
Let this thy *Vestal*, Heav'n, atone for all:
Her *Arethusian* Stream remains unsoil'd,
Unmixt with Forreign Filth and undefil'd,
Her Wit was more than Man, her Innocence a Child.[20]

The very texture of words like "profligate", "prostitute", and "lubrique", with their clotted double consonants and lingual sounds, seem to enhance the emotion of contemptuous disgust. We almost picture Dryden picking his way through the garbage of Covent Garden.

The poem concludes with a vision of the Last Judgement and the General Resurrection. I do not think that there is any element of deliberate burlesque here. The literalistic picture of the reconstitution of the bodies of the dead, which must strike oddly to most modern readers, seems to have had a curious fascination for this period. It occurs in Cowley's ode *The Resurrection*, and a little later in Young's *The Last Day*. But what is noteworthy in Dryden's poem is the daring vindication of the special status of poets and poetry:

The Sacred Poets first shall hear the Sound,
And foremost from the Tomb shall bound:
For they are cover'd with the lightest ground;
And, streight, with in-born Vigour, on the Wing,
Like mounting Larks, to the New Morning sing.
There *Thou*, sweet Saint, before the Quire shalt go,
As Harbinger of Heav'n, the Way to show,
The Way which thou so well hast learn'd below.[21]

The figure of Anne Killigrew in this ode can be related to that of St Cecilia in the two cantata-odes which Dryden wrote for her festival. When Dryden came to write *Alexander's Feast* in 1697 he had forefeited his Laureateship and court favour. The celestial music of Saint Cecilia is by implication contrasted with the

[20] *Op. cit.*, 56–70, p. 34.　　　　　[21] *Op. cit.*, 188–95, p. 38.

technical virtuosity of the court poet Timotheus. The irony of
this poem has not, I think, often been noticed:

> A present Deity, they shout around:
> A present Deity, the vaulted Roofs rebound.
> > With ravish'd Ears
> > The Monarch hears,
> > Assumes the God,
> > Affects to nod,
> > And seems to shake the Spheres.[22]

The comic effect of the last three lines should be unmistakeable:
Edward Young was wildly off the mark when, supposing Dryden
used them to convey a feeling of dignity, he framed the whole of
his long and disastrous *Ocean: an Ode* upon them. Alexander is a
typical heroic figure – he had indeed been a central character in
Lee's *The Rival Queens*, the most extravagant of all heroic tragedies. But here he is placed in a slightly absurd light, and he is
also wicked. It is not he but Timotheus who guides the action
of the poem, as he displays the power of music by arousing and
allaying the various passions in the King. It should be noted that
all these passions are really ignoble ones. Even Alexander's pity
for the fallen Darius is a sentimental self-indulgence:

> With down-cast Looks the joyless Victor sate,
> > Revolving in his alter'd Soul
> > > The various Turns of Chance below;
> > And, now and then, a Sigh he stole,
> > And Tears began to flow.[23]

It all ends up in an orgy of senseless destruction:

> The Princes applaud, with a furious Joy;
> And the King seiz'd a Fambeau with Zeal to destroy;
> > *Thais* led the Way,
> > To light him to his Prey,
> And, like another *Hellen*, fir'd another *Troy*.[24]

On this appalling scene Dryden suddenly drops the curtain,

[22] *Alexander's Feast*, 36–41. Dobrée, p. 26.
[23] *Op. cit.*, 84–8, p. 27.   [24] *Op. cit.*, 148–50, p. 29.

and invokes the Saint in whose honour the poem is really written.
But there is irony even in the famous concluding lines:

> He rais'd a Mortal to the Skies;
> She drew an Angel down.[25]

Timotheus only raised a mortal to the skies by flattering his self-
conceit. After 1688 Dryden had good cause to say "put not your
trust in princes". He had striven to support the idea of a divinely
ordained monarchy in the persons of Charles II and James II,
and had raised those mortals to the skies. But now that cause was
lost, and England had become, and has remained ever since,
effectively a republic.

In the foregoing pages I have tried to show how the baroque
heroic ideal represented for Dryden the realisation in poetic terms
of a transcendent order. But in his work it is continually struggling with an ironic and more modern spirit which is destructive of
it. There is a kind of good-humoured serenity in his final work,
The Secular Masque, written in the year of his death, 1700. It is a
fitting farewell to the complex and turbulent seventeenth century.
Diana represents the more extroverted age of the last years of
Elizabeth and of James I, Mars the troubled times of Charles I
and the Civil War, Venus the Restoration but

> All, all of a piece throughout:
> Thy Chase had a Beast in View;
> Thy Wars brought nothing about;
> Thy Lovers were all untrue.
> 'Tis well an Old Age is out,
> And time to begin a New.[26]

The new age did begin, and a new poet, Alexander Pope, was
waiting in the wings. But, although he carried the Augustan
ideals of style established by Dryden to greater perfection, he had
in some ways a narrower range and a less masculine intellect than
his illustrious master.

[25] *Op. cit.*, 169–70, p. 29.
[26] *The Secular Masque*, 91–6. Dobrée, p. 285.

D. W. Jefferson

ASPECTS OF DRYDEN'S IMAGERY[1]

I

One of the weaknesses of Mark Van Doren's otherwise excellent study of Dryden's poetry is its belittlement of the imagery:

> In no piece did Dryden ever display a happy gift for turning up images. He speaks from time to time of difficulties encountered in curbing a luxuriant fancy. But it is plain that the difficulties were never really great.[2]
>
> Dryden was most at home when he was making statements. His poetry was the poetry of declaration. At his best he wrote without transforming passion. When Shakespeare's imagination was kindled his page thronged with images. When Donne was most possessed of his theme he departed in a passionate search for conceits. When Dryden became fired he only wrote more plainly.[3]

The question of Dryden's imagery is connected, of course, with that of his "metaphysical" qualities. It has always been recognised that there is a metaphysical element in his poetry, but it has usually been regarded as something vestigial, occurring mainly in early work, and not essential to his mature style. Literary historians tend to regard him as the great representative of the reaction against the school of Donne; which he was, but not in

[1] Reprinted, with revisions, from *Essays in Criticism*, Vol. IV (1954) pp. 20–41.
[2] *John Dryden: A Study of His Poetry*, 3 edn., New York (1946) p. 36.
[3] *Op. cit.*, p. 71.

every respect. He reacted against metaphysical tortuousness and obscurity, but he did not lose the metaphysical act of using images suggestively and wittily.

It is in his mature work – especially the rhymed heroic plays and the satires – that the more interesting, the more essentially metaphysical images appear. This is the Dryden with whom we shall be concerned here. The poet of *Astraea Redux* and even *Annus Mirabilis*, whatever his merits at this stage of his development, had not quite found himself; he had not discovered what he wanted to say or how to say it. The earlier Dryden used imagery rather more profusely than the later, often with the confused and pointless ingenuity of the decadent metaphysicals, under whose influence he remained for too long. Dr Johnson, quoting a long passage from *Astraea Redux*[4] found in it "such a cluster of thoughts unallied to one another as will not easily be found". *Annus Mirabilis* is better; the imagery is more pleasing, more neatly developed, and there are some good passages of description. But on the whole it is an immature work. It lacks qualities which are essential to the real Dryden: boldness of treatment and imaginative breadth. Its weakness lies in an excess of detailed effects, which are on too small a scale for the size of the poem. We cannot say, in Mr Eliot's words, that the small is made great or the trivial magnificent. Dr Johnson said, in reference to some metaphysical poetry: "Sublimity is produced by aggregation, littleness by dispersion." Sublimity may be too grand a word to apply to Dryden, but he certainly had a natural gift for weighty and imposing effects, and in *Annus Mirabilis* he has not yet learnt to achieve them. It is the minute parts of the work – the individual strokes of wit and fancy, and the descriptive touches, often tedious – that exercise our attention at the expense of the total design. A great style can only be evolved in response to a great stimulus. Dryden needed a subject-matter to bring his powers into action, to rescue him from "littleness" and develop his essential largeness.

Dryden's rather late development as a poet seems to be due to the simple fact that during his early years he had nothing to say. Until his early thirties he produced, as far as we know, only occasional poetry, small in quantity and unambitious in scope.

[4] 151 f.

He was of a generation in which the spiritual contraction following the Elizabethans began to make itself felt. The poetry of love, death, and religious feeling, the tragic drama, the lyric: all these things were losing their vitality; and the imagination of poets had not yet come to terms with the new, less exalted subject-matter – politics, religious controversy, philosophies, social life, personalities – to which the Augustans were to become happily adjusted. Dryden was largely responsible for this adjustment, but it was the work of his late maturity. He was successful here only after some years of significant development in another sphere of activity: the drama.

The Restoration was an age of emotional impoverishment in poetry, but it was easier in the theatre than elsewhere, by a bold externality and artificiality, to give a kind of life to emotions which had ceased to be real.[5] And there were opportunities here for subtlety and intelligence. The age had its two sides: it was sceptical, materialistic, in certain important respects uninspired: but it liked grandeur, bold and triumphant assertion, emotional display. Dryden was very conscious of these opposites and of their interplay. While entering to a large extent into the contemporary taste for display and assertion, he showed an ironical awareness of the meaning of these things in his own and his age's psychology. In his treatment of the popular themes there is often a reservation, a withholding of himself, which gives the right limitation to the effect.

Many of Dryden's plays are of little importance: he could produce a comedy, a comedy-romance, or a tragi-comedy or anything else that current taste demanded, always maintaining an adequate literary level, but not always putting much of himself into it. The rhymed heroic plays are exceptional in that they offered a subject-matter through which his sensibility and intelligence found ample expression; the subject-matter in the handling of which he discovered himself fully as a poet.

[5] Professor Bonamy Dobrée has supplied the necessary defence of "artificiality" in Restoration plays in *Restoration Tragedy* (1929) p. 93, and elsewhere.

2

I have tried elsewhere[6] to show that in these plays Dryden's attitude to his theme, though apparently serious, is modified by a lurking comic intention; that heroic virtuosity, while filling his mind with bold and colourful ideas and giving him an opportunity for rhetoric, also stimulated his wit, tempting his essentially plastic genius to indulge in effects of exaggeration and distortion. The tendency towards absurdity which makes the idea of the invincible hero so vulnerable to burlesque is deliberately cultivated along with the element of dignity, which is always allowed to remain dominant for dramatic purposes. The villains are given a kind of depraved or hollow splendour, which always has a comic aspect.

The passage in which Almanzor realises that he is in love, usually condemned as an example of Dryden's worst bombast, is a fair example of this mixture:

> I'me pleas'd and pain'd since first her eyes I saw,
> As I were stung with some *Tarantula*:
> Armes, and the dusty field I less admire;
> And soften strangely in some new desire.
> Honour burns in me, not so fiercely bright,
> But pale as fires when master'd by the light.
> Ev'n when I speak and look, I change yet more;
> And now am nothing that I was before.
> I'm numm'd, and fix'd, and scarce my eye-balls move;
> I fear it is the Lethargy of Love!
> 'Tis he; I feel him now in every part:
> Like a new Lord he vaunts about my Heart,
> Surveys in state each corner of my Brest,
> While poor fierce I, that was, am dispossest.
> I'm bound; but I will rowze my rage again:
> And though no hope of Liberty remaine,
> I'll fright my Keeper when I shake my chaine.[7]

[6] "The Significance of Dryden's Heroic Plays", *Proceedings of the Leeds Philosophical and Literary Society* (*Literary and Historical Section*), Vol. v, Part III (1940).

[7] *The Conquest of Granada*, I. III, 328–44. [The text used for the plays is Dryden, *Dramatic Works*, ed. Montagu Summers, London (Nonesuch Press) 1931–2.]

The conventional symptoms of love are parodied and exaggerated, the imagery being deliberately made crude. Although there are serious lines, the last is frankly comic. This speech may be compared with that of Maximin, the imperial villain of *Tyrannick Love*, who also finds himself inconveniently in love. Again there is a grotesque violence in the imagery, but the heroic quality is absent:

> This Love that never could my youth engage,
> Peeps out his coward head to dare my age.
> Where hast thou been thus long, thou sleeping form,
> That wak'st like drowsie Sea-men in a storm?
> A sullen hour thou chusest for thy birth:
> My Love shoots up in tempests, as the Earth
> Is stirr'd and loosen'd in a blust'ring wind,
> Whose blasts to waiting flowers her womb unbind.[8]

These two passages show that Dryden could use images piquantly to introduce a grotesque element into a character. He excelled in images of comic portentousness:

> It is a murd'ring will!
> That whirls along with an impetuous sway;
> And like chain-shot, sweeps all things in its way.[9]

The above is a description of a "heavy father".

> Her tears, her smiles, her every look's a Net.
> Her voice is like a Syren's of the Land;
> And bloody Hearts lie panting in her hand.[10]

The ineffectiveness of Boabdelin, the wretched king of Granada, is continually being enhanced by the images of spurious grandeur in his own speeches:

> On your Allegiance, I command you stay;
> Who passes here, through me must make his way.
> My life's the *Isthmos*; through this narrow line
> You first must cut, before those Sea's can joyn.[11]

---

[8] *Tyrannick Love*, III, 1–8.
[9] *The Conquest of Granada*, I, v, 134–6.
[10] *Op. cit.*, I, III, 71–3.
[11] *Op. cit.*, I, I, 130–3.

> Let my Crown go; he never shall return;
> I, like a Phoenix in my Nest will burn.[12]

or by the insulting images in Almanzor's:

> The word which I have giv'n shall stand like Fate;
> Not like the King's, that weathercock of State.
> He stands so high, with so unfixt a mind,
> Two Factions turn him with each blast of wind.[13]

> How did he dare my freedom to restore?
> He like some Captive Lyon uses me;
> He runs away before he sets me free.[14]

But these passages will have more point for us when they are related to another kind of imagery, which may be said to have a thematic "metaphysical" content.

The fact that the heroic plays are so remote from reality in characterisation and action enabled Dryden to play very freely with his material. He could use every situation for his own purpose, so that whether the characters are trying to terrorise or seduce, whether they are expressing overweening pride in themselves or scorn of others, or making general remarks about life, love, honour, priests, or the proper relation between a despot and his subjects, their speeches are all opportunities for him to compose for his own pleasure, to exercise his wit and say the things he wanted to say, under cover of a conventionally vehement and flamboyant action.

One of the favourite *motifs*, occurring frequently in speeches of invective, is a comic conception of the human species, of the processes appertaining to its creation and generation, and of the relation between soul and body. In *Aureng-Zebe* Morat speaks resentfully of his position as a younger son:

> . . . for when great Souls are given,
> They bear the marks of Sov'reignty from Heav'n.
> My Elder Brothers my fore-runners came;
> Rough-draughts of Nature, ill-design'd and lame.
> Blown off, like Blossoms, never made to bear;
> Till I came, finish'd; her last-labour'd care . . .[15]

[12] *Op. cit.,* II. I, ii, 186–7. [13] *Op. cit.,* I. III, 9–12.
[14] *Op. cit.,* I. V, 391–3. [15] *Aureng-Zebe,* V, 27–32.

Birthright's a vulgar road to Kingly sway;
'Tis ev'ry dull-got Elder Brother's way.
Dropt from above, he lights into a Throne;
Grows of a piece with that he sits upon;
Heav'n's choice, a low, inglorious, rightful Drone.[16]

But Aureng-Zebe says of him:

When thou wert form'd, Heav'n did a Man begin;
But the brute Soul, by chance, was shuffl'd in.[17]

Nourmahal, in the same play, amazed that so faithful a copy of
her own charms as Indamora can exist, asks her to speak:

Speak, if thou hast a Soul, that I may see,
If Heav'n can make throughout, another Me.

and is reassured by her response that so far as "soul" is concerned
the younger woman is inferior:

The Palm is, by the Foes confession, mine;
But I disdain what basely you resign.
Heav'n did, by me, the outward model build;
The inward work, the Soul, with rubbish fill'd.[18]

The Emperor in *Aureng-Zebe*, on one of his subjects:

That crawling Insect, who from mud began,
Warm'd by my Beams, and kindl'd into Man.[19]

On his subjects as a whole:

The Vulgar, a scarce animated Clod[20]

and

The little Emmets with the humane Soul[21]

His definition of children:

Children (the blind effect of Love and Chance,
Form'd by their sportive Parents' ignorance)[22]

Boabdelin on his ebbing fortunes:

[16] *Op. cit.*, v, 66–70.   [17] *Op. cit.*, iii, 306–7.   [18] *Op. cit.*, v. 278–83.
[19] *Op. cit.*, ii, 126–7.   [20] *Op. cit.*, iii, 182.   [21] *Op. cit.*, iii, 185.
[22] *Op. cit.*, iii, 209–10.

Of all Mankind, the heaviest Fate he bears
Who the last Crown of sinking Empire wears.
No kindly Planet of his Birth took care:
Heav'ns Out-cast; and the Dross of every Starr![23]

This type of imagery is not peculiar to the heroic plays. An early instance is found in the last line of a stanza from *Annus Mirabilis*:

Not so the *Holland* Fleet, who tir'd and done,
Stretch'd on their decks like weary Oxen lie:
Faint sweats all down their mighty members run,
(Vast bulks which little Souls but ill supply.)[24]

Examples are found later in the well-known description of Shaftesbury in *Absalom and Achitophel*:

A fiery Soul, which working out its way,
Fretted the Pigmy Body to decay:
And o'r inform'd the Tenement of Clay.[25]

and of Shaftesbury's son:

Got, while his Soul did hudled Notions try;
And born a shapeless Lump, like Anarchy.[26]

The description of the Dissenters in *The Hind and the Panther* is perhaps his most notable use of this imagery for comic purposes:

. . . nor will the Muse describe
A slimy-born and sun-begotten Tribe:
Who, far from steeples and their sacred sound,
In fields their sullen conventicles found:
These gross, half-animated lumps I leave;
Nor can I think what thoughts they can conceive.
But if they think at all, 'tis sure no high'r
Than matter, put in motion, may aspire.

[23] *The Conquest of Granada*, II. i, ii, 17–20.
[24] *Annus Mirabilis*, 277–80. *The Poems of John Dryden*, ed. James Kinsley, Oxford (Clarendon Press) 1958, Vol. I, p. 64.
[25] *Absalom and Achitophel*, 156–8. Kinsley, Vol. I, p. 221.
[26] *Op. cit.*, 171–2. Vol. I, p. 221.

> Souls that can scarce ferment their mass of clay;
> So drossy, so divisible are They,
> As wou'd but serve pure bodies for allay:
> Such souls as *Shards* produce, such beetle things
> As onely buz to heav'n with ev'ning wings;
> Strike in the dark, offending but by chance,
> Such are the blind-fold blows of ignorance . . .[27]

This may be referred to as "body-soul" imagery. It may be linked up with passages in which Dryden takes pleasure in overturning human standards in favour of the sensual self-sufficiency of the brute creation:

> Reason's nice taste does our delights destroy:
> Brutes are more bless'd, who grossly feed on joy.[28]

> Or let thy Orders with my reason sute
> Or let me live by Sense a glorious brute.[29]

Nourmahal's invitation to incestuous love is flavoured by a similar play of ideas:

> And why this niceness to that pleasure shown,
> Where Nature sums up all her joys in one;
> Gives all she can, and, labouring still to give.
> Makes it so great, we can but taste and live;
> So fills the Senses, that the Soul seems fled,
> And thought it self does, for the time, lie dead.[30]

Another theme, related to the "body-soul" theme, is that of "matter". Matter was, for Dryden, a stimulating idea. It suggested weight and bulk, the elements of material splendour and importance, but it could also suggest brute inertness and, by association, stupidity: the predominance of the physical over the spiritual in man. What is interesting in Dryden is that these different implications are liable to be present at the same time. In conveying an impression of the grandiose, he leaves us with just the faintest sense of the ridiculous, while grossness and dullness are invested with mock dignity. In his description of the Dutch

---

[27] *The Hind and the Panther*, I, 310–24. Kinsley, Vol. II, p. 478.
[28] *Aureng-Zebe*, V., 560–1.   [29] *Op. cit.*, III, 45–6.
[30] *Op. cit.*, IV, 119–24.

(quoted above) physical hugeness becomes ridiculous in association with spiritual poverty. The union of hugeness with absurdity is found in the celebrated passage on Shadwell in *Mac Flecknoe*, but here an element of spurious dignity is present:

> Besides his goodly Fabrick fills the eye,
> And seems design'd for thoughtless Majesty:
> Thoughtless as Monarch Oakes, that shade the plain,
> And, spread in solemn state, supinely reign.[31]

The oak is usually a symbol of grandeur and permanence, but here there is the suggestion of monumental inertia. Shadwell becomes impressive in his towering stupidity, and he casts an ample shadow of intellectual darkness all around him. Comparable with this is the description of Titus Oates in *Absalom and Achitophel*:

> Yet, *Corah*, thou shalt from Oblivion pass;
> Erect thy self, thou Monumental Brass:
> High as the Serpent of thy mettall made,
> While Nations stand secure beneath thy shade.[32]

The suggestion of brazen effrontery and baseness of composition conveyed by the metal image is united with that of size and conspicuousness to produce an ominous effect. The metal image in Montezuma's dying speech has the effect of making heroism limited and material:

> Still less and less my boyling Spirits flow;
> And I grow stiff as cooling Mettals do:[33]

In describing the symptoms of love Morat represents it as encountering tough material resistance:

> Love softens me; and blows up fires, which pass
> Through my tough heart, and melt the stubborn Mass.[34]

The following passages introduce another theme:

ABDELMELECH. His Victories we scarce could keep in view,
 Or polish 'em as fast as he rough drew.

[31] *Mac Flecknoe*, 25–8. Kinsley, Vol. I, p. 265.
[32] *Absalom and Achitophel*, 632–5. Kinsley, Vol. I, p. 233.
[33] *The Indian Emperor*, v, ii, 249–50.
[34] *Aureng-Zebe*, v., 155–6.

ABDALLA. Fate after him, below with pain did move,
     And Victory could scarce keep pace above:
     Death did at length so many slain forget,
     And lost the tale, and took 'em by the great.[35]

     Would you so please, Fate yet a way would find;
     Man makes his fate according to his mind.
     The weak low Spirit Fortune makes her slave;
     But she's a drudge, when Hector'd by the brave.
     If Fate weaves common Thrid, he'l change the doom:
     And with new purple spread a Nobler loom.[36]

Dryden enjoyed giving a grotesque account of the operation of
abstract agencies such as fate and fortune. The superman, in the
second passage, overrides the heavenly powers, orders them about
or does their work for them. What is involved in such imagery
is a comic view of the universe and of the influences governing it,
which links up with his well-known anti-clerical spirit and
truculent scepticism.

   If we keep in mind these themes many passages in the heroic
plays which have usually been dismissed as foolish rant acquire a
piquancy. The following lines spoken by Maximin are in a vein
which may be described as the "comic gigantesque". They
depend for their effect partly on Dryden's brilliance in inventing
arguments appropriate to abandoned states of mind, and partly on
portentous imagery:

     I'le find that pow'r o're wills which Heav'n ne're found.
     Free will's a cheat in any one but me.
     In all but Kings 'tis willing slavery.
     An unseen Fate which forces the desire,
     The will of Puppets Danc'd upon a wyre.
     A Monarch is
     The Spirit of the World in every mind;
     He may match Wolves to Lambs and make it kind.
     Mine is the business of your little Fates:
     And though you war like petty wrangling States,
     You're in my hand; and when I bid you cease,
     You shall be crush'd together into peace.[37]

[35] *The Conquest of Granada*, I. II, 24–9.   [36] *Op. cit.*, I. II, 231–6.
[37] *Tyrannick Love*, IV, i, 297–308.

The comic gigantesque enters into Almanzor's invective against
Abdalla:

> If I would kill thee now, thy fate's so low
> That I must stoop 'ere I give the blow.
> But mine is fix'd so far above thy Crown,
> That all thy men,
> Pil'd on thy back, can never pull it down[38]

Some of Dryden's images of light may be considered in relation
to the "matter" theme. Only he could have written:

> And ye small Starrs, the scattered seeds of light,[39]

Light is often seen as something limited and ineffective, with
material rather than spiritual associations:

> You importune it with a false desire:
> Which sparkles out, and makes no solid fire.[40]

> Think you my aged veins so faintly beat,
> They rise no higher than to Friendship's heat?
> So weak your Charms, that, like a Winter's night,
> Twinkling with Stars, they freez me while they light?[41]

> Dim, as the borrow'd beams of Moon and Stars . . .[42]

> My manhood, long misled by wandring fires,
> Follow'd false lights; and when their glimps was gone,
> My pride struck out new sparkles of her own . . .[43]

Dryden may be regarded as a kind of negative scholastic. In
playing with the themes of body, matter and soul, he showed an
awareness of scholastic notions, and therefore of medieval
philosophical values, but he used these ideas in such a way as to
travesty the old conception of man. He was further removed
from the world of medieval thought and feeling than Donne; he
belonged to the age which denied scholasticism: but it was in the

---

[38] *The Conquest of Granada*, I, III, 511–15.
[39] *The Indian Emperor*, II, i, 12.
[40] *Aureng-Zebe*, II, 298–9. [41] *Op. cit.*, II, 86–9.
[42] *Religio Laici*, 1. Kinsley, Vol. I, p. 311.
[43] *The Hind and the Panther*, I, 73–5. Kinsley, Vol. II, p. 472.

scholastic world that his mind had been formed. His metaphysical images are flavoured by the current materialist beliefs. In some seventeenth century philosophies the soul was denied altogether, or dubiously located in a gland. For Hobbes, man was "matter in motion". (Dryden uses this phrase in the passage, quoted above, on the Dissenters.) Dryden was probably never seriously a materialist, but materialism exerted a profound influence on him; more on his sensibility, perhaps, than on his thought. It appealed to his temperament, it fed his cynicism, and the idea of "matter" was one on which his imagination could work. Seventeenth-century materialism by itself was not likely to inspire poetry of any kind. In Dryden's case it operated as a stimulus, as a modifying influence, on a mind already formed by scholastic thought. There was a piquancy for him in the contrast between the two worlds of ideas.

The attitude to life which finds expression in Dryden's poetry is not easy to sum up briefly. The word "cynicism" does not describe it satisfactorily, though one is driven to use it in the absence of a more exact expression. His negative comments on life often convey rather the equanimity of one who has absorbed discouraging experiences and remains fundamentally on good terms with himself and with the world. There is a certain ironical deliberateness in his acceptance of lower levels. Since materialism, the denial of spiritual values, was what his age had to offer, he asserted it with marked, almost malicious, emphasis. Two ideas, opposite in tendency, seem to come together in his poetry: the comic impotence of spiritual values, and the comic grossness of materialism.

In referring to human beings as misconceived, comic abortions, monstrosities of matter without soul, Dryden was not, of course, stating a philosophy. It was simply an idea which pleased him, and stimulated his imagination. The grotesque images are often applied to persons whom it was legitimate to present as absurd or distorted; or they are used in the speeches of comic characters to convey their debased views of life or of their fellow creatures. It is the Emperor, not Dryden, who describes the people as a "scarce animated clod". Everywhere Dryden is protected by his context, and this gives him a strategic advantage. He indulges his delight in thinking ignobly of the soul without committing himself to a view of the nature of man; and, of course, it is only a certain side of him which is expressed in such a view.

The play of attitudes conveyed in his "body-matter-soul" imagery has something of the value of a criticism of life, which we may apply to the life of Dryden's epoch. As was remarked earlier, it was an age of contrasts: on the one hand, the cultivation of splendour; on the other, a marked tendency towards the prosaic. To appreciate the former we must keep in mind certain continental developments which are not fully paralleled in England, but which had their influence on the English sensibility: the glorification of despotism and the brilliance of Baroque art.

The courtly and aristocratic life which Dryden saw around him must have had its dubious features. Smoke from the glass factories filled the rooms of palaces, the King was disgracefully short of money, politics could descend to the indignity of a Titus Oates. Temperamentally a Royalist, Dryden seems sometimes to be merely humouring the pretensions of monarchy or taking a half-satirical pleasure in its undesirable or foolish aspects. In his exploitation of "Baroque" values, (*Alexander's Feast* is a good example) there is a jovial abandon which suggests he did not take them altogether seriously. He responded positively to his age, with its love of display and its cult of heroism, but he was aware that in it man had suffered another fall, a grotesque one: the philosophers were looking for his soul and could not find it.

Primarily through his imagery, then, Dryden succeeded in evolving an imaginative approach to his rather intractable environment. The theme of "matter", the common factor in human glory and human dullness or baseness, linked the contrasting elements of Restoration life together in his imagination. In this way he was able to make the materials of his age available to poetry, and adjust poetry to the limitations of his age.

There is an important difference between the rhymed heroic plays and *All for Love*.[44] Of the former it may be said that their seriousness is always modified by the presence, or the lurking possibility, of some non-serious element. They are not, in fact, really serious. It is characteristic that Aureng-Zebe's reflexions on death ("Distrust

---

[44] I have discussed *Don Sebastian* and some later plays in "All, all of a piece throughout" in *Restoration Theatre*, ed. J. R. Brown and B. Harris, *Stratford-upon-Avon Studies* 6 (1965) pp. 159–76.

and darkness of a future state") should be entirely lacking in emotional or intellectual importance, so that there is a smooth transition to veiled comedy when Nourmahal appears with her incestuous intentions. This deliberate limitation of seriousness, the reduction of beauty to prettiness, the exclusion of disturbing elements, sometimes have an ironical value in Dryden: things are made pleasing which ought to be more than pleasing, and this is a subtle way of debasing them. Dryden had only a limited capacity for seriousness, and was most at ease in works where seriousness could be modified and adulterated. But sometimes he tried to rise above himself and produce something unequivocally serious. This was his object in *All for Love*. Writing this play meant suppressing much that is piquant in his art. We cannot say that it was untypical of Dryden to do this; on the contrary, it was in keeping with his character that he should try to get away sometimes from his own ironical, sceptical temperament. A few passages, here and there, with the "body-soul" theme may be noted in *All for Love*:

> Poor I was made
> Of that course matter which, when she was finish'd,
> The Gods threw by for rubbish.[45]

> He was a Bastard of the Sun, by *Nile*,
> Ap'd into Man; with all his Mother's Mud
> Crusted upon his Soul.[46]

> And this you see, a lump of sensless Clay,
> The leavings of a Soul.[47]

The magnificence is flavoured by a "gigantesque" touch:

> Suppose me come from the *Phlegraean* Plains,
> Where gasping Gyants lay, cleft by my Sword:
> And Mountain tops par'd off each other blow, –
> To bury those I slew: receive me, goddess:
> Let *Caesar* spread his subtile Nets, like Vulcan;
> In thy embraces I would be beheld
> By Heav'n and Earth at once,
> And make their envy what they meant their sport.

[45] *All for Love*, III, 458–60.   [46] *Op. cit.,* V, 175–7.   [47] *Op. cit.,* V, 468–9.

Let those who took us blush; I would love on
With awful State, regardless of their frowns,
As their superior god.[48]

3

It was mainly in the heroic plays that Dryden developed the imagery which forms, as it were, the nucleus of his poetic conception of life, and the nucleus of his satire, in so far as his satire is a thing of the imagination. His superiority in satire over his predecessors lies mainly in his large approach to his material and complete imaginative adjustment to it. The world of politics is in many respects a little world, full of confusing details. Marvell, for the most part, was unable to rise above this littleness and confusion. His *Last Instructions to a Painter* is composed chiefly of obscure references to insignificant people and their forgotten deeds. But viewed in another light it is a world in which the imagination can expand; if not with images of real greatness, at least with those of inflated self-importance, over-weening ambition, and egregious roguery. Dryden's imagination learnt to respond to such conceptions in the heroic plays.

It is interesting to see how Dryden's characteristic imagery appears, in modified form, in his religious poems. There are some passages of unqualified seriousness in *The Hind and the Panther*, but one of the great virtues of this poem is that Dryden does not pretend to be any more spiritual than he is. After a moving statement of unworthiness and penitence ("Thy throne is darkness in the abyss of light") he is able quite naturally to make the transition to earthier levels of feeling, at which the objects of his satire are seen in the old grotesque terms. And his comic imagery is liable to be present even in his treatment of serious religious themes. As with heroism so with religion Dryden's attitudes are ambivalent. It was through the fideistic apologetics that he was converted,[49] which means that reason capitulated to faith: the desperate short cut for a nature fundamentally rather sceptical and unspiritual. In moods of submission and penitence he confesses

[48] *Op. cit.,* III, 14–24.
[49] L. I. Bredvold's *The Intellectual Milieu of John Dryden,* Ann Arbor, Mich. (1934) is illuminating on this point.

D

his unspirituality as a defect: but, as a reaction after such moods, it was natural that his mind and imagination should be pulled in another direction, towards the old world of habits. His solution to this mental situation was that of a true metaphysical poet: he pulled his religion after him, and made it accommodate itself to those habits. He achieved, as it were, a sort of revenge against religion for being difficult and mysterious, by making it almost grossly palpable, and by introducing a suggestion of travesty. But it was a pleasant revenge, and only to be regarded as a witty indulgence:

> One portion of informing fire was giv'n
> To Brutes, th' inferiour family of heav'n:
> The Smith divine, as with a careless beat,
> Struck out the mute creation at a heat:
> But, when arriv'd at last to humane race,
> The god-head took a deep consid'ring space:
> And, to distinguish man from all the rest,
> Unlock'd the sacred treasures of his breast . . .[50]

Here the creation of man is treated soberly, the comic imagery being transferred to the creation of the brutes. But the imaginative link is with his old comic conception of man's creation or generation. There is a suggestion of violence in the following image, contrasting with the solemnity of the theme:

> Can they who say the Host should be descry'd
> By sense, define a body glorify'd?
> Impassible, and penetrating parts?
> Let them declare by what mysterious arts
> He shot that body through th'opposing might
> Of bolts and barrs impervious to the light,
> And stood before his train confess'd in open sight.[51]

It is characteristic that he should round off a serious, even poignant, expression of faith with a robustly unspiritual image:

> Rest then, my soul, from endless anguish freed;
> Nor sciences thy guide, nor sense thy creed.

[50] *The Hind and the Panther*, i, 251–8. Kinsley, Vol. ii, p. 476.
[51] *Op. cit.,* i, 93–9. Vol. ii, p. 472.

Faith is the best ensurer of thy bliss;
The Bank above must fail before the venture miss.[52]

Typical of his delight in reducing mental processes to absurdity is the following:

Perhaps the *Martyn*, hous'd in holy ground,
Might think of Ghosts that walk their midnight round,
Till grosser atoms tumbling in the stream
Of fancy, madly met and clubb'd into a dream.[53]

In the passage where he compares the Church of Rome with the Church of England from the point of view of effectiveness in dealing with heretics[54] we have an entertaining transition from the serious to the serio-comic and thence to the comic. The Church of Rome is described with images of solid, palpable splendour ("Entire, one solid shining Diamond"), but in the fight with the heretics there is an element of the gigantesque, with the habitual slight suggestion of comedy. In the description of the "Egyptian Sorcerers", with their majestic ineffectiveness, we are back in the atmosphere of the heroic plays.

His characteristic imagery occasionally appears in his translations, which were the work of the last years of his life. Sometimes he goes beyond his original to introduce a favourite idea; for example, in the fifth and sixth lines of the following passage, for which there is no warrant in Persius's satire, we have the theme of majesty comically associated with inertia and a reference to "fate" as the hardworking subordinate of a lazy Jupiter:

He'll stare, and O, Good *Jupiter!* will cry;
Can'st thou indulge him in this Villany!
And think'st thou, *Jove* himself, with patience then,
Can hear a Pray'r condemn'd by wicked men?
That, void of Care, he lolls supine in state,
And leaves his Bus'ness to be done by Fate?
Because his Thunder splits some burly Tree,
And is not darted at thy House and Thee?[55]

---

[52] *Op. cit.*, i, 146–9. Vol. ii, pp. 473–4.
[53] *Op. cit.*, iii, 513–6. Vol. ii, pp. 516–17.
[54] *Op. cit.*, ii, 526 *ff.* Vol. ii, pp. 498 *ff.*
[55] *Second Satire of Persius* ii, 43–50, 22–5 orig. Kinsley, Vol. ii, pp. 753–4.

The first book of *Metamorphoses*, in which an account is given of the beginning of things, offered him a number of opportunities to indulge his amused view of the universe, by adding his own flavour to Ovid's descriptions.

These metaphysical effects in Dryden bear a distinct resemblance to some of those in Pope which Dr Leavis has described so well in his essay in *Revaluation*. Pope also has his grotesque images of the soul. The majestic portentousness of the Bentley passage (*Dunciad* IV) is reminiscent of those places in Dryden where grandeur is modified by absurdity; and the mixed effect of dirtiness and prettiness in the Sporus portrait is an example of a similar poetic principle. In both writers this imagery represents an adjustment of the comic imagination, but also of the poetic imagination, to the materials of their age. In both, wit is accompanied by a precise sense of the limits within which, in that age, certain kinds of modifications of seriousness could be achieved. Dr Leavis has underestimated a little Dryden's place in the "line of wit" and Pope's indebtedness to him in this connexion.

II. THE POETRY

Arthur W. Hoffman

AN APPRENTICESHIP IN PRAISE[1]

As Mark Van Doren remarks in his influential survey of Dryden's poetry, "no critic has felt that he could afford to commend Dryden in general without proving that he had taken into account the worst of him in particular."[2] There is, however, something defensive and seemingly ungenerous about such a procedure, though a critic must establish his own credit in order to establish the credit of the poet. The procedure may seem to be at odds with Dryden's own conception that critics are properly the defenders of poets and the main business of the critic is to exhibit the excellences of the poet. Yet it is certain that to understand Dryden's excellences we must explore his variousness, confronting that variety when it is sad as well as when it is rich and happy. Dryden was, as Congreve remarked, an improving poet to the last, and many of his later improvements are achieved by setting earlier mediocrities in a new key or transposing a vain extravagance into a new context where it is filled with meaning.

The circumstance that Dryden began as a poet in an extended series of poems of compliment, many of them addressed to rulers of state and to major public events, is of the first importance as a groundwork for his subsequent development. In 1649 he produced his elegy *Upon the Death of the Lord Hastings*; in 1650 his complimentary lines *To John Hoddesdon, on His Divine Epigrams*; in 1658 his *Heroique Stanzas to the Glorious Memory of Cromwell*; in 1660 *Astraea Redux*, celebrating the return of Charles II; in the same year the complimentary poem *To My Honored Friend, Sir*

---

[1] [Reprinted from *John Dryden's Imagery*, Gainesville (University of Florida Press) 1962, pp. 1–19.]

[2] *John Dryden: A Study of His Poetry*, 3rd edn. New York, 1946, p. 30.

Robert Howard; in 1661 *To His Sacred Majesty, a Panegyrick on His Coronation*; in 1662 *To My Lord Chancellor*, celebrating the statesmanship of Edward Hyde, Earl of Clarendon; in the same year a complimentary epistle *To My Honored Friend, Dr. Charleton*; probably in 1663 the lines addressed *To the Lady Castlemaine, upon Her Incouraging His First Play*; and in 1666 (published 1667) *Annus Mirabilis: The Year of Wonders, 1666*, a poem that considerably exceeds the frame of the usual poems of compliment but that is important in this series for its attempt to bring king and people together within the same focus of compliment.

Under the lengthened shadow of Dr Johnson's well-known strictures on obsequious flattery of the great, it has been more the custom to deplore the motives than to explore the style and content of these poems. Dr Johnson, in a characteristically pungent passage, managed at once to acknowledge and to lament Dryden's facility in this vein

> . . . in the meanness and servility of hyperbolical adulation I know not whether, since the days in which the Roman emperors were deified, he has been ever equalled, except by Afra Behn in an address to Eleanor Gwyn. When once he has undertaken the task of praise he no longer retains shame in himself, nor supposes it in his patron. As many odoriferous bodies are observed to diffuse perfumes from year to year without sensible diminution of bulk or weight, he appears never to have impoverished his mint of flattery by his expences, however lavish. He had all forms of excellence, intellectual and moral, combined in his mind, with endless variation; and when he had scattered on the hero of the day the golden shower of wit and virtue, he had ready for him, whom he wished to court on the morrow, new wit and virtue with another stamp. Of this kind of meanness he never seems to decline the practice, or lament the necessity: he considers the great as entitled to encomiastick homage, and brings praise rather as a tribute than a gift, more delighted with the fertility of his invention than mortified by the prostitution of his judgment. It is indeed not certain that on these occasions his judgment much rebelled against his interest. There are minds which easily sink into submission, that look on

grandeur with undistinguishing reverence, and discover no defect where there is elevation of rank and affluence of riches.[3]

It seems proper to urge a discrimination of the biographical judgments involved in Johnson's comments. It is difficult at our distance in time to judge Dryden's motives, and the motives are inessential to a judgment of the poetry. If the poetry offers lines that are sounding brass or tinkling cymbal, we may well discover their hollowness by confronting them squarely without resort to the indirection of biographical inference. Men with the best motives in the world have written execrable poetry, and that men with execrable motives may yet write well is an unpalatable fact that critics must swallow in their progress towards familiarity with what W. H. Auden calls "the treason of all clerks". In his poem *In Memory of W. B. Yeats*, Auden puts the point succinctly:

> Time that is intolerant
> Of the brave and innocent,
> And indifferent in a week
> To a beautiful physique,
>
> Worships language and forgives
> Everyone by whom it lives;
> Pardons cowardice, conceit,
> Lays its honours at their feet.[4]

The earliest poem in the series of complimentary pieces, the elegy *Upon the Death of the Lord Hastings*, is comparatively free from the tincture of suspect motives of policy and advantage. It is, it should be remembered, a schoolboy's poem, and the conjecture is reasonable that it was produced, along with other poems by Westminster boys that appeared in the Hastings volume, under the direction of the famous master, Dr Busby. The poems by Dryden's schoolfellows were in Latin and imitated Latin models. Dryden's poem, in English, is altogether more ambitious, and

[3] *Lives of the Poets*, ed. G. B. Hill, 3 vols, Oxford, 1905, I, pp. 399–400.
[4] *The Collected Poetry of W. H. Auden*. New York (Random House) 1945. The phrase "the treason of all clerks" occurs in the last line of the next to last stanza of "At the Grave of Henry James" (p. 130); the quoted stanzas are the second and third of the third part of the poem (p. 50).

Busby was apparently willing, with some natural granted and expected allowance, to have it stand beside the work of Denham, Marvell, Herrick, and Brome. The formal plan and capacity of the poem have been admirably set forth by Miss Ruth Wallerstein, who, after careful study of all the poems in the Hastings volume, finds Dryden's elegy no mean production, even in such company. Miss Wallerstein remarks: ". . . he shows a far deeper sense of the elegy as a formal genre than anyone who wrote for the King volume except Milton, and than any other contributors to the Hastings volume except Denham and Herrick and Marvell." Later she said: "Dryden's *Hastings* has not the personal and emotional tone to win our interest as does, say, Shelley's early poetry: but in scope, in ordnance, in its selections and rejections, in its wonderful sense of artistic purpose, it is the prophecy of a major poet and of a new age."[5] Miss Wallerstein recognises that the poem is callow and in some ways naïvely imitative, revealing in its stiffness that the poetic talent here displayed is only beginning to exercise itself. But she is not led astray into fixed contemplation of certain faults of style, which have stuck in the eyes of many earlier critics. Dr Johnson, of course, boggled at the conceits of the poem, especially those having to do with smallpox. Scott, in one motion, recognised and deplored the antecedents of some of the stylistic features of the poem which he calls ". . . a servile imitation of the conceits of Cleveland and the metaphysical wit of Cowley, exerted in numbers hardly more harmonious than those of Donne".[6]

The poem has drawn fire not only from Scott but also from Mark Van Doren for its tunelessness. Van Doren says: 'Metrically it was chaos. Gray remarked to Mason that it seemed the work of a man who had no ear and might never have any."[7] With respect to the conceits and with respect to metrics there are some observations to be made not more out of charity than out of simple fairness. A poet of eighteen does not usually invent at one blow a new style; he employs the style or styles available to him.

[5] Ruth Wallerstein, *Studies in Seventeenth-Century Poetic*, Madison (University of Wisconsin Press) 1950, pp. 115–42.

[6] *The Works of John Dryden*, ed. Sir Walter Scott, revised and corrected by George Saintsbury, 18 vols. Edinburgh, 1882–93, XI, p. 93.

[7] *John Dryden*, p. 81.

Dryden did not originate the bad conceit; he adopted a conceited style that had reached the stage of decay. He did not have to invent his conceits on smallpox. Cartwright had written on the subject of smallpox, and other elegists of Hastings, as Miss Wallerstein points out, found the topic inevitable and went at it in the received style. Needham wrote:

> Those eyes which Hymen hop'd should light his Torch,
> Aethereal flames of Fevers now do scorch,
> And *envious Pimples* too dig Graves apace,
> To bury all the Glories of his face.[8]

Charles Cotton wrote:

> Bathe him in Tears, till there appear no trace
> Of those sad Blushes in his lovely face:
> Let there be in't of Guilt no seeming sence,
> Nor other Colour then of Innocence.[9]

The roughness of Dryden's numbers is, as Scott recognised, not without example. A comparable roughness can be found in many passages of Donne's *Anniversaries*. There is something about the method by which Dryden's poem moves that imitates a characteristic method of Donne's, and there is something about that method of movement that entails roughness. The method is interrogative and argumentative, querying and postulating, lead-ing up to conceits by way of questions, using the conceits as postulates and deriving corollaries. A pseudo logic is developed to force the reader to follow the conceit, and since the primary objective of the poet is to tie the mind of the reader effectively to the development and progress of the conceit, no exterior consider-ations of tuneful harmony or smooth movement can enter it; the only appropriate harmony in such poetry is one which does not get in the way of but enforces the conceit. Metre is cast upon a Procrustean bed, wracked and torn, and is most whole when most torn provided only that the conceit itself justifies the torture. It is perfectly clear that Dryden's conceit – and, we may add, the conceit as Dryden received it – seldom justifies the torture:

[8] Quoted by Wallerstein, p. 126.
[9] *Ibid.*

Was there no milder way but the Small Pox,
The very Filth'ness of *Pandora's* Box?
So many Spots, like *næves*, our *Venus* soil?
One Jewel set off with so many a Foil?
Blisters with pride swell'd; which th'row's flesh did sprout
Like Rose-buds, stuck i' th' Lily-skin about.
Each little Pimple had a Tear in it,
To wail the fault its rising did commit:
Who, Rebel-like, with their own Lord at strife,
Thus made an Insurrection 'gainst his Life.
Or were these Gems sent to adorn his Skin,
The Cab'net of a richer Soul within?[10]

The point to be made here is that the conceited metaphysical style at its best is closely allied to a very special and domineering treatment of metrics. If one grants that the metaphysical style was irretrievably sinking under the sheer weight of too many bad conceits, then one must concede that the *raison d'être* of a particular treatment of metrics was disappearing. In Dryden's progress as a poet, the rejection of the conceit and the rejection of harsh numbers went hand in hand.

Before leaving the subject of Dryden's metrics in this poem and proceeding to consideration of the poem as opening the vein of compliment, I want to include a suggestion offered by Miss Wallerstein because it is pertinent not only to this poem but also to subsequent developments in Dryden's early poetry which this study attempts to shed some light on:

> It is true that the versification lacks that resonance which "fortune rarely gives the young". But Scott, reading it with an ear attuned to the heroic couplet, saw only its defect. To me the rhythm suggests a probable attempt to mediate between speech rhythms and the formal movement of the new couplet. If so, it follows Denham, and it is Dryden's first try at the principle which was to create his great verse.[11]

When one considers this elegy's method of creating its focus

---

[10] *Upon the Death of the Lord Hastings*, 53–64. *The Poems of John Dryden*, ed. James Kinsley, Oxford (Clarendon Press) 1958, Vol. 1, p. 2.
[11] Wallerstein, pp. 135–6.

of praise, one notices, of course, the employment of conceit and paradox to define and elevate the figure at the centre of the poem. But besides the familiar Donnian method of "proving" the tremendous consequences of a death and thereby establishing the magnitude and quality of the deceased, there is a parallel procedure, or the beginning of a parallel procedure. Mixed in with the paradoxical method there are the materials of a more straightforward substantiation of the focus of praise:

> O had he di'd of old, how great a strife
> Had been, who from his Death should draw their Life?
> Who should, by one rich draught, become what ere
> *Seneca, Cato, Numa, Cæsar*, were:
> Learn'd, Vertuous, Pious, Great; and have by this
> An universal *Metempsuchosis*.[12]

The alignment of a series of classical exemplars of qualities which in the next line are enumerated in a parallel series is here subsumed within the conceit of metempsychosis, a conceit familiar in Donne, but the foundation is laid in the neat ranking and equation for an analogic structure independent of the conceit, and the later Dryden is full of allusive analogies to classical figures which, without the schoolboyish enumeration of the appropriate qualities, make the name serve as a compact metaphor of a quality, and link the name by overt simile to the particular focus of praise. The classical names become, for Dryden, designations of the many provinces in the moral realm, and the full range of ethical discriminations is ordered by way of the models. Theological figures and conceits, such as the one which in the passage above embraces the ethical evaluation, are suppressed, and the appearance of theology or metaphysics in a poem comes to be managed in a different fashion.

The Hastings elegy makes it clear that Dryden, at this stage, was uncertain about the couplet. His uncertainty persisted for some time and expressed itself in several experiments in quatrains, testing the usefulness of the example offered by Davenant's *Gondibert*. As a result, we have Dryden's *Heroique Stanzas* (for Cromwell) and his *Annus Mirabilis* in quatrains. It seems probable, though not strictly demonstrable, that uncertainty about the conceit and uncertainty about the couplet went hand in hand and

[12] *Upon the Death of the Lord Hastings*, 67–72. Kinsley, Vol. 1, p. 2.

were quite significantly related. In the Hastings elegy he was employing the couplet at one remove from Donne's manner and at several removes from his own ultimate practice. Donne sometimes concluded a movement with a heavily end-stopped first line of a couplet and began anew with the second line. This Dryden did not do in his elegy, but most of the other devices for tailoring the verse to the measure of the conceit Dryden did follow. He employed run-over lines casting a word into a distinct, emphatic prominence at the beginning of the second line:

> Must all these ag'd Sires in one Funeral
> Expire?[13]

He hammered out lines in which the stresses wrestled down the iambic norm while the words themselves, common words, were deliberately played at tug-of-war with the dignified, solemn side of the elegy's complex of feeling and tone, producing a not very happy version of the metaphysical inclusion of extremes of language and feeling:

> Must Drunkards, Lechers, spent with Sinning, live
> With such helps as Broths, Possits, Physick give?
> None live, but such as should die?[14]

He employed sentence structures that listened to a drum different from that heard by the line or couplet. He even ended a sentence and started another in the middle of a line, as Donne sometimes did, and generally made grammatical divisions disruptive of line and couplet:

> Must *Vertue* prove *Death's* Harbinger? Must She,
> With him expiring, feel Mortality?
> Is *Death* (Sin's wages) Grace's now? shall Art
> Make us more Learned, onely to depart?
> If Merit be Disease, if Vertue Death;
> To be Good, Not to be; who'd then bequeath
> Himself to Discipline? Who'd not esteem
> Labour a Crime, Study Self-murther deem?[15]

> But that transcends thy skill; thrice happie all,
> Could we but prove thus Astronomical.[16]

---

[13] *Op. cit.* 73–4, p. 2.   [14] *Op. cit.,* 85–7, p. 3.
[15] *Op. cit.,* 5–12, p. 1.   [16] *Op. cit.,* 41–2, p. 2.

He is far from any steady idea of a studied use of caesura to exploit the various balances of a line, and, of course, farther still from the interanimation of half-lines within a full, complex, formally structured couplet. Now and again, perhaps, the conceited manner is employed with a stiff neatness that suggests the conciseness and compactness of lines in some of Dryden's later couplets:

> Beauty and Learning thus together meet,
> To bring a *Winding* for a *Wedding-sheet*?[17]

> The Nations sin hath drawn that Veil, which shrouds
> Our Day-spring in so sad benighting Clouds.[18]

But he is not trying to achieve any sustained or frequent effects of balance or antithesis, and the ironies and distinctions as well as the accumulation and power of his later couplets can scarcely be anticipated here.

Almost ten years later in the *Heroique Stanzas* to Cromwell Dryden wrote quatrains (rhymed *abab*) of astonishing smoothness. As Mark Van Doren remarks: "In this poem . . . Dryden wielded with positive assurance a mighty line which was much his own."[19] The evidence all but compels acceptance of Van Doren's conjecture that the intervening period must have been devoted to a good deal of practice in verse. Neither the lines to Hoddesdon (1650) nor those to Honor Dryden (1655) prepare us for the competence of the *Heroique Stanzas*. I am not sure, as Professor Van Doren seems to be, that we need to suppose a great *variety* of experiment, but to do without the supposition of very considerable poetic practice seems difficult. Of course, we must remember the element of deliberation in the rough metre of the Hastings elegy; Dryden did not there choose to show how smoothly and yet powerfully he could handle a line, but wrote purposefully rugged verse in a received style. We must not fall into the error of seeing a sheer difference in competence where the issue is complicated by a deliberate difference in style and method.

The conceit appears in the *Heroique Stanzas*, but remarkably tempered and subdued – subdued, that is, to the verse pattern. The striking feature here is the frequent successful employment of the method of overt analogy, the appropriate, carefully cut and

[17] *Op. cit.*, 3–4, p. 1. [18] *Op. cit.*, 49–50, p. 2. [19] *John Dryden*, p. 82.

limited, but finely illuminating comparison. First, to illustrate what is now happening to the conceit, we may consider an example such as that in the twenty-seventh stanza:

> When such *Heröique Vertue* Heav'n sets out,
> The Starrs like *Commons* sullenly obey;
> Because it draines them when it comes about,
> And therefore is a taxe they seldome pay.[20]

The conceit here is swiftly and economically generated, developed, and completed. The short simile, *like Commons*, quickly introduces the full spread of the conceit, yoking the astronomical to the political figure, and *taxe* in the last line intensifies by its specification the extravagance implicit in the conceit. The conceit, however, does not dominate the verse structure; the stanza that presents the conceit retains its integrity. The syntactical structure employed to present the conceit is so contrived that each verse line carries a straightforward and distinct part of the statement: statement, consequence, explanation of consequence, conclusion (*When*, first line; [*then*], second line; *Because*, third line; *therefore*, fourth line). The fluidity and sustained movement of this quatrain are prophetic; they are virtues effectively capitalised when Dryden attains his matured couplet style.

The smooth management of the full-dress conceit is important, but more important in the general movement of the poem is the easy but apt analogy, either empirical or conventional. There are a great many of these similes, varying in length from the minimal two words to two lines. The poem gets under way with one of these figures in its opening stanza:

> And now 'tis time; for their Officious haste,
> Who would before have born him to the sky,
> Like *eager Romans* ere all Rites were past
> Did let too soon the *sacred Eagle* fly.[21]

Another simile, in the sixth stanza, illustrates the smooth accommodation of the empirical and the traditional, gliding from the empirical image for wars to the conventional *sun* symbol of the ruler:

[20] *Heroique Stanzas*, 105–8. Kinsley, Vol. i, p. 11.
[21] *Op. cit.*, 1–4, p. 6.

And Warr's like mists that rise against the Sunne
Made him but greater seem, not greater grow.[22]

The figure is developed without impeding the verbal movement which remains clear and strong. The same sustained verbal movement can be seen in the two comparisons in the thirteenth stanza:

Swift and resistlesse through the Land he past
Like that bold *Greek* who did the East subdue;
And made to battails such Heroick haste
As if on wings of victory he flew.[23]

Variety and fertility characterise the images applied to Cromwell, variety rather than managed pattern. A partial clue to the imagery of the poem is provided in the initial suggestion of a Roman apotheosis. Much of the imagery and illustration that follow is drawn from classical figures and customs, both Greek and Roman, and the astronomical comparisons, of which there are quite a few, seem to be initiated and prepared for by the ceremonial apotheosis enskying the soul of the hero at the beginning.

Astraea Redux, less than two years later (1660), celebrating the return of Charles II, shows an important development in the application of imagery and allusion to praise. Indeed, the poem is in such a variety of ways significant of things to come that it is a convenient base for a number of illustrations looking toward Dryden's later technique.

The pungency of Dr. Johnson's attack on what he called Dryden's facility in flattery has perhaps drawn attention away from the fact that a structure of compliment can be a burden of obligation. The very excesses, the most ambitious flights of praise creating the heroic model, while they elevate the person praised to a lofty pinnacle, can have also the effect of exposing him. And Dryden, when he had brought the process of compliment to a certain altitude, liked suddenly to disclose that an atmosphere rarefied is also difficult to survive in and that the light of such a region, while it can create a transfiguring nimbus, can also search and probe with brilliant shafts. So, for example, what this poem has made of Charles' exile, a learning by suffering, is advanced as a commitment for the future:

[22] *Op. cit.,* 23–4, p. 7.   [23] *Op. cit.,* 49–52, p. 8.

E

Inur'd to suffer ere he came to raigne
No rash procedure will his actions stain.
To bus'ness ripened by digestive thought
His future rule is into Method brought.[24]

Just beneath the surface of compliment are perilous rocks upon which kings have foundered. The poem takes cognizance of the peculiar perils to the king of restoration after the kingless Commonwealth, restoration to a throne which the people had but recently discovered they had power to shake, and possibly these lines are also an implicit recognition of regal errors in the recent past. All this is carried off as a compliment, yet a real and present peril affecting the conduct of kingship at this particular juncture is being recognised, and just back of the veil of compliment the lines present a warning face.

A similar grave demand emerges from the light of compliment in a passage where the movement of praise is near its summit and powerfully ascending:

And welcome now (*Great Monarch*) to your own;
Behold th' approaching cliffes of *Albion*;
It is no longer Motion cheats your view,
As you meet it, the Land approacheth you.
The Land returns, and in the white it wears
The marks of penitence and sorrow bears.
But you, whose goodness your discent doth show,
Your Heav'nly Parentage and earthly too;
By that same mildness which your Fathers Crown
Before did ravish, shall secure your own.
Not ty'd to rules of Policy, you find
Revenge less sweet then a forgiving mind.
Thus when th' Almighty would to *Moses* give
A sight of all he could behold and live;
A voice before his entry did proclaim
Long-suff'ring, Goodness, Mercy in his Name.
Your Pow'r to Justice doth submit your Cause,
Your Goodness only is above the Laws;
Whose rigid letter while pronounc'd by you
Is softer made. . . .[25]

---

[24] *Astraea Redux,* 87–90. Kinsley, Vol. 1, p. 18.
[25] *Op. cit.,* 250–69, pp. 22–3.

The passage is certainly not wanting in compliment, hyperbole, and the most honorific comparison. At the advent of the *Great Monarch* the land itself moves penitently toward him. The monarch is like God in the proclaimed virtues which herald his approach. But the virtues become conditions of the return. It is *goodness* that is the sign of the lineal and true king. It is *mildness* that will secure the throne. It is a time for *a forgiving mind* to rise superior to a mean and factional policy of revenge. God Himself, in His appearance to Moses, was proclaimed in terms of *Long-Suff'ring, Goodness, Mercy.* The king's power is represented as submitting itself to justice (and it is, after all, the return of Astraea which the poem has for its subject); it is the king's goodness, not the king's power that is above the laws. A king is a true king and god-like when his character tempers the severity rather than enforces the rigour of the laws. The whole pattern of compliment thus has a tempering and restricting undertone; even the conceit which puts the land's submission and penance at the extreme and seems to abase the people at the advent of the great monarch has this undertone:

As you meet it, the Land approacheth you.[26]

The conditional possibility latent in *As* perhaps reflects the fact that the King's return, thoroughly welcome though it was to almost all the strife-wearied people, was not besought by a grovelling popular submission but was based on terms. The Declaration of Breda, worked out by Clarendon, had made it possible for Charles to return without the assistance of foreign arms. The king moving toward the land and the land toward the king made an accurate image of the rapprochement. *Th' approaching cliffes of Albion* are white in token of penance, but as they are cliffs they may also carry the suggestion of the difficulties that attend monarchy in this realm.

The method of extending and at the same time limiting is to be remarked not only as applied to the character of the king, but also as applied to the narrative action in which the royal figure is engaged. Poetry, as Aristotle observed, differs from history; history is occupied with particulars, whereas the poetic account constitutes an action that is universal. This difference is clearly

26 *Op. cit.,* 253, p. 22.

visible in Dryden's poetry throughout his long career because his poetry is so frequently occasional and takes its rise from immediate historical events. Consequently the process of transmuting historical sequence into poetic action is a prominent feature of his poetry. It is the explicitness of the historical material that makes the process peculiarly visible, and there are occasions when the historical material is so bulky and unwieldy that it proves intransigent to the myth-making power with the result that the transmutation is never satisfactorily completed. Dryden did, however, develop an extraordinary ability to assimilate complex sequences and tangles of history; *Absalom and Achitophel* is an astonishing example of resourcefulness in turning history into myth. In *Astraea Redux* the outlines of the typical procedure may be observed.

There is, first, a titular myth – the return of the goddess of justice, Astraea brought back. In this case, the titular myth is classical. Second, the content of the myth as it is developed in the poem is both classical and Christian, or biblical. (In the case of *Absalom and Achitophel* the titular myth is biblical, the content both classical and Christian). The goddess of justice who resided on earth during the Saturnian golden age was driven out by the wickedness and impiety of the brazen and iron ages. As the constellation Virgo, the goddess with her sword and scales has taken her place in the heavens. The return of the goddess to earth will occur when, in the revolution of time, the golden age returns. Such a renewal of time had been attributed to the reign of Augustus, and Dryden completes the cycle in his poem by presenting the return of Charles as the beginning of a new Augustan age. The mythical fabric is enhanced with a variety of classical material, much of it fairly close to the myth of Astraea. So, for example, Charles' exile is compared to the flight of Jove, and the English rebellion becomes the revolt of the Titans in which "bold Typhoeus" violated heaven and forced Jove to flee. "The rabble" are compared, in their blindness, to the Cyclops, another of the giant brood. These classical materials are drawn principally from Virgil's *Fourth Eclogue*, or *Pollio*, from the sixth book of the *Aeneid*[27] from the first and thirteenth books of Ovid's *Metamorphoses*, and possibly from Hesiod's *Theogeny*. Virgil's

[27] In Dryden's translation, *Aeneis*, VI, 1073 *ff*. Kinsley, Vol. III, p. 1229.

Pollio is here, as so frequently in seventeenth-century and eighteenth-century treatments of the classical golden age, a crucial source because it is so closely analogous to the Christian Messianic tradition, and because the connexion had long been recognised not only as a literary parallel but as a mystical linking of Christian and classical Sibylline prophecy. The argument prefacing Dryden's translation of the *Pollio* concludes with this statement: "Many of the Verses are translated from one of the Sybils, who prophesie of our Saviour's Birth".[28] Accordingly Dryden's treatment of the cyclical myth of the golden age is conventional in its admission of Christian material. For the phase of banishment Dryden uses Astraea's and Jove's exiles as the classical analogues of Charles' exile, and for the biblical analogues he uses David's exile, and Adam's banishment from paradise:

> Thus banish'd *David* spent abroad his time,
> When to be Gods Anointed was his Crime.[29]

> Such is not *Charles* his too too active age,
> Which govern'd by the wild distemper'd rage
> Of some black Star infecting all the Skies,
> Made him at his own cost like *Adam* wise.[30]

Dryden's account of the return, filled with the millenary suggestions of the *Pollio*, becomes quite explicitly Messianic in its imagery, employing a celestial omen that Charles' contemporaries had connected with him as the pivot on which to turn to a strong allusion to the birth of Christ, the Saviour and the divine King:

> That Star that at your Birth shone out so bright
> It stain'd the duller Suns Meridian light,
> Did once again its potent Fires renew
> Guiding our eyes to find and worship you.[31]

A more explicitly Messianic passage is the following:

> Heav'n would no bargain for its blessings drive
> But what we could not pay for, freely give.

[28] Kinsley, Vol. ii, p. 887.
[29] *Astraea Redux*, 79–80. Kinsley, Vol. i, p. 18.
[30] *Op. cit.*, 111–14, p. 19.
[31] *Op. cit.*, 288–91, p. 23.

The Prince of Peace would like himself confer
A gift unhop'd without the price of war.
Yet as he knew his blessings worth, took care
That we should know it by repeated pray'r;
Which storm'd the skies and ravish'd *Charles* from thence
As Heav'n it self is took by violence.[32]

The sequence of the mythical action is supported by a pattern of imagery. The initial scene of disorder is presented by "black Clouds", furious "Winds", "Stiff gales", "some black Star infecting all the Skies". The restoration of order is characterised by the dispersion of "Those Clouds that overcast your Morne"; the winds now calmed and, in their joy and submission, even too faint; the star of Charles' birth renewing its fires; the land, returning, wearing white; and "times whiter series . . . / Which in soft Centuries shall smoothly run". Not only the extreme conditions, but also the transition from one to the other is reflected in the imagery and managed with special adroitness in two passages:

Well might the Ancient Poets then confer
On Night the honour'd name of *Counseller*,
Since struck with rayes of prosp'rous fortune blind
We light alone in dark afflictions find.[33]

Yet as wise Artists mix their colours so
That by degrees they from each other go,
Black steals unheeded from the neighb'ring white
Without offending the well cous'ned sight:
So on us stole our blessed change; while we
Th' effect did feel but scarce the manner see.
Frosts that constrain the ground, and birth deny
To flow'rs, that in its womb expecting lye,
Do seldom their usurping Pow'r withdraw,
But raging floods pursue their hasty thaw:
Our thaw was mild, the cold not chas'd away
But lost in kindly heat of lengthned day.[34]

This pattern of imagery is consistent with both classical and

[32] *Op. cit.,* 137–41, p. 19. [33] *Op. cit.,* 93–6, p. 18.
[34] *Op. cit.,* 125–36, p. 19.

Christian models. The storms and the black star are close to the tempests and black fire of Virgil's *Aeneid*; black fire is fire that comes from below and is contrasted by Virgil to the flashing fire of Jove's thunderbolt that comes from above. Dryden affirms the suggestion of hellish dominion in the period of disorder by presenting also a Christian version of it; "Legion" is the image he uses for those who have possessed the "once sacred house". The allusion to Night as counsellor is classical and together with the reference to blindness may suggest the great exemplars of sight out of blindness, Tiresias and King Oedipus, but as the second passage develops the transition from black to white, from darkness to light, the change is capped with a Messianic allusion, and thus the Isaiahan prophecies are also drawn into the background. The title of the Messiah here is the Prince of Peace, which occurs in the sequence "Counselor . . . the Prince of Peace".[35] The imagery may derive its colour, then, from Isaiahan as well as classical shadings; the transition from dark to light, for example, is part of the Messianic vision: "The people that walked in darkness have seen a great light: they that dwell in the land of the shadow of death, upon them hath the light shined".[36] And the picture of the restored king's government, in its closeness to Virgil's *Pollio*, is also close to Isaiah; Dryden writes:

> Abroad your Empire shall no Limits know,
> But like the Sea in boundless Circles flow.[37]

Such lines are associated with a generalised prophetic strain; the prophet's version is familiar: "Of the increase of his government and peace there shall be no end."[38]

The whole pattern of classical and biblical allusion which creates the special myth of this poem ranges from very overt references to much more tacit correspondences and parallels. Since the more tacit sort of reference is so important to Dryden's poetic method throughout his career, it may be well to cite an additional example of this device. It has already been suggested that his general pattern of imagery supporting the mythical action can be paralleled in the *Aeneid*; the presentation of Charles, the chief actor,

[35] Isaiah 9: 6. [36] Isaiah 9: 2.
[37] *Astraea Redux*, 298–9. Kinsley, Vol. 1, p. 23.
[38] Isaiah 9: 7.

is also managed in a way to suggest occasionally the heroic figure of Aeneas. The section from line 43 to line 58 makes Charles a Roman figure, suffering for himself and his people, enduring with fortitude the vicissitudes of storms at sea. The amassing of details contributes to the effect, but the contour of the language clinches the suggestion:

> He toss'd by Fate, and hurried up and down,
> Heir to his Fathers Sorrows, with his Crown,
> Could tast no sweets of youths desired Age,
> But found his life too true a Pilgrimage.[39]

Toss'd by Fate echoes Virgilian language and constructions – *fato profugus* and *vi superum . . . iactatus* – that are the signature of Aeneas' trials by sea.[40]

Perhaps the most significant general conclusion that emerges from close attention to the imagery and diction of this early poem is that in his poems of compliment Dryden was, from the beginning, occupied with the accommodation of the classical and the Christian images of the hero. This problem of creating the hero along the lines of two traditions had been confronted by Chaucer in *The Knight's Tale*, by Spenser in *The Faerie Queene*, and was to be faced anew by Milton in *Paradise Lost*. The conceptions of the convergences and divergences of the two traditions varied from age to age and from poet to poet; in the seventeenth century Puritanism gave a new acuteness to the problem, and in Milton it is the sense of divergence that grows sharper and more insistent, with the result that instead of an accommodation of two heroic images there is, in *Paradise Lost*, supersession of an older heroic image by a new image of the Christian hero.[41]

It is interesting to find Dryden, much later in his career, in the dedication of his translation of Virgil, saying: "I must acknow-

---

[39] *Astraea Redux*, 51–4. Kinsley, Vol. 1, p. 17.

[40] The Aeneas-Charles parallel was drawn by Waller in a poem called *Of the Danger of his Majesty . . . Escaped*, 89–93, *The Poems of Edmund Waller*, ed. G. Thorn Drury, 2 vols. London ("The Muses Library") n.d., 1, pp. 1–7.

[41] This development in Milton's epic is perhaps analogous to the superseding of the older Homeric heroic image in Virgil's *Aeneid*. Amid the flames of Troy, in Book II of the *Aeneid*, Aeneas is torn loose from the older image of the hero and made to undertake the exploration and development of a new heroic meaning.

ledge that *Virgil* in Latine, and *Spencer* in English, have been my Masters."[42] The context of this expression of indebtedness suggests that Dryden was speaking primarily of a debt to Spenser in matters of versification, but it seems reasonable to suggest that his awareness of Spenser probably also included awareness of Spenser's way of accommodating the classical and Christian heroic images. It is, in fact, hard to imagine a seventeenth-century English poet aware of his tradition who would not be aware of the problem or who would not find that he had to work out his own ways of meeting the problem. It happened that Dryden met the problem early and frequently on the rather special ground of the poem of compliment addressed to public figures. Consequently it was public virtue of which he had to make the image. Besides the strong classical tradition which had developed the genre and continued strongly to influence its form, there was the fact that heroic images in the mould of chiefs of government were more easily drawn from classical than from Christian sources. On this ground – the ground of compliment to public leaders – it would have been hard to do without the classical traditions. What he could not easily do without, Dryden proceeded emphatically to do with, and probably the will behind this emphasis derives strength, and, in Dryden's case, more and more strength as time goes by, from royalism and anti-Puritanism. The hero is made in the classical as well as the Christian image as a way of disavowing the Puritan rejection of the classical tradition as fabulous, lying, and heathen. *Eikon Basilike* and the martyrology of Charles I were an affront to the Puritan spirit; they were idolatry. This idolatry, this powerful concentration of Christian symbolism upon the figure of the king flourished at the restoration of the martyred king's son. In the poems of compliment, classical imagery of the hero added paganism to idolatry and thus wrote the full royal signature. A rapprochement of classical and Christian, an emphatic mingling of the two in the royal presence, was an expression of the Cavalier spirit.

Much of what has been said here about *Astraea Redux* is anticipatory in mood, looking forward to subsequent developments. The features of this poem which identify it with the early stages of Dryden's development should be acknowledged.

[42] *The Dedication of the Aeneis*, Kinsley, Vol. III, p. 1048.

Attention certainly should be called to the way he manages couplets in this poem. The obtrusive conceit and the rough Donnian metres of the Hastings elegy have disappeared, but the influence of writing the *Heroique Stanzas* in quatrains in 1658 lingers on in the couplets of *Astraea Redux*. Frequently the unit of organisation from a syntactical point of view is quite domineeringly a unit of four lines in which only a mild pause occurs at the end of the first couplet.[43] Dryden has not yet learned to turn around within the strict confines of the couplet; he can do it, but not consistently, not steadily through a long performance. Six years later, in *Annus Mirabilis*, he yields explicitly to the quatrain form of organisation – and, with the expansion allowed for by the four-line organisation, there occurs a renewed efflorescence of the conceit. These hesitations, variations, and uncertainties in his early development are a partial explanation of the fact that Dryden never did completely commit himself to the couplet. He finally developed sanctioned forms to accommodate the tendency that he could not or would not eradicate. One form, for which he claimed Spenser's example, was the Alexandrine or hexameter conclusion of a couplet, and the other, frequently used with an Alexandrine final line, was the triplet. To the end of his career, he remained almost addicted to these devices of expansion. Often he used them powerfully and effectively. It seems a reasonable conjecture, at any rate, that the older Dryden's fondness for these devices had its roots in his early work as a poet, and that the overriding of the couplet in *Astraea Redux* was to be tamed and licensed but never extirpated. It became, in fact, an indulgence that Dryden enjoyed, and what Dryden enjoyed often made his best verse.

[43] For examples of this four-line organisation in *Astraea Redux*, see 1–20, 31–4, 51–4, 73–6, 111–14, 131–4, 141–4, 147–50, 153–6, 165–8, 195–8, 211–22, 276–9, 288–91.

Bruce King

ABSALOM AND ACHITOPHEL: A REVALUATION

Contrasting Dryden with Ben Jonson, F. R. Leavis says that whereas Jonson brings the life and manners of his time into relation with the ideal, Dryden has "no spiritual antennae" which would attune his sensibility to finer shades of feeling.[1] I think Leavis gives Dryden less credit than he deserves. *Absalom and Achitophel* is an almost perfect fusion of traditional Christian values and the poised, experienced urbanity which typifies the aristocratic court tradition. If Dryden's achievement has not been fully appreciated, it is because our knowledge of the poem's political occasion misdirects our response away from its imaginative patterns. *Absalom and Achitophel*, like many of the best Augustan satires, is an "anatomy", in which examples are related to a broad inclusive theme; it satirises a cast of mind, of which politics, behaviour and personalities are exemplifications; and it holds up other attitudes as models of correct social and moral conduct.

The main theme of *Absalom and Achitophel* might be described

---

[1] F. R. Leavis, *Revaluation*. London, 1962, p. 32. Leavis refers to Dryden's "pamphleteering verse" and "satiric pamphlets". I have found useful on *Absalom and Achitophel*: Morris Freedman, "Dryden's Miniature Epic", in *Journal of English and Germanic Philology*, LVII (1958) pp. 211–19; Barbara Kiefer Lewalski, "The Scope and Function of Biblical Allusion in *Absalom and Achitophel*", in *English Language Notes*, III (1965) pp. 29–35; Arthur W. Hoffman, *John Dryden's Imagery*, Gainesville (University of Florida Press) 1962, pp. 72–91; A. B. Chambers, "Absalom and Achitophel: Christ and Satan", in *Modern Language Notes*, LXXIV (1959) pp. 592–6; and parts of Bernard Schilling, *Dryden and the Conservative Myth*, New Haven (Yale University Press) 1961.

as the dangers of the imagination. Man is influenced by his
appetitive nature, which inflames his imagination and makes him
restless, ambitious, envious, and desirous of change. The spur to
such desires is pride. Adam, Eve, and Satan imagined that they
could improve their condition and as a result of such ambition
fell. Mankind since the fall has been particularly subject to the
dangers of the imagination:

> . . . when to sin our bias'd nature leans,
> The careful Devil is still at hand with means;
> And providently pimps for ill desires.[2]

Restlessness, fanaticism, and ambition destroy the moderate
contentment and happiness possible in this world, bring further
disquietudes, and are the causes of evil. Life is a test: "But life
can never be sincerely blest;/Heav'n punishes the bad, and proves
the best."[3] *Absalom and Achitophel* is organised around a contrast
between two ways of life. Extravagance, restlessness, ambition,
pride, intolerance, and zeal are contrasted with moderation, order,
tolerance, patience, humility, and forgiveness. The destructive is
contrasted with the fruitful; the disturbers of society contrasted
with the socially useful; cupidity contrasted with charity; evil
contrasted with good.

The way the anatomy works can be shown by the links between
images of mental processes and thematic motifs. Images of "headstrong", "moody", "murm'ring" align the Jews with the "warm
excesses" of Absalom and "turbulent" wit of Achitophel (in
contrast with David, indulgent and undisturbed). "Adam-wits"
telescopes man's essential condition throughout the ages. The
Jews are like Adam in misusing their freedom: but, as the ironic
allusion to the fortunate fall makes clear, they are also the descendants of Adam, capable of redemption but prone to sin: "These
Adam-wits, too fortunately free,/Began to dream they wanted
liberty."[4] "Wits" reminds us that the fall was caused by inordinate
ambition, and links original sin to the dangers of an over-imagi-
native mind throughout the ages. The Jews, Achitophel, Absalom
and Zimri are led into rebellion by delusions of the imagination.

---

[2] *Absalom and Achitophel*, 79–81. All quotations are from *The Poetical Works
of Dryden*, ed. George R. Noyes, Cambridge, Mass., 1950.

[3] *Op. cit.,* 43–4.   [4] *Op. cit.,* 51–2.

Such words as "dream", "desires", "thought", "humour", "wonder'd" are associated with rebellion and disobedience. The best of the malcontents "thought the pow'r of monarchy too much"; they are "mistaken men". Others "thought to get preferment", justify spoils by "inspiration", or are "dreaming saints"; Zimri is "ten thousand freaks that died in thinking". Absalom is "deluded", "impatient", and of high "hopes". The people "imagine a disease" and "murther monarchs for imagin'd crimes". Just as the Jebusites "were thought God's enemies" and the priests "think" it is their duty to make their religion prevail, so the Plot is "bad in itself, but represented worse".

An overactive mind is likely to be fired with delusions, and cause unnatural extremes of behaviour. Absalom's "warm excesses" are "purg'd by boiling o'er" in murder. He has "a spark too much of heavenly fire". His "soul disclaims the kindred of her earth". The Plot is "rais'd in extremes, and in extremes decried". Achitophel is a "fiery soul", a "daring pilot in extremity", "for a calm unfit", "pleas'd with the danger". Zimri rails and praises "in extremes". He is "over-violent, or over-civil". Such "wild desires" are a form of madness. Achitophel's great wit is "to madness near allied". Zimri is a "blest madman", the Sanhedrins are infected with "public lunacy" and share "the madness of rebellious times", "so high the madness grows".

Discontented, overactive minds cause social and moral anarchy. The Jews "thought they might ruin him they could create"; Achitophel "resolv'd to ruin or to rule the State"; "the triple bond he broke", "the pillars of the public safety shook". Achitophel's followers bend the "springs of property", and wind them so hard they "crack'd the government". The Enthusiasts "'gainst form and order . . . their pow'r imploy,/Nothing to build, and all things to destroy."[5] If they win, government "must fall". They are "engines bent,/ To batter down the lawful government."[6] They plot "to ruin Church and State". Absalom, like Samson, would "shake the column". Such anarchical instincts are in opposition to divine order. "No king could govern nor no God could please" the Jews. The Jebusites' gods are "disgrac'd, and burnt like common wood". The Jews "by natural instinct . . . change their lord". "God was their king, and God they durst depose".

[5] *Op. cit.*, 531–2.   [6] *Op. cit.*, 917–8.

Shimei "Heav'n's anointed dar'd to curse"; he declares "against the monarch of Jerusalem". The Jews would "make heirs for monarchs, and for God decree". They would "at once divine and human laws control". They try to "impose an heir upon the throne". "God cannot grant so much as they can crave".

In *Absalom and Achitophel* the persons and events are the immediate embodiment of a cosmic drama. They incarnate great archetypes which recur throughout history. They are related to their archetypes through broad analogies, local metaphors, allusion, imitative action, Christian symbolism, and other forms of correspondence. Often several moments of time are seen as symbolically equivalent. The narration utilises the Christian view of time which treats all history as recapitulatory of archetypal events.[7] *Absalom and Achitophel* shadows: the rebellion of Lucifer against God; the Creation of the world; the fall of Adam and Eve; major events in the Old Testament; the coming of the Messiah; and the triumph of God over His Adversary at the end of time. The ambiguous time scheme of the poem in which various ages are superimposed upon each other, and the continual flashbacks and jumps forward in time, are, like the narrative dislocations in *Paradise Lost*, an attempt to recreate imaginatively the simultaneity of all history, from the Creation to the Second Coming, as symbolically implicit within Genesis. *Absalom and Achitophel* imaginatively includes many ages of biblical history. The era could be before Aaron ("ere priestcraft"), before Moses ("no law denied"), or during the time of Abraham ("use of concubine and bride"). "Israel's monarch" could refer to David or to the Messiah.

The beginning of the poem involves a witty pun on the meaning of Genesis, *i.e.* generation. David is an easy-going, sensual monarch, promiscuous and indulgent. His reign is a Paradise recalling man's prelapsarian state before sin or law existed. Within this Paradise David is both like the God of Creation and Adam. The Genesis context is established with the first three words of the poem, "In pious times" recalling "In the beginning". David

---

[7] Expert guidance to traditional Christian imaginative habits can be found in: Arnold Williams, *The Common Expositor*, Chapel Hill, N.C., 1948; C. A. Patrides, *Milton and the Christian Tradition*, Oxford, 1966; Gordon Worth O'Brien, *Renaissance Poetics and the Problem of Power*, Chicago, 1956.

like the Holy Spirit at Creation "his vigorous warmth did variously impart". His relation to Absalom is in particular like that of God to Adam. David's procreation of Absalom is humorously described as "inspir'd by some diviner lust". He looks on beaming at his "image" and gives Absalom a bride. However, David is also like Adam at Creation, enjoying the promptings of instinct, scattering "his Maker's image thro' the land", and in a particularly important allusion is said to embody Adam's dominion over the earth, "wide as his command".

David is the embodiment of God's goodness and mercy. His indulgence and mildness[8] are in themselves an expression of divine love. He is merciful[9] and pardons those who have sinned against him.[10]

What millions has he pardon'd of his foes,
Whom just revenge did to his wrath expose?
Mild, easy, humble, studious of our good;
Enclin'd to mercy, and averse from blood;
If mildness ill with stubborn Israel suit,
His crime is God's beloved attribute.[11]

As a figure of divine love David takes on a Christ-like function. He is "shepherd" and his "flock" is Israel. Like Christ he suffers the scorns of his enemies,[12] is betrayed for gold[13] and will be rejected by the Jews as their king.[14] At the end of the poem he asserts his rightful claim to the throne. Such behaviour was expected of the Messiah as is shown by Christ's claim to have come to fulfil the law. David at the end of the poem shadows Christ the suffering servant,[15] the restorer of the peace between man and God, the judge, and the founder of a new age and a new order of time.[16]

David's speech may not seem like a very dramatic conclusion to the story; however, if read with an awareness of its central imaginative patterns, it is the most intense and exciting of the scenes. David is "Heav'n's anointed", "God's anointed", the

[8] *Absalom and Achitophel*, 77, 381.   [9] *Op. cit.*, 939, 943.
[10] *Op. cit.*, 941   [11] *Op. cit.*, 323–8.   [12] *Op. cit.*, 275, 400.
[13] *Op. cit.*, 405–6.   [14] *Op. cit.*, 409–10.   [15] *Op. cit.*, 933, 998.
[16] The imitation of Virgil's *Fourth Ecologue* at the conclusion of the poem is appropriate as it was allegorised by medieval commentators into a prophecy of the coming of Christ.

Godhead's image, and finally "by Heav'n inspir'd" becomes a vehicle for the divine will. "Inspired" does not mean personal inventiveness; it means that a spiritual power is speaking through someone. In his moment of inspiration David incarnates divine mercy and justice. His vision is like the mind of God which foreseeing the uses to which man will put his freedom knows that at the end of time He must "the sword of justice draw".[17] His words are both prophecy and action.

David's speech, while appropriate to his own situation, shadows several analogies. At one imaginative level the events in the poem are seen against man's archetypal choice in Eden. Absalom and Israel have, like Adam, fallen through disobedience and pride. The king, like God, has his "revenge delay'd" and is willing to forgive the offenders. He would, like Christ in *Paradise Lost*[18] bring the first tears of Adam and Eve to God as a sign of man's penitence. David laments:

> But O that yet he would repent and live!
> How easy 't is for parents to forgive!
> With how few tears a pardon might be won
> From nature, pleading for a darling son![19]

If free will is to have any meaning, man must, however, be expelled from Eden before he can be redeemed:

> Why am I forc'd, like Heav'n, against my mind,
> To make examples of another kind?
> Must I at length the sword of justice draw?
> O curst effects of necessary law!
> How ill my fear they by my mercy scan![20]

Just as the divine mind foresees that man's fall will result in a greater good and the eventual conquest of death, so David perceives a new era when "those dire artificers of death shall bleed".

[17] *Op. cit.*, 1002. David embodies God's mercy, peace, justice and truth (see Ps. 85:10 and Patrides, p. 131). If in the earlier part of the poem he is mild, good, gracious, at line 811 he is "righteous" (*i.e.* just). For the sword of justice see Rev. 19:15.

[18] Book xi.   [19] *Absalom and Achitophel*, 957–60.

[20] *Op. cit.*, 1000–4.

Within the Edenic analogy the poem has moved from the Creation of the world to man's expulsion from Paradise and the prophecy of God's eventual triumph over Satan. David's speech is a moment both in and out of time, when past and future intersect with the present and exist simultaneously. If the poem has at one imaginative level remained in Eden, it has at another imaginative level moved forward in time not only through Genesis, Exodus[21] and David's reign in the Book of Samuel, but through the New Testament to the events foreseen in the Book of Revelations.[22] The threat of anarchy, the appearance of a false Messiah, miracles,[23] the active intervention of Satan are signs of the final days of the world before God is revealed at the Last Judgment. The image of "offending age" also adds to the analogy between the rebellion against David and the era of sin which precedes Christ's rule. Just as the Beast and Anti-Christ seduce the nations of the world into false worship,[24] so the people misled by Achitophel attempt to impose Absalom on the throne. God, however, finally reveals Himself, "let Law then shew her face". His enemies fight among themselves and are defeated in a final battle[25] between the faithful and the followers of the Beast.[26] The final lines of the poem with their many echoes of Revelations identify the end of the rebellion against David with the beginning of the kingdom of Christ:

He said. Th' Almighty, nodding, gave consent;
And peals of thunder shook the firmament.
Henceforth a series of new time began,
The mighty years in long procession ran:
Once more the godlike David was restor'd,
And willing nations knew their lawful lord.[27]

And the seventh angel sounded the trumpet: and there were great voices in heaven, saying: The

[21] *Op. cit.,* 55.
[22] On one imaginative level the poem never leaves Genesis. Even David's remark "I am not good by force" (950) ironically alludes to the Creation (which is "good"), an act freely performed by God out of his mercy and goodness. (See Patrides, p. 35.)
[23] *Op. cit.,* 320.   [24] Rev. 13:14.   [25] Rev. 17:14–16.
[26] *Absalom and Achitophel,* 1012–24.
[27] *Op. cit.,* 1026–31. "He spake, and it was done" (Ps. 33:9), *i.e.* the Creation. Also see Rev. 20:2–3 and 21:5.

F

monarchy to Israel. His restoration is linked to mankind's ultimate restoration. David's forgiving, merciful nature typifies the new law which will be brought by Christ to replace the old.[37] In rejecting David the Jews shadow their later rejection of the Messiah.[38] But they cannot change the divine scheme. The Messiah will come and man will be "restor'd". David's final triumph shadows both the victory of God against Satan in heaven ("For lawful pow'r is still superior found") and at the end of time.

If David is an agent of divine goodness and mercy, Achitophel is the embodiment of Satanic pride and ingratitude. When he first appears in the poem it is as leader of the King's opponents who have already been dismissed from court; the analogy is to the fallen angels led by Satan, the Adversary:

Some by their friends, more by themselves thought wise,
Oppos'd the pow'r to which they could not rise.
Some had in courts been great, and thrown from thence,
Like fiends were harden'd in impenitence.
Some, by their monarch's fatal mercy, grown
From pardon'd rebels kinsmen to the throne,
Were rais'd in pow'r and public office high;
Strong bands, if bands ungrateful men could tie.
Of these the false Achitophel was first;
A name to all succeeding ages curst.[39]

Achitophel's epitaph "false" recalls Satan's deception of Eve which caused mankind's fall. "Curst" alludes to the curse put on

[37] David is also a type of Adam, the father of mankind (942, 958, 961), who is the archetype of all heads of families, biblical patriarchs, leaders of tribes (906) and monarchs. David's legal right to govern (1031) derives from Adam's dominion over the earth (9) and from Noah (301–2), who as the only head of family left alive at the time of the Flood restored monarchy to the world. (According to Renaissance political theory, the right to govern was inherited by biblical patriarchs and later monarchs from Noah's sons.) If Adam can impute original sin to future generations, he can bind mankind to inherited monarchy (769–71). Adam was given dominion without any reservations. If you reject his right to covenant for future generations (767), you reject original sin, the promise of redemption, and God's justice (773). The least achieved imaginative patterns in the poem are those passages treating the contractual origins of monarchy.

[38] *Absalom and Achitophel*, 758, 790, 1006. See John 19:7.

[39] *Op. cit.*, 142–51.

the serpent in Genesis. Like Lucifer who through pride rebelled, although he would in the fullness of time have been made godlike, Achitophel is too proud to await his rewards:

> Disdain'd the golden fruit to gather free,
> And lent the crowd his arm to shake the tree.
> Now manifest of crimes contriv'd long since,
> He stood at bold defiance with his prince.[40]

Like fallen Lucifer, who through hatred of God wanted to rule or ruin creation, Achitophel is "in friendship false, implacable in hate;/Resolv'd to ruin or to rule the State".[41] Just as the Devil in the hope of destroying God's work tempts Eve into disobedience, so Achitophel hopes to plunge Israel into disorder and anarchy[42] by tempting Absalom into rebellion. If David as monarch is an image of the divine order, Achitophel, the archrebel, is an agent of Satanic disorder. Even Achitophel's procreation of a son recalls the tradition that Satan's proud thoughts of rebelling against God were the beginning of Sin and that the union of Satan and Sin gave birth to Death: "Got, while his soul did huddled notions try;/And born a shapeless lump, like anarchy".[43]

Achitophel's temptation of Absalom recalls both Satan's temptation of Eve with promises of divinity and his unsuccessful temptation of the Messiah. Absalom is described as the second Moses and a saviour. A star shines at his nativity and his coming has been prophesied.[44] The Messianic implications of Achitophel's speech are both obvious and ironic:

> How long wilt thou the general joy detain,
> Starve and defraud the people of thy reign?
> Content ingloriously to pass thy days
> Like one of Virtue's fools that feeds on praise;

[40] Op. cit., 202–5. The images of "tree" and "golden fruit" look forward to Absalom's temptation where "thy fruit must be/Or gather'd ripe, or rot upon the tree" (250–1). The connexion is that both falls result from a desire to be godlike before one's time. Adam and Eve would in the course of time have advanced in the heavenly hierarchy and replaced the fallen angels.

[41] Op. cit., 173–4. [42] Op. cit., 224–7.

[43] Op. cit., 171–2. An echo of Ps. 51:5: "Behold I was shapen in iniquity: and in sin did my mother conceive me".

[44] Op. cit., 238–9.

Till thy fresh glories, which now shine so bright,
Grow stale and tarnish with our daily sight.[45]

It is in keeping with Achitophel's false nature that every value
should be inverted. The glory and praise due to the Redeemer
are treated as trivial; virtue is seen as foolish. The divine scheme of
atonement, redemption, and restoration is used as propaganda
for immediate political action. It is ironic that while Achitophel
uses traditions of Christian prophecy to tempt Absalom, he also
tries to convince him of a world without providence, a world in
which the deity is helpless before the chance occurrences of the
human will.[46] Christ the son of God who dies to redeem man is
mocked ("Behold him setting in his western skies"). Good is
what is successful. Daring activity alters fate. It is a world of
Machiavellian scheming rather than the slow unfolding of divine
will through time: "For human good depends on human will".[47]
Everything about Achitophel inverts the natural order. He is
"pleas'd with the danger, when the waves went high,/He sought
the storms; but, for a calm unfit":[48]

Else why should he, with wealth and honor blest,
Refuse his age the needful hours of rest?
Punish a body which he could not please;
Bankrupt of life, yet prodigal of ease?[49]

The utter inversion of values is shown by Achitophel's comparison
of David to Satan.[50] Achitophel's values of activity, expediency,
and worldly success are related to his pride, restlessness, and
turbulent imagination. That which makes him disobedient to his
king and God also makes him reject their vision of order.

Absalom, "too full of angels' metal in his frame,/Unwarily [is]
led from virtue's ways".[51] "Metal" is a pun on "mettle" meaning
ardour. The promptings of his own mind lead him into temptation: "Yet O that fate, propitiously inclin'd,/Had rais'd my birth, or
had debas'd my mind".[52] While "praise", "flattery", "ambition",

[45] *Op. cit.,* 244–9.   [46] *Op. cit.,* 253, 262–5.
[47] *Op. cit.,* 255. For the seventeenth-century context of Dryden's irony, see
Ruth Nevo, *The Dial of Virtue,* Princeton, N.J., 1963.
[48] *Absalom and Achitophel,* 160–1.
[49] *Op. cit.,* 165–8.   [50] *Op. cit.,* 273–5.
[51] *Op. cit.,* 310–11.   [52] *Op. cit.,* 363–4.

and the "desire of pow'r" influence him, he falls, like Eve, through the desire to be godlike. He succumbs to temptations of glory and kingdom: the main temptations Christ resisted. His claims to divinity are presumptuous pride.[53] The allusions to his birth are important as they disqualify his claims to both the political and spiritual kingdoms.[54] Whereas the son of God is born of "woman's seed" to atone for the sins of man, Absalom's soul

> . . . disclaims the kindred of her earth;
> And, made for empire, whispers me within,
> "Desire of greatness is a godlike sin."[55]

Absalom is a warrior hero fit for pagan epics;[56] it is David, of course, who displays Christ-like patience, fortitude, and submission to divine providence.[57]

Absalom's progress is both a parody of Christ's triumphal entry into Jerusalem and a shadowing of the Beast and his followers. He imitates and debases the traditions associated with the Messiah. His tears, sighs, pity, and compassion are to gain sympathy for his cause; he denounces his father, seeks a kingdom of this world, urges his own cause and tries to insinuate himself into the people's hearts. True values are inverted: a son opposes his father;[58] a man is worshipped as a god: "Each house receives him as a guardian god,/And consecrates the place of his abode".[59] The political and social chaos which would result if Absalom's followers were victorious recalls the changes in the natural world[60] and the predatory state of nature which resulted from Adam's sin: "government itself at length must fall/To nature's state, where all have right to all".[61] "Deluded" Absalom is the perfect example of why the Restoration distrusted "enthusiasm" and defined it as the mistaken belief that one is divinely inspired.

The malcontents that Achitophel unites in support of Absalom are those of all ages who fall into disobedience through pride in

---

[53] *Op. cit.*, 969–72.   [54] *Op. cit.*, 16, 361–70.   [55] *Op. cit.*, 370–2.
[56] *Op. cit.*, 23, 221, 382.   [57] *Op. cit.*, 325–7, 948.
[58] *Op. cit.*, 720. A sign of the Last Days. See Mark 13:12.
[59] *Op. cit.*, 735–6.   [60] *Op. cit.*, 805–10.
[61] *Op. cit.*, 793–4.

their own ideas.[62] Whereas God creates order out of chaos, Satan and his followers are the party of misrule, inverted values, anarchy and destruction. They are against monarchy because they are against order.[63] Zimri is the epitome of mankind in its fallen state: restless, dissatisfied, opinionated, intemperate, impaired in judgment, impaired in enjoyment, and subject to every vanity of human wishes. He squanders his wealth and his estate; he is deceived and gets every value wrong: "Nothing went unrewarded but desert". Jonas makes "treason law". Shimei "did wisely from expensive sins refrain,/And never broke the Sabbath, but for gain".[64] He misuses the law. During his office, "treason was no crime". His following of mass opinion is the opposite of finding communion in Christ:

> When two or three were gather'd to declaim
> Against the monarch of Jerusalem,
> Shimei was always in the midst of them.[65]

It is too often assumed that Dryden's satiric portraits are merely attempts to settle old scores or propaganda to discredit the political opposition. Because *Absalom and Achitophel* is treated as a political document rather than a self-sufficient poem, its imaginative patterns are overlooked. Achitophel's party illustrates the inversion of social, cultural and religious values. The linkage between religion and the quality of social life is made explicit:

> Chaste were his cellars, and his shrieval board
> The grossness of a city feast abhorr'd:
> His cooks, with long disuse, their trade forgot;
> Cool was his kitchen, tho' his brains were hot.[66]

The anticipations of Pope's *Moral Essays* should not blind us to the more inclusive nature of Dryden's theme. The pun on "brains" associates Shimei's miserliness, social irresponsibility and perverted

[62] *Op. cit.,* 495–500, 529–32. "But a whole Hydra more/Remains of sprouting heads" (541–2). See Rev. 13:1. The heads and horns of the first beast are usually understood as all the enemies of God from the beginning to the end of the world.

[63] *Op. cit.,* 775–6.

[64] *Op. cit.,* 587–8.

[65] *Op. cit.,* 601–3.

[66] *Op. cit.,* 618–21.

religiosity (the lack of communion is especially damning)
with the delusions of Zimri, Absalom, and Achitophel. The
portrait of Corah completes the wide range of perverted cultural
and religious values. He takes upon himself the signs, characteristics and predictions of the prophets. But his truths are
lies and his prophecies false. Unlike the apostles he is not a witness
bearing evidence; rather he uses his imagination to make up
stories which suit "the temper of the times". Instead of men
bearing witness for Christ, Corah prostitutes the meaning of
witness: "For *witness* is a common name to all".

Contrasted to the mob which Absalom commands is the "small
but faithful band" who support David. They are a shadowing
of those, throughout the ages, who stand with Christ, especially in
the Last Days ("worst of days"). They also represent the cultural
and religious norms from which Absalom's followers are the
extreme deviants. Barzillai is loyal to his prince even in times of
trouble. He advises but does not flatter. Unlike Zimri he knows
the proper use of wealth and position and he patronises the arts.
Honour, lineage, duty, and service meet in Barzillai and his son.
These are among the proper ends of man in society and reflect the
perfection of the divine order. Barzillai's son offers us a contrast
to Achitophel's son:

> All parts fulfill'd of subject and of son:
> Swift was the race, but short the time to run.
> O narrow circle, but of pow'r divine,
> Scanted in space, but perfect in thy line![67]

The Sagan of Jerusalem and Zadoc the priest who shuns "pow'r
and place" provide a contrast to the bad priests, false prophets,
and hypocrites portrayed earlier. The Sagan's

> . . . weighty sense
> Flows in fit words and heavenly eloquence.
> The prophets' sons, by such example led,
> To learning and to loyalty were bred.[68]

He is also a patron of the arts. David's followers embody the
virtues necessary for the social and moral good of mankind.
They represent the right use of money and position, religion and

[67] *Op. cit.*, 836–9.   [68] *Op. cit.*, 868–71.

law, family and bravery. They are counsellors not politicians, men of independent judgment rather than followers of mass opinion. They live orderly, regulated lives.

Careful consideration of the portrait of Achitophel and the portraits of David's supporters would disprove the assumption that it was not until his later works that Dryden achieved sufficient unity of cultural vision to initiate the Augustan compromise. The cultural and religious assumptions which underlie the work of Swift, Pope, and Johnson are also the values implicit in *Absalom and Achitophel*. A proper imaginative response to the poem includes the recognition of tacitly assumed values. It is only necessary to consider the role played by the narrator in *Absalom and Achitophel* to understand how completely the assumptions are the result of poetic creation.

While not hiding his opinions the narrator assumes the stance of an urbane, impartial observer. His few gestures towards the traditional pose of the epic poet as inspired visionary are self-mocking: "Titles and names 't were tedious to rehearse/Of lords, below the dignity of verse";[69] or perfunctory: "Here stop, my Muse, here cease thy painful flight;/No pinions can pursue immortal height".[70] But it is the narrator who, despite his witty scepticism, sees the story in terms of a timeless cosmic drama. David's reign is Edenic, Achitophel is Satanic and Absalom a fallen Adam, because the narrator sees them as such. It is the narrator who reports Achitophel's temptation of Absalom "in such words as these", and who associates Absalom's fall with the desire to emulate God:

> Desire of pow'r, on earth a vicious weed,
> Yet, sprung from high, is of celestial seed:
> In God 't is glory; and when men aspire,
> 'T is but a spark too much of heavenly fire.[71]

The narrator creates a continuum of sensibility ranging from the most tolerant and worldly to the intensely Christian. A concern with manners and good sense is aligned with the visionary. It is the narrator who, at the beginning of the poem, sees David's promiscuity as patriarchical and who also sees the analogy as comically absurd ("Scatter'd his Maker's image").

[69] *Op. cit.*, 569–70.   [70] *Op. cit.*, 854–5.   [71] *Op. cit.*, 305–8.

The narrator's sensibility is reflected in the varying tones of his voice. The unjustifiable discontent of the Israelites is revealed in the sound of "a headstrong, moody, murm'ring race". Achitophel's innate character is created by the restless, unbalanced movement of the lines in which he is described:

> For close designs and crooked counsels fit;
> Sagacious, bold, and turbulent of wit;
> Restless, unfix'd in principles and place;
> In pow'r unpleas'd, impatient of disgrace:
> A fiery soul . . .[72]

A similar disturbed, irregular movement of verse occurs whenever people or ideas associated with chaos, pride, and deluded imagination appear in the poem. The imitative nature of the verse changes with each example, since all threats to order are not equally dangerous or intense: but the cumulative effect of such passages as they operate upon the reader's sense of form and relation is thematic in the musical sense. The epigrammatic is especially common. Perhaps the best example is the disorderly catalogue and tumbling rhythms which describe Zimri:

> In the first rank of these did Zimri stand;
> A man so various, that he seem'd to be
> Not one, but all mankind's epitome:
> Stiff in opinions, always in the wrong;
> Was everything by starts, and nothing long;
> But, in the course of one revolving moon,
> Was chymist, fiddler, statesman, and buffoon:
> Then all for women, painting, rhyming, drinking,
> Besides ten thousand freaks that died in thinking.[73]

The social, moral, and mental disorder which Zimri represents is typical of Achitophel's followers, and proceeds from the same causes, but it is transposed into comedy. Instead of jagged, restless rhythms, the verse tumbles clownishly. It is not necessary to examine the various ways in which the portrait of Zimri echoes the portrait of Achitophel; the relationship is felt in similarities of sound and movement of the verse. Similar associations are conveyed by:

[72] *Op. cit.,* 152–6.   [73] *Op. cit.,* 544–52.

What standard is there in a fickle rout,
Which, flowing to the mark, runs faster out?
Nor only crowds, but Sanhedrins may be
Infected with this public lunacy.[74]

Contrasted to the disharmonious music of Achitophel and his followers, there are the steady, orderly, assured tones which signify the King and his supporters:

The sober part of Israel, free from stain,
Well knew the value of a peaceful reign.[75]

And David's mildness manag'd it so well,
The bad found no occasion to rebel.[76]

"Thus long have I, by native mercy sway'd,
My wrongs dissembled, my revenge delay'd."[77]

leading to:

Henceforth a series of new time began,
The mighty years in long process ran.[78]

The movement of the verse is continually varied in accordance with the immediate subject-matter; the stylistic alignments and linkages are organic and a reflexion of content. When Absalom is tempted, the hissing "s" sounds associate Achitophel with the serpent in Eden.[79] The narrator's opinions may guide our attitudes, but it is the local characteristics of the verse which carry the burden of significance. Meaning derives from tone, rhythm, imagery, and analogy rather than statement. The cultural and moral values emerge from the verse, rather than being imposed upon it.

The modulations of the speaker's voice allow Dryden to be objective in his treatment of his material. Throughout the poem the narrator seems only tentatively committed, recognising faults in all parties: "What faults he had, (for who from faults is free?)/ His father could not, or he would not see".[80] Or the narrator, while committed, pauses to recognise the validity of the main

[74] Op. cit., 785–8.   [75] Op. cit., 69–70.   [76] Op. cit., 77–8.
[77] Op. cit., 939–40.   [78] Op. cit., 1028–9.   [79] Op. cit., 228–31.
[80] Op. cit., 35–6.

arguments advanced by the other side.[81] The urbane, cool wit of the narrator creates a buffer of civilised emotions between the action portrayed and our normal immediate response. It creates the aesthetic distance necessary for the poem as art object rather than propaganda. By assuming an air of disinterested reasonableness, by letting the most important characters speak for themselves, and by viewing the particular and momentary against the timeless universal, Dryden has created the conditions in which the narrator's vision may be felt as the expression of deeply held cultural values rather than personal opinion.

The importance of parody in *Absalom and Achitophel* is not that this or that passage imitates a line of Virgil or Milton. Imitation, allusion and parody assume a highly educated audience and establish a community of cultivated values. The poem, with its humorous allusions to Creation, its patterns of analogy and, at its conclusion, its shadowing of the Last Days, also pays sophisticated homage to centuries of Christian biblical study and meditation. Dryden took over the imaginative habits of mind of seventeenth-century millenarianism, rooted in centuries of prophecy and eschatology, and tempered them with Augustan court values of good sense, urbanity, and knowledge of human nature. The result is not a mere ironic turning of certain religious arguments against political opponents; the poem creates cultural values. Christian patience and trust in divine providence find their social expression in a concern for order, good sense, and a humane, civilised, fruitful life.

Absalom and Achitophel is one of the most sustained imaginative creations in English poetry. It fully achieves the placing of its subject within a cosmic as well as cultural dimension. Its imaginative patterns are perfectly realised, its wit relevant to its themes.[82]

---

[81] *Op. cit.,* 759–64.

[82] The mass section (106–27) is often misunderstood. The mass (113) need not be Roman Catholic; it can be any Christian mass. The food images ("eat", "drink", "swallow'd", "unchew'd", "crude", "taste", "brew'd", etc.) are a sign of gluttony. Gluttony is a traditional Christian symbol for disorderly passions (110). Gluttony, in the form of Eve's desire for the apple, brought sin and death into the world. (See *Paradise Lost*, IX, 791–2, and James 1:15.) The food images are related to fruit and tree images also associated with the fall. The "nation's curse" (108) derives from the gluttony (107) of the priests. That which is "swallow'd . . . unchew'd and crude" (113) has a

Its local effects are congruent with the whole, and the imaginative organisation is held together by an original use of traditional analogies. While the attitudes implied by the narrator's voice contribute to our acceptance of the poem's values, our response is assured by image patterns and analogies which put people and events into a larger perspective. *Absalom and Achitophel* has a vertical integration – relating society to the spiritual – unusual in any poem after the mid-seventeenth century. It is almost Elizabethan in its correspondences between the microcosm and the macrocosm, the particular and the universal.

"dangerous consequence" (135). The good-natured joke at the expense of transubstantiation (119–20) continues the gluttony / food imagery. Those shocked by Dryden's wit should remember that an even greater "teacher" "rak'd . . . the stews" (127) for converts. The "fever" (136) caused by gluttony creates unrest and threatens the government (141). It brings "disease" (926) on the nation.

Elias J. Chiasson

DRYDEN'S APPARENT SCEPTICISM IN *RELIGIO LAICI*[1]

Professor Bredvold's view of Dryden as a philosophic sceptic in the general tradition of Pyrrho, Sextus Empiricus, and Montaigne, or as a "fideist" after the fashion of certain Roman Catholic apologists,[2] continues to be the generally accepted one. Samuel Monk, in summing up the direction that Dryden studies have taken, says: "Dryden's naturally sceptical temper found support in the various scepticisms of Montaigne, of the Royal Society, and of Catholic apologetics."[3] It is this scepticism, so the story goes, which drove Dryden to the shelter of the Roman Catholic Church.

Mindful of Dryden's later conversion, Bredvold is certain that Dryden's position, even when he wrote *Religio Laici*, had no real affinities with Anglicanism. He says: "If the question of his sincerity is to be raised, it would therefore seem more discerning to raise it in connection with his Anglicanism in the . . . [*Religio Laici*], rather than with his conversion a few years later". That this is his point is clear, for he says that in 1682 Dryden was "far along on the road to the Roman communion . . ."[4]

The purpose of this article is to show that there is no need to posit anything so special as pyrrhonistic scepticism or Catholic

[1] [Reprinted from *The Harvard Theological Review*, Vol. LIV (1961) pp. 207–21.]
[2] L. I. Bredvold, *The Intellectual Milieu of John Dryden*, Ann Arbor, Mich. (1934).
[3] Samuel Holt Monk, "Dryden Studies: A Survey", *E.L.H.*, XIV (1947).
[4] Bredvold, *Intellectual Milieu*, p. 121.

fideism to explain Dryden's position,[5] and that Dryden belongs to that tradition of Christian humanism which had, in varying degrees and with varying speculative or practical emphases, been common to patristic, medieval, and Renaissance Christendom. In its broadest extension, such a humanism denotes a world view which distinguishes between the order of grace and the order of nature, which subordinates the second to the first, and which recognises not the destruction but the perfection of nature by grace. Such a view does not permit exalting the supernatural at the expense of the natural, on the one hand, or exalting the natural at the expense of the supernatural on the other, or even, while accepting both orders, insisting on their divergence. Tertullian during the patristic period, the Averroists and William of Occam during the medieval period, Luther and Calvin at the Reformation, various sceptics of the sixteenth century, and the "Baconians" and Deists of the seventeenth and eighteenth centuries illustrate that at no time was such a unified view of life universally embraced.[6]

But from the time of Hooker to the Restoration and beyond, Anglicans continued to assert the central imperatives of this Christian humanism. After the Restoration, certain changes occur which presage but do not yet officially announce the disappearance of that "massive but flexible tradition. . . ."[7]

The Cambridge Platonists, for example, continued to insist on the closest and most intimate relation between religion and philosophy. Truth, whatever its course, from reason or revelation, has its origin in God. Recognising the limitations of man's cognitive faculties as a result of the Fall,[8] they affirmed the necessity of supplementing "the truth of natural inscription" with the "truth of divine revelation . . ."[9] Viewing reason as the

---

[5] A. W. Secord, *J.E.G.P.*, xxiv (1935) p. 463, reviewing Bredvold's book is convinced of Dryden's fideism, but is less careful than Bredvold in defining it as "the medieval distinction between reason and faith". Such a definition would make Catholicism generally and a whole array of Anglicans fideistic.

[6] Among the pertinent studies of this question are: D. Bush, *The Renaissance and English Humanism*, Toronto (1939); G. G. Walsh, *Medieval Humanism*, New York (1942); H. Haydn, *The Counter-Renaissance*, New York (1950); H. Baker, *The Wars of Truth: Studies in the Decay of Christian Humanism in the Earlier Seventeenth Century*, Cambridge, Mass. (1952).

[7] Baker, *Wars of Truth*, p. 98.

[8] John Smith, *Selected Discourses*, Cambridge (1859) p. 61.   [9] *Ibid.*

distinctive quality of man, they affirmed, much like Hooker and the medieval tradition, that reason is the very voice of God.[10] Encouraged by the conviction, central to any Christian humanism, that "all Truth is Catholic", they turned to the pagan philosophers for much of their inspiration. The contemporary need, as Cudworth saw, in view of the antagonisms which surrounded him,[11] was a "philosophy of religion confirmed and established by philosophical reasons . . ."[12] Here faith anticipates and completes the findings of reason, and philosophy is the handmaid of religion.[13] Since Truth, whatever its source, is ultimately grasped by reason, there can be no conflict between faith and reason, or between revealed and natural truth. As Whichcote observes, "Our reason is not confounded by our religion, but awakened, excited, employed, directed, and improved . . ."[14] With a Dryden-like metaphor Culverwel points to the relationship which properly exists between reason and revelation: "The light of Reason doth no more prejudice the light of faith, then the light of a Candle doth extinguish the light of a Star."[15] Whichcote suggests a similar relationship by his choice of verbs: "Reason discovers what is natural, and reason receives what is supernatural."[16]

The Latitudinarians preserved a similar distinction between nature and grace. For while it is true that most Latitudinarians tended to "frame a reasonable system of belief and then demonstrate that it was actually the same as the traditional faith",[17] they constantly emphasised that natural religion must be supplemented

[10] Benjamin Whichcote, *Moral and Religious Aphorisms*, London (1753) p. 76.
[11] The contemporary need was to counter the twin dangers of Puritan bibliolatry and Hobbistic materialism.
[12] Ralph Cudworth, *The True Intellectual System of the Universe*, London (1845) Preface.
[13] Smith, *Selected Discourses*, p. 442.
[14] Whichcote, *Select Sermons*, London (1698) p. 298.
[15] Quoted in M. L. Wiley, *The Subtle Knot*, Cambridge, Mass. (1952) p. 93.
[16] Whichcote, *Aphorisms*, p. 99.
[17] G. R. Cragg, *From Puritanism to the Age of Reason*, Cambridge (1950) p. 68. However, S. L. Bethell, *The Cultural Revolution of the Seventeenth Century*, London (1951) p. 15, takes issue with G. N. Clark's assertion that post-Restoration writers "tried to justify Christianity itself not on the ground that it was divinely revealed but on the ground that it was reasonable". On the contrary, says Bethell, "Seventeenth-century thought, both earlier and later, has a subtlety and precision that eludes such broad-meshed categories".

by the disclosures of revelation. Stillingfleet is typical in defending revelation by an appeal to reason and arguing that there are cogent "grounds for divine revelation from natural light", but at the same time insisting that "the immediate dictates of natural light are not to be the measure of divine revelation . . ."[18] The sermon tradition from Isaac Barrow through Robert South to Tillotson illustrates the habit of mind we have been describing. Barrow, in a sermon delivered in 1661, exhorts us to obtain Wisdom "by the faithfull exercise of our Reason, carefull observation of things, diligent study of the Divine Law, watchfull reflexion upon our selves, vertuous and religious practice; *but especially, by imploring the Divine influence, the original spring of light, and the fountain of all true knowledge* . . ."[19] A similar spirit may be found in South's sermon preached in 1691. "Let a Man", he says, with imagery which suggests the manner of Dryden, "carefully attend to the *Voice* of his *Reason*, and all the Dictates of Natural Morality . . . For though Reason . . . is, indeed, but a weak, and diminutive *Light*, compared to Revelation . . . it ought to be no disparagement to a Star, that it is not a *Sun*".[20] Tillotson is equally convinced that there is "a natural and immutable and eternal reason for that which we call goodness and virtue", to which man may arrive "under the influence of God's grace and assistance which is never wanting to our sincere indeavours . . ."[21]

The conclusion therefore would seem to be that the Anglican tradition (to which Dryden properly belongs) preserved, with varying emphases, the traditional balance between reason and faith. If because of the absence of a principle of infallibility, which could settle certain controversial questions by means of dogmatic pronouncements, Anglicanism was to make its appeal finally to reason, the nature of this reason must not be disregarded.[22]

[18] Edward Stillingfleet, *Origines Sacrae*, London (1666) Bk. ii, Ch. v, *passim*.

[19] This sermon and one by South and Tillotson respectively are conveniently reproduced in *Seventeenth-Century Verse and Prose*, eds. White, Wallerstein, Quintana, New York (1952). For the present quotation see *op. cit.*, ii, p. 186.

[20] *Op. cit.*, ii, p. 185.

[21] *Op. cit.*, ii, p. 204.

[22] Throughout the Anglican tradition there was general agreement that, in the words of Donne (*Works*, ed. H. Alford, ii, p. 7), "no natural man can do anything towards a supernatural work . . ."

G

At this point it is essential, if we hope to understand Dryden, to make distinctions not always made in present Dryden criticism. For example, it must not be too readily assumed that controversialists, both Anglican and Catholic, are the most reliable judges of the precise drift of each other's opinion. One must furthermore also avoid labelling as "fideistic" positions which seem quite consistent with positions which, when held by another, one calls rationalistic.[23] To exaggerate the rationalism of the seventeenth-century Anglican, for example, would be as unsatisfactory as to exaggerate the fideism of seventeenth-century Catholicism.[24] To say that Anglicans unhesitatingly made their appeal to reason demands, as we have seen, a clear understanding of the nature of that reason. Similarly, the mere exploitation by a Catholic of the importance of the principle of infallibility is not *necessarily* fideistic. Nor is it a mere seventeenth-century apologetic device, but perhaps the central difficulty which complicates the reunion of Catholicism with what it views as the separated brethren.

The difficulty of Anglicans with Catholic infallibility was not, generally speaking, a reflexion of greater Anglican confidence in the power of human reason, but a resistance to the *exclusive* character of Catholic claims. Certainly in the seventeenth century, Anglicanism, Sectarianism, and Catholicism were agreed on the

[23] Bredvold is especially confusing on this point. On p. 81, Bredvold says that Hooker and Chillingworth "appealed unhesitatingly to reason". And yet Hooker (*Polity*, III, viii, 18) insists that men's reason in divine matters must not be thought of as working independently of "the aid and assistance of God's most blessed Spirit". Furthermore, it is difficult to see why Chillingworth's professed willingness to adopt Roman Catholicism if infallibility were indeed a fact (*Anglicanism*, eds. P. E. More and F. L. Cross, p. 113), as well as Sherlock's (cited in Bredvold, p. 94), is consistent with the sturdy rationalism of Chillingworth and Sherlock, and yet that a similar suggestion in Dryden is conclusive evidence of his hankering for authority.

[24] Bredvold's treatment of Edward Worsley (*Intellectual Milieu*, p. 94) illustrates the unsatisfactoriness of such exaggerations. Worsley, a Catholic apologete, defends himself against the allegation of impugning reason by conceding that "Reason euer precedes Faith, and is grounded vpon those rational motiues which Induce to Belieue" but that "Faith, precisely considered as Faith, relies vpon a quite Different Obiect, God's pure Reuelation . . ." Bredvold regards this as a "tangle of logic" and as a typical example of fideistic apologetic, in spite of the fact that, as this paper shows, this position is common to Hooker and Laud and the majority of Anglicans.

necessity for some principle which would protect the faith against the obvious fallibility of human reason. Hooker is typical of the Anglican anchoring of the truth in reason – not reason *sans phrase*, but reason protected by tradition and Scripture and illuminated by the Grace of God.[25] The Sectarians, less dependent on tradition and relying primarily on revelation, found their stay in the *inner light*. Catholics, convinced that both Protestant positions were either gross or more subtle varieties of reliance on the individual reason, insisted on the competence of the Church to examine the findings of reason, revelation, and tradition, and to enforce dogmatically the results of this examination. Methodologically these three concepts of infallibility do not differ greatly. Much of the difficulty was caused not by the concept itself, but by the precise location of this infallible power. To a thoroughgoing rationalist, any one of the three would be an illegitimate restriction of the power of reason.

Before proceeding to an examination of *Religio Laici*, one might cite a passage from Dryden's life of Plutarch in which Dryden sets forth what he conceives to be the highest achievement and yet the serious limitations of the unregenerate, pagan mind (ancient or modern). "I have ever thought", he says, "that the wise men in all ages have not much differed in their opinions of religion; *I mean as it is grounded on human reason*: for reason, *as far as it is right*, must be the same in all men; and *truth being but one*, they must consequently think in the same train." The wise pagans "doubtless believed the identity of the one Supreme Intellectual Being, which we call God". Of Plutarch he says that Plutarch "could not know" the way to salvation "without revelation, and the revelation was not known to him". Plutarch therefore suffered the general pagan disability of being able to believe "no more than" could be deduced "from the principles of nature . . ."[26] The references to the oneness of Truth, and the hierarchical balance of reason and revelation required for its attainment suggest Hooker and the Cambridge Platonists and the general tradition

[25] Hooker, *Polity*, III, viii, 18.
[26] John Dryden, *Works*, ed. Scott-Saintsbury, XVII, p. 33. This passage is quoted in Bredvold, *Intellectual Milieu*, p. 114, as evidence of Dryden's "rationalism" in spite of Dryden's clear distinction between revelation and reason.

which we have described, not the variety of scepticism generally alleged.

Dryden does not substantially change his position in *Religio Laici*. For while in the extended image which opens the poem Dryden does deprecate the complete sufficiency of reason, his apparently melancholy conclusion that "reason's glimmering ray" can but "guide us upward to a better day" is but the orthodox Christian-humanistic position, already described, that reason without faith cannot come to the fullness of Christian truth. There is, as yet, no real reason to suppose that Dryden is rejecting reason as operative on its own object. Since reason does have the power "to guide us upward to a better day", it can scarcely be said to be inoperative, unless one wishes to say that it is inoperative in Hooker, the Cambridge Platonists, and such men as Barrow and South.

As he does in his life of Plutarch, Dryden in the *Religio Laici* makes the traditional concession that reason can arrive at God's existence ("one first principle must be") while insisting on the impossibility of reason arriving at His Nature ("But what or who, that UNIVERSAL He . . . Not even the Stagirite himself could see"). Dryden would undoubtedly have agreed with Laud: "The *quod sit*, that there is a God, blear-eyed reason can see; but the *quid sit*, what it is, is infinitely beyond all the fathoms of reason . . ."[27] Laud is typically Anglican on this point: "Though reason without grace cannot see the way to heaven nor believe this Book in which God hath written the way, yet grace is never placed but in a reasonable creature . . ."[28] Like Laud, Dryden makes a distinction between reason and faith. Reason can establish the preambles of faith; it requires a grace to believe the Truth presented.

Dryden's reference to Hooker in the Preface to *Religio Laici*[29] would suggest that he conceived himself to be in a tradition which

[27] *Anglicanism*, eds. P. E. More and F. L. Cross, Milwaukee, Wis. (1935) p. 100.

[28] *Op. cit.*, p. 102.

[29] I find it impossible to conclude, with Bredvold (*Intellectual Milieu*, p. 119), that the Preface to *Religio Laici* makes it clear that Dryden had "Hooker and other Anglican 'philosophizing divines' in mind . . ." As a matter of fact, Dryden there associated himself with "venerable Hooker" in resisting the extreme individualism of the sectarians.

by no means repudiated the place of reason in the discovery of religious truth. His reference to the "light of nature as the next in dignity" is scarcely a repudiation of the power of reason. What he is specifically opposed to is the Deists' professed ability "to be able to find out that there is one supreme agent or intellectual agent which we call God; that praise and prayer are his due worship; and the rest of those deducements . . .". Such religious sophistication (and here Dryden includes the pagans) Dryden, after the manner of some of the Fathers, attributes to "the faint remnants or dying flames of revealed religion in the posterity of Noah . . ." Here Dryden is certainly more restrictive than Hooker who would have allowed a greater competence to the human mind. Nevertheless the Pauline reference prevents us from concluding that Dryden sees the unregenerate pagan mind as completely powerless with respect to religious and moral duties. If Dryden's belief in the oneness of Truth, referred to earlier, can be appealed to, his restrictiveness here will seem less severe. It is furthermore to be remembered that Dryden's restrictions on what is attainable "by our discourse" is immediately followed by the caveat: "I mean as simply considered, and without the benefit of divine illumination". Like Hooker,[30] Dryden defines faith as "the seal of heaven impressed upon our human understanding".

The brunt of Dryden's attack is directed not against reason but against the rationalism of the Deists, that is to say, against the absence in their system of a concept of grace – flowing from the fact of the Incarnation. Against the deistic confidence in the rationally conceived common notions, Dryden asserts the primacy of the faith. His claim that "Reason saw not, till Faith sprung the light" and that therefore "'Tis Revelation what thou think'st Discourse" does not fracture the synthesis of reason and faith, for in Dryden reason does see, though admittedly only after the act of faith. He merely asks that the Deists recognise the

---

[30] Even Hooker, who cannot be suspect of disregarding or understressing the rights of reason, insists (*Polity*, III, viii, 15) that "other motives and inducements be they never so strong and consonant unto reason, are notwithstanding uneffectual of themselves to work faith concerning this principle [i.e. the reliability of Scripture], if the special grace of the Holy Ghost concur not to the enlightening of our minds".

unconscious debt that they owe to a long tradition of religious experience. In pursuit of his argument, Dryden asks why, if the common notions of prayer "to one sole God" and an afterlife of happiness or reprobation are available to the unregenerate reason, why the pagans, Plato, Aristotle, Plutarch, Seneca, or Cicero ("those giant wits") were so contradictory and confused about such matters.

That Dryden's intention is not to reject the order of nature is clear from his admission that man is capable of a natural movement towards remorse, a movement which, however, is inadequate because of the disproportion between God offended and man offending: "See then, the Deist lost: remorse for vice/ Not paid, or paid, inadequate a price." In other words, Dryden is insisting on the traditionally accepted meaning of the Incarnation as a dramatic instance of the mercy of God with which man can co-operate but which he must not attempt to supplant with his own private ethic, no matter how noble. This is the traditional view, tirelessly reiterated,[31] that "no natural man can do anything towards a supernatural work".[32]

Dryden then proceeds to assert the necessity of Scripture if man is to know this particular economy of grace. He does so in the context of the formidable argument of the Deists, based on the fact that since Revelation was of a certain time and place, pagans – past and present – remain out of this so-called economy of grace which the orthodox insist upon. Dryden feels the cogency of this argument, but rejects the implications the Deists would draw, insisting, as the overwhelming majority of Christian theologians would insist, that salvation outside the economy of the Incarnation is impossible. Buttressing himself with a natural movement of charity and with an assertion of St Paul[33] that the pagans, not knowing the law, are a law unto themselves, Dryden says: "tho' no name be for salvation known, /But that of his eternal Son's alone;/ Who knows how far transcending goodness

[31] This is not to deny, of course, the subtle changes which were occurring in the *way* in which the relationship between nature and grace was being viewed. *Cf.* Bethell, *The Cultural Revolution*, p. 58, for a description of the *narrowing* of the concept of reason that is responsible for the grave differences in tone which complicate the apparent agreement between Hooker and Tillotson.

[32] John Donne, *Works*, ed. H. Alford, London (1839) II, p. 7.

[33] Rom. II, 14.

can/ Extend the merits of that Son to man?" Dryden's Pauline emphasis, which Rand refers to as the very foundation of Christian humanism,[34] strongly suggests that Dryden's "scepticism" is of a very special kind indeed. Dryden's assertion that "those who followed Reason's dictates right" "may [also] see their Maker's face" corrects the impression that he perhaps made earlier about the exclusive character of Christian ethics, while preserving (by means of the subjunctive *may*) the view of salvation as a gift. This is, of course, far from submission to the Deists. Their precise point was that the common notions (rationally derivable) can perform a function which Dryden, like most Anglicans, restricts to a very special economy – the economy of grace, the only known centre of which lies in the mystery of the Incarnation.

Dryden then moves to a discussion which Bredvold sees as most explicitly pointing to Dryden's scepticism. This is the digression in praise of the translator of Father Simon's *Critical History of the New Testament*, and is devoted, in large measure, to the problem of finding "a generally accepted method for interpreting, for purposes of church discipline and morality, the truth which God reveals in His Scripture".[35] This, as we have seen, was a problem perennial to any system of Christianity which lays no claim to being infallible. But there is no evidence, in spite of Bredvold, that Dryden was unduly affected by the attempt of Father Simon to undermine the Protestant confidence in Scripture. He falls back, as other Anglicans had done, on the assurance that on all needful points Scripture is plain. The poem at this point, as a matter of fact, reflects the serenity of Dryden in the face of the potent Catholic argument that admitted difficulties of interpretation point to the necessity of an infallible Church. To suppose, with Bredvold, that the couplet, "Such an omniscient Church we wish indeed,/ 'T were worth both testaments; and cast in the creed" is a reflexion of Dryden's disturbance at the fundamental lack of authority within Protestantism is to read *Religio Laici* in the light of the later *Hind and the Panther*. To suggest that a poem which is consistently critical of the Deists, the Puritans, and the Catholics, is suddenly startled into a tone of yearning for the bosom of the Catholic Church is to suggest a

[34] E. K. Rand, *Founders of the Middle Ages*, Cambridge, Mass. (1929) p. 35.
[35] Baker, *Wars of Truth*, p. 191.

Romantic not a Neo-Classic poem. As a matter of fact, this precise attitude, which reflects not yearning for but dismissal of the reality behind the principle of Catholic infallibility, can be found in Anglicans whose intellectualism is not at all suspect. Chillingworth, for example, says: ". . . if I knew any one Church to be infallible, I would quickly be of that Church".[36] William Sherlock, whom Bredvold does not place on the road to Rome, says in *A Discourse Concerning a Judge of Controversies in Matters of Religion* (1686): "Now could they prove that the Church of Rome is infallible, this indeed would be an irresistible Reason to return to her Communion . . ."[37]

Like any other Anglican, Dryden cites Father Simon's argument for the necessity of an infallible judge of tradition only to reject it. But typical of Anglicanism, he falls back to a position which methodologically is much like that of Rome. For, says he, "In doubtful questions 't is the safest way/ To learn what unsuspected ancients say;/ For 't is not likely we should higher soar/ In search of heav'n than all the church before." Bredvold's comment on this conservatism in Dryden is that Dryden here yielded "an obedience to the Church of England by law established, more strict than it theoretically could claim and more blind than that Church, in its fear of being identified with Popery, would want to claim".[38] While Bredvold may be correct on the theoretical right of Anglicanism to *demand* the allegiance of the faithful, because of the individualistic principle which informs it, many Anglicans, among them Hooker, Donne, Laud, and countless others,[39] did not hesitate to make this demand, especially against

[36] *Anglicanism*, p. 113.
[37] Quoted in Bredvold, *Intellectual Milieu*, p. 94.
[38] *Op. cit.*, p. 126.
[39] Donne's view of the self-elected saints as the white spots of leprosy in the Church, and Browne's recognition that every "man is not a proper Champion for Truth" as well as Burton's fear of the "fopperies" of private judgment, can be matched by Taylor's comment on the sectarian insistence that conscience is above law: "And so Suspicion; and Jealousie, and Disobedience, and Rebellion are become Conscience; in which there is neither knowledge, nor revelation, nor truth, nor charity, nor reason, nor religion." For these references see Donne, *The Works*, IV, p. 511; Browne, *Religio Medici* (Everyman edn.) p. 8; Burton, *Anatomy of Melancholy* (Bohn Library) III, p. 372; Taylor, "Ductor Dubitantium," in L. P. Smith, *The Golden Grove*, Oxford (1930) p. 145.

the excessive individualism of the Sectarians. To think of Dryden's attitude as a hankering for authority which removed him from the central tendancy of Anglicanism is to mistake the nature of Anglicanism. This is as misleading as Bredvold's view that the Catholic position "that reason appeals to evidence but faith accepts authority" was but a distinction "which the Protestants refused to recognize as valid".[40] For while Hooker (to quote but one instance) defines ecclesiastical law as that "which out of the law either of reason or of God men probably gathering to be expedient, they make it a law",[41] Hooker means by reason not the private reason of the individual but rather the corporate reason of the Church. He insists that that "which the Church by her ecclesiastical authority shall probably think and define to be true or good, must in congruity of reason overrule all other inferior judgments whatsoever".[42]

Like Hooker Dryden does not fall back on the authority of the Church prematurely. For in Dryden the place of reason in the elucidation of the divine test is by no means ignored. Dryden's assertion is clear that if the simple soul "Plods on to heaven, and ne'er is at a loss", nevertheless there are some born to instruct as others to be taught who "must study well the sacred page". The function of such elucidators is to discover "Which doctrine this, or that, does best agree/ With the whole tenor of the Work divine/ And plainliest points to Heaven's reveal'd design." His specific charge against the Puritans is that in them reason has been replaced by the inner light: "Each was ambitious of th' obscurest place,/ No measure ta'en from knowledge, all from GRACE./ Study and pains were now no more their care;/ Texts were explain'd by fasting and by prayer:/ This was the fruit the private spirit brought,/ Occasion'd by great zeal and little thought." The distinction that Dryden makes between knowledge and grace by no means suggests any thorough-going repudiation of the activity of reason in religion. Indeed Dryden is anxious to "stem" both the "tides of ignorance" (Puritans) and "pride" (Roman Catholics). It is true that temperamentally Dryden is satisfied with religion in its more simple expression. In the Preface to the *Religio*, he tells us that the Apostles' Creed is the

[40] Bredvold, *Intellectual Milieu*, p. 94.
[41] Hooker, *Polity*, i, iii, i.   [42] *Op. cit.*, v, viii, 5.

one best fitted to his weak understanding. But this is an attitude by no means foreign to Anglicanism.[43]

Dryden's opposition to Puritan "ignorance" suggests very strongly that he would be at one with Hooker in insisting that "the benefit of nature's light" must not be "thought excluded as unnecessary, because the necessity of a diviner light is magnified".[44] It would seem clear that to Dryden, as to Hooker, reason is not merely a supplement but a "necessary instrument, without which we could not reap by the Scripture's perfection that fruit and benefit which it yieldeth".[45] Furthermore the nature of Dryden's criticism hardly suggests a lack of confidence in reason. He speaks of pre-Reformation times as times "o'er grown with rust and ignorance" when "want of learning" was exploited by priestcraft. Such ignorance gives way to "a knowing age" which refused to accept Roman claims of infallibility. This is quite in the spirit of Hooker who refuses "to be tied and led by authority", and who rejects the notion "that authority of men should prevail with men either against or above Reason, is no part of our belief".[46]

But again like Hooker, when this anti-authoritarianism was pushed within Protestantism by the Puritans, Dryden demurs. Hooker has insisted that "ten thousand general councils" cannot overweigh "one demonstrative reason alleged, or one manifest testimony cited from the mouth of God himself to the contrary . . ."[47] But faced with the Protestant "genius for schism",[48] he also insists that even in matters of doctrine where no clear proof is presented, if it can be shown that "a number of the learnedest divines" are unified on a particular point, a "somewhat reasonable man" would submit. For although it would not be clear "what reason or what Scripture" had led to such unanimity, the reasonable man would be deterred from opposition by a recognition of "the common imbecilities which are incident into our nature".[49] Dryden, aware that this "good" of the Reformation has had "full

---

[43] Cf. *Anglicanism*, pp. 121 – 31, for representatives of those who prefer the Apostles' Creed rather than the more theologicially explicit Creeds without, however, intending to undermine the content of those Creeds.

[44] Hooker, *Polity*, I, xiv, 4.   [45] *Op. cit.*, III, viii, 10.

[46] *Op. cit.*, II, vii, 6.   [47] *Op. cit.*, II, vii, 5.

[48] Herschel Baker's phrase, *Wars of Truth*, p. 193.

[49] Hooker, *Polity*, II, vii, 5.

bad a consequence" whereby "he was gifted most that loudest
bawl'd", falls back on the proposition that in "doubtful questions
't is the safest way/ To learn what unsuspected ancients say".
Moreover, "if after hearing what our Church can say", reason
still demurs, Dryden like Hooker, both of them persuaded of
"the common imbecilities . . . incident into our nature", recommends that the "private Reason 't is more just to curb/ Than by
disputes the public peace disturb". Hooker, in his conflict with
the Puritans, had already cited the desirability of "some definitive
sentence, which being given may stand, and a necessity of silence
on both sides afterwards imposed".[50]

The conclusion to be drawn is that while Dryden sharply
criticises the Deists' substitution of the common notions for the
central fact of Christianity – the Incarnation – this cannot with
any justification be called scepticism, unless Christianity by
definition is a scepticism. For Dryden, reason is of course powerless to achieve our salvation despite the fact that as "the Light
of Nature" it is "the next in dignity" to the light of Revelation.
But if, as Saint Paul and Anglicans generally say, the pagans are
saved by the merciful application of the Incarnation to them,
and not by virtue of their natural light, Dryden's criticism of the
Deists' claims should not be thought of as unusual. Further, if
Dryden prefers his religion simple, he is at one with a number of
Anglicans whose central intellectualism is not generally suspect.[51]
His opposition to Roman Catholicism is on what he sees as
rational grounds; his criticism of the Puritans is on the grounds
of their lack of intellectual credit. His traditionalism can be
matched at many points within Anglicanism, and constitutes no
evidence of scepticism in him. Indeed, it would seem that scepticism in the *Religio Laici* can be found only at the cost of exaggerat-
ing the rationalism of seventeenth-century Anglicanism, and of

---

[50] *Op. cit.,* Pref., vi, 4.

[51] Bredvold, *Intellectual Milieu*, p. 87, quotes the Independent John Owen's
answer to the Franciscan John Vincent Canes, the first of whom Bredvold
considers rationalistic, the second fideistic: "This Protestants think sufficient
for them, who as they need not to be wise above what is written; nor to know
more of God, than he hath so revealed of himself, that they may know it . . ."
This seems to be essentially the position of Dryden, and so it is difficult to see
how a sturdy rationalism in Owen can become metamorphosed into conclusive evidence of Dryden's hankering for authority.

too readily assuming that seventeenth-century Roman Catholic "fideism" has no recognisable methodological affinities with this Anglicanism. One is led to the further conclusion that if Dryden had not become a Catholic, and had not written *The Hind and the Panther*, the evidence of his turning to Rome and of his leanings to scepticism would, with respect to the *Religio* have remained quite unsuspected.

Dryden's opposition to Deism, Sectarianism, and Catholicism represents, therefore, not a lack of confidence in human reason but an attempt to reassert a basic Christian humanism which he found to be endangered by the secularism of the Deists, the anti-intellectualism of the Sectarians, and the excessive claims of the Catholics. That he will eventually recognise Catholicism to be a Christian humanism which most adequately resolves the traditional tensions between nature and grace has no bearing on his position at the time of the *Religio Laici*. At this point, he is securely within the tradition of Anglican Christian humanism.

A. D. Hope

ANNE KILLIGREW, OR THE ART OF
MODULATING[1]

There is a skill in poetry which has an analogy with the technique of modulation in music. A long poem of any kind cannot be sustained indefinitely at the highest level and a poet's problem is to learn to maintain the tone of the poem as a whole, while modulating skilfully from one level to another. Now that long poems are rarely attempted it is not only an art which is in danger of being lost, but one which readers and critics often fail to recognise and appreciate. Perhaps the most astonishing feat of modulation in the whole of English poetry is Dryden's ode: "To the Pious Memory of the Accomplished Young Lady Mrs Anne Killigrew, Excellent in the Two Sister Arts of Poesie and Painting."

She was born in 1660, the daughter of the Reverend Henry Killigrew, chaplain of the Duke of York, an irascible clergyman who wrote some poetry himself, in Latin. She grew up to be virtuous, accomplished, handsome, and charming, and became one of the Maids of Honour to Mary of Modena, the Duchess of York. She wrote poetry and she drew and painted and in both gained some reputation within the circle of the court, though she records with some indignation a malicious rumour that she was not really the author of her poems, which began to appear when she was twenty. She complains that the Matchless Orinda (Katherine Philips) had been accepted as a poet even though she too was a woman;

[1] [Reprinted from *The Cave and the Spring*, Adelaide (Rigby Ltd.) 1965, pp. 129–43.]

Th' Envious Age, only to Me alone
Will not allow, what I do write, my Own,
But let them rage, and 'gainst a Maide Conspire,
So Deathless Numbers from my Tuneful Lyre
Do ever flow; so Phebus I by thee
Divinely inspired and possest may be;
I willingly accept *Cassandras* Fate,
To speak the Truth, although believed too late.[2]

It is obvious throughout her poems that she had quite a good opinion of herself as a poet and it is equally obvious that there was little reason for anyone to think that she had not written them entirely herself. She threw off epigrams, she wrote complimentary addresses to ladies of the court and to young gentlemen whom she admired, and to more mature gentlemen who admired her. She wrote pastoral dialogues, moral essays in verse, poems on her own paintings, pindaric odes, lyrics about love, and even began an heroic poem on Alexander the Great but dropped it, realising that her powers were unequal to the task. The specimen of her verse that I have quoted is quite typical. She had some competence, a little wit, small experience and less originality but her verses have a modest charm, and some personal feeling comes through the conventional language and ideas. There is nothing in the poems that a nice girl with a taste for poetry could not have managed to write. When she was twenty-five or twenty-six she caught smallpox, like the Matchless Orinda with whom she chose to compare herself, and died of it. The following year her family collected her poems and published them with an engraving of a self-portrait, a Latin epitaph, and an ode in her memory by John Dryden. Dryden is said never to have met her, but he was a friend of the family. At any rate he could not have been the poet accused by gossip of writing her verses for her.

My Laurels thus an Others Brow adorn'd,
My Numbers they Admired, but Me they scorn'd:
An others Brow, that had so rich a store
Of Sacred Wreaths, that circled it before;

---

[2] *Poems by Mrs Anne Killigrew*, London. Printed for Samuel Lowndes, 1686, p. 47.

Where mine quite lost, (like a small stream that ran
Into a Vast and Boundless Ocean)
Was swallowed up, with that it joyn'd and drown'd
And that Abiss yet no Accession found.[3]

There were, of course, plenty of other poets at court. Yet it
could have been pleasant to think of Dryden's Boundless Ocean
paying its debt to her little brook in the great ode.

For a great ode it is. Johnson said of it, and justly at the time,
"His poem *on the death* of Mrs Killigrew is undoubtedly the
noblest ode that our language ever has produced". For manner
indeed it has perhaps never been surpassed. The problem that it
raises is not with the manner but the matter. Anne was undoubtedly a poet, but Dryden has surely overpraised her. If we
take the matter of the poem seriously it seems to be little more than
a piece of complimentary nonsense. George Crabbe, in his preface
to *Tales of the Hall*, remarked:

> If there be any combination of circumstances which may be
> supposed to affect the mind of a reader, and in some degree
> to influence his judgment, the junction of youth, beauty and
> merit in a female writer may be allowed to do this; and yet
> one of the most forbidding of titles is "Poems by a very
> Young Lady".[4]

Anne Killigrew's volume is a little better than this, but it is
still very small beer. It is difficult to believe that what the "noblest
ode" proposes as its theme can consist of fulsome praise of such
a very minor accomplishment.

One way out of the difficulty is to ignore Dryden's ostensible
subject altogether and to say that while he pretends to be writing
about Anne Killigrew he is really writing about the art of poetry.
That is what E. M. W. Tillyard does in his *Five Poems 1470–
1870*.

Dryden does indeed tell us things about Anne Killigrew,
that she was virtuous and gifted; that she wrote verse and
painted landscapes and royal portraits; that she died of the

---

[3] *Op. cit.*, p. 46.
[4] *Tales of the Hall. The Poetical Works of George Crabbe*, ed. A. J. Carlyle and
R. M. Carlyle. London (Oxford University Press) 1908, p. 340.

small-pox. But the two hundred lines spent in saying this are, as information, nearly all padding, while what astonishes and delights is the wealth of imaginative invention and the glory of the verbal music.[5]

But this will not do at all. More than half the poem consists of information which is plainly misinformation, for Dryden appears to be saying that Mistress Killigrew was really a superb poet and painter when he must have known better, and all the readers of the volume must have known that he knew it. I do not see how a poem which is half padding and absurd hyperbole can be really good, and to hold that verbal music and imaginative invention alone can make a good poem out of trivial material and false sentiments is to make poetry itself trivial. What is said and the way it is said must have a relation that the judgment can seriously accept. Johnson has perhaps indicated the secret of Dryden's method when he says:

> When he describes the Last Day, and the decisive tribunal, he intermingles this image:
> > When rattling bones together fly,
> > From the four quarters of the sky.
> It is indeed never in his power to resist the temptation of a jest.[6]

Johnson was close enough to Dryden and still within the world of taste to which the grand manner was natural. I think he could be trusted to distinguish whether this is jest or earnest. To Johnson this sounded like a deliberate joke, and the seriousness of the ode, I think, includes and, in fact, depends on a strain of humorous irony which runs all through it. By means of this irony Dryden manages to use the form and the language of a great Baroque ode to raise a few compliments about a charming girl to the proportions of a meditation on and a celebration of the power of poetry. And, in spite of his seeming to do the exact opposite, by the underlying humorous irony he never loses the proportion due to each of two subjects – one, the reach and force

[5] E. M. W. Tillyard, *Five Poems 1470–1870*. London (Chatto and Windus) 1948, p. 49.
[6] Samuel Johnson, *Lives of the English Poets*. London (Oxford University Press) 1961, Vol. I, p. 328.

of genius; the other, the girl who touched the edge of the great world of art and letters but was in no sense a genius. What he contrives to do is to make us feel that she belongs to that world in which genius rules and that this is her gift, her distinction: *that she shared in it*. What is important is that art is important; and because Anne Killigrew had her modest share in its world she is entitled to a share in its praise. Dryden's celebration of the art of poetry has a double force. What he says about poetry is exemplified and made vivid by a superb example of the thing he is celebrating. And the magnificence of the poetry is the source of a delicate irony by which he compels dissent from, or at least qualification of, what he seems to be saying about Anne as a poet. Another source of this irony is that the information he gives of her work is at variance with the praise he loads it with. Far from padding out the poem, the information is integral to its theme and essential to a modulation of its tone.

Another aspect of the poem which Tillyard neglects is the importance of its being a funeral ode. Had Dryden tried to write in this strain while Anne Killigrew was alive – deprived of the contrast of heaven and earth, he would have found his task more difficult. But, as it is, the Christian religion is his means of supporting his theme. Anne Killigrew alive was an ordinary human being, a "nice" girl, pious and accomplished, but she is now, he believes, in heaven. Just as we can speak seriously of a quite ordinary person translated and transfigured by the mystery of death and the assumption of eternity, so we can speak of a minor poetess passing into and partaking of the eternity and immortality of the whole world of art. It requires some tact to picture Mr Bones the Butcher playing a harp beside the Glassy Sea, but this is what any Christian must be able to do, and is able to do because the mortal butcher and the immortal soul are both one and distinguishable. The mortal Miss Killigrew can be pictured without incongruity putting on the immortality of that world in which her gifts and interests gave her some part. Dryden uses her Christian apotheosis with great tact to support Anne Killigrew's literary apotheosis and so manages to give a precise indication of the nature of her achievement without making us too uneasy about his placing her with Homer and Virgil. "The writer of an epitaph", as Johnson remarked, "should not be

considered as saying nothing but what is strictly true. Allowance
must be made for some degree of exaggerated praise. In lapidary
inscriptions a man is not upon oath."

But the poem is not merely a funerary ode, it is also a dedicatory
poem to a book of poems, a fact which at the time also allowed
for a certain conventional exaggeration. In 1692, Dryden published "Eleonora: A Panegyrical Poem Dedicated to the Memory
of the Late Countess of Abingdon", who had died at the age of
thirty-three. Dryden, who had never met her, wrote the panegyric
at the request of her husband. In his preface addressed to the earl
he defends the extravagance of his praise and the language in which
it is couched:

> We, who are Priests of *Apollo*, have not the Inspiration
> when we please; but must wait till the God comes rushing
> to us, and invades us with a fury, which we are not able to
> resist: . . . Let me not seem to boast, my Lord; for I have
> really felt it on this Occasion and prophecy'd beyond my
> natural power. Let me add and hope to be believ'd, that the
> Excellency of the Subject contributed much to the Happiness
> of the Execution: And that the weight of thirty Years was
> taken off me, while I was writing. I swom with the Tyde,
> and the Water under me was buoyant. The Reader will
> easily observe, that I was transported, by the multitude and
> variety of my Similitudes, which are generally the product of
> a luxuriant Fancy; and the wontoness of Wit. Had I call'd
> in my Judgment to my assistance, I had certainly retrench'd
> many of them. But I defend them not; let them pass for
> beautiful faults amongst the better sort of Critiques: For the
> whole Poem, though written in that which they call Heroique
> Verse, is of the Pindarique nature, as well in the Thought as
> the Expression; and, as such, requires the same grains of
> allowance for it. It was intended, as Your Lordship sees in
> the Title, not for an Elegie, but a Panegyrique. A kind of
> Apotheosis, indeed; if a Heathen Word may be applyed to a
> Christian use.[7]

These words apply with even more force to the ode on Anne

7 Preface to *Eleonora*, 15–33. *The Poems of John Dryden*, ed. James Kinsley.
Oxford (Clarendon Press) 1958, Vol. ii, pp. 582–3.

Killigrew. It is Pindaric in form as well as in nature; it is a panegyric more than an elegy; it is Anne Killigrew's Apotheosis and in it the poet is plainly transported by the multitude and variety of his similitudes which he neither intends nor expects his readers to take in too literal and sober a sense. Nevertheless the exuberance of its praise is tempered with a perfectly just insinuation of the defects of the young woman's poetry even though these defects are turned into compliments, a device Dryden had used shortly before in his exquisite elegy on the young poet John Oldham. He candidly indicates that Oldham's verse was rough and unskilled though he turns the fault to a compliment, calling it "A Noble Error".

To do this in the ode on Anne Killigrew without giving offence and without involving himself in contradiction, required the greatest tact and skill and the power to modulate from a tone of the most elevated fervour to one that might be described as one of familiar and ironic tenderness. He prepares for this in the first stanza which, more than any part of the poem, deserves Johnson's attribution of Horace's encomium on Pindar: *Fervet, immensaque ruit.*

This note of ironic tenderness appears immediately in the opening stanza:

> Thou youngest Virgin-Daughter of the Skies,
> Made in the last Promotion of the Blest;
> Whose Palmes, new pluckt from Paradise,
> In spreading Branches more sublimely rise,
> Rich with Immortal Green above the rest:[8]

It is, of course, very delicately insinuated. The words: "Made in the last Promotion of the Blest" can be taken perfectly seriously. Yet they invite us to think of death and the soul's reception into Heaven in terms of official advancement, in a military, ecclesiastical, or civil hierarchy, which are faintly inappropriate. I think there is little doubt that Dryden's turn of phrase is touched with irony which is very slightly comical: the notion of the saved souls being "promoted" in batches is put forward with a grave smile; and when the magnificent first stanza has run its course and Dryden has thoroughly established the feeling about her, not as

[8] *Ode to Anne Killigrew,* 1-5. Kinsley, Vol. 1, p. 459.

one of the local girls, but as an immortal soul, he returns to this note as he comes to her poetry and pictures her before her death as being "on probation":

> When thy first Fruits of Poesie were giv'n;
> To make thy self a welcome Inmate there:
> While yet a young Probationer,
> And Candidate of Heav'n.[9]

He covers this smiling image with the general tone of the baroque manner so that he does not seem to be actually making fun of her.

The second stanza, tracing the progress of the soul of Anne Killigrew through its previous tenements, Homer, Virgil, Sappho, and the Rev Henry Killigrew, is at first sight in the vein of the most absurd convention of high-flown compliment though it is not quite as absurd, for the occasion, as it would be if written today. Moreover, Dryden has prepared us for the idea in the first stanza:

> Here then a Mortal Muse thy Praise rehearse,
> In no ignoble Verse;
> But such as thy own voice did practise here.[10]

This is surely playful. Dryden could not possibly be serious in suggesting that Anne Killigrew could have written anything approaching the superb bravura passage with which his ode begins. But, as the author of a dedicatory ode, he can pay her the compliment of pretending that it is possible. The main thing is that Dryden is not *only* playing, which would be out of place in the circumstances. He is seriously proposing the theory of the unity of the world of literature. The myth of the progress of the poet's soul does not simply mean that the soul which just now occupied the "beauteous frame" of Miss Killigrew was the same which once filled the frames of Homer and Virgil – it has rolled through "all the mighty poets" and it rolls still through all the true poets whether mighty or not, including Dryden himself. The soul which animated Virgil might by corollary be one which had animated previously some ancient Anne Killigrew. Minor

---

[9] *Op. cit.*, 19–22, p. 460.
[10] *Op. cit.*, 16–18, p. 460.

poet or great poet, the spirit of poetry is one; and the last line stresses this:

Return, to fill or mend the Quire, of thy Celestial kind.[11]

It is as a member of the choir that she can be said to inherit the spirit of Homer and Sappho without being a poet of their rank.

Stanza three combines the notion of the confraternity of Art with that of the confraternity of Christendom. The elevated feeling, the long complex rhythmic sentence with its exulting energy and the baroque exaggeration with a slightly comic undertone are maintained. The picture of the angels too busy celebrating Anne's birthday to work the usual miracles is obviously humorous, yet

> And if no clust'ring Swarm of Bees
> On thy sweet Mouth distill'd their golden Dew[12]

is both serious and exquisite, so that it does make us feel that Dryden is perfectly serious about poetry and in saying that Anne has a place in it. All the same there is, I think, a deliberate lowering of tone from stanza one through stanza two and stanza three – a continuous and skilful modulation. Dryden is, in fact, bringing his poem down from heaven to earth and he has to get down to earth because he is now approaching the touchy part of the job: that of describing Anne's actual achievements. After this high-flown praise he is in danger of having either to contradict himself or to be insincere. He does neither. He chooses the one thing he can unreservedly praise, the innocence and purity of her verse, and he introduces this with a tirade on himself and the other poets writing for the contemporary stage. He would not have expected his readers to have taken him too literally, yet it may have been fitting. Dryden had been converted to the Roman Catholic Church the year before. He was engaged in writing *The Hind and the Panther*. He had given up writing for the stage for the time being. His cast of mind at the time was serious and preoccupied with questions of religion. There is no reason to doubt his sincerity. Yet it is difficult to feel that the repentance, however sincere, can be unmixed with irony.

[11] *Op. cit.,* 38, p. 460.
[12] *Op. cit.,* 50–1, p. 461.

What can we say t' excuse our *Second Fall*?
Let this thy *Vestal*, Heav'n, attone for all!
Her *Arethusian* Stream remains unsoil'd,
Unmixt with Forreign Filth and undefil'd,
Her Wit was more than Man, her Innocence a Child![13]

One can imagine neither that Dryden seriously thought the immorality of the Restoration stage equivalent to the Fall of Man itself, nor that he was unaware of the blasphemy involved in carrying on the comparison to the point where Anne Killigrew represents the central figure in a second Atonement for Sin. The comparison cannot be taken quite seriously, though the notion of the prostitution of the sacred arts of course can and indeed must be. In any case "the steaming Ordures of the stage" presents so gross an image that it would be wholly out of place if Dryden was to be taken here as maintaining a really high and serious tone. And there must be irony, too, in "Her Wit was more than Man, her Innocence a Child". Not only do Anne's few immature poems do nothing that anyone could take seriously as redressing, let alone atoning for, the whole Restoration drama, but Dryden and his readers would be perfectly aware that literature is produced not by innocence but by experience. What he is doing here is broadening the ironic tone and in a sense coarsening the effects in preparation for his next stanza.

> Art she had none, yet wanted none:
> For Nature did that Want supply,
> So rich in Treasures of her Own,
> She might our boasted Stores defy:
> Such Noble Vigour did her Verse adorn,
> That it seem'd borrow'd, where 'twas only born.[14]

Dryden, as his critical writings show, knew perfectly well that Nature does not and cannot "supply" lack of art. At best it can do something to compensate for the lack. What he appears to be saying here is very like what he said of John Oldham's unskilful versification, that Anne's poetry was artless stuff but had a certain natural vigour and charm. The same is true of his treatment of her love poetry.

[13] *Op. cit.,* 66–70, p. 461.   [14] *Op. cit.,* 71–6, pp. 461–2.

Ev' Love (for Love sometimes her Muse exprest)
Was but a *Lambent-flame* which play'd about her Brest:
Light as the Vapours of a Morning Dream,
So cold herself, whilst she such Warmth exprest,
'Twas *Cupid* bathing in *Diana's* Stream.[15]

Under the exquisite image, the sympathetic evocation of the
Morning Dream cut off so soon, the comment is clear: her love
poems show that she did not really know what she was talking
about.

Next he turns to her paintings with a return to hyperbole, but
without the tone of elevation. The exaggeration is good-
humoured and jolly and has an overtone of the condescension
with which one may praise amateur efforts without implying that
they are good:

Born to the Spacious Empire of the *Nine*,
One would have thought, she should have been content
To manage well that Mighty Government:
But what can young ambitious Souls confine?[16]

There is a good-humoured chuckle in that "One would have
thought", and Dryden hardly bothers to conceal it in his description of her paintings:

Her Pencil drew what e're her Soul design'd,
And oft the happy Draught surpass'd the Image in her Mind.[17]

That he hints her success to have been a somewhat hit-or-miss
affair, the following lines describing her subjects leave little
doubt. The tone and movement of the verse, with its jog-trot of
octosyllabic couplets, is one of tolerant amusement. The subjects
of her sketches are those with which talented young ladies have
always filled romantic sketch-books.

The *Sylvan* Scenes of Herds and Flocks,
And fruitful Plains and barren Rocks,
Of shallow Brooks that flow'd so clear,
The Bottom did the Top appear[18]

[15] *Op. cit.*, 83–7, p. 462.   [16] *Op. cit.*, 88–91, p. 462.
[17] *Op. cit.*, 106–7, p. 462.   [18] *Op. cit.*, 108–11, p. 462.

And so on. The concluding comment is open enough:

> So strange a Concourse ne're was seen before,
> But when the peopl'd Ark the whole Creation bore.[19]

In fact this part of the poem descends to parody, though parody of the gentlest kind. It must seem odd to find Dryden breaking the accepted form of his ode, the irregular Pindaric stanza, at this point and introducing a passage of descriptive octosyllabic couplets. But readers of Anne Killigrew's volume would recognise that he here breaks into an imitation of her own style in her poems describing her pictures. For example that entitled "On a Picture Painted by her self, representing two nimphs [*sic*] of DIANA'S, one in a posture to Hunt, the other Batheing".

> We are Diana's Virgin-Train
> Descended of no Mortal strain;
> Our Bows and Arrows are our Goods,
> Our Pallaces, the lofty Woods,
> The Hills and Dales, at early Morn
> Resound and Eccho with our Horn;
> We chase the Hinde and Fallow-Deer,
> The Wolf and Boar both dread our Spear;
> In Swiftness we out-strip the Wind
> An Eye and Thought we leave behind[20]

And so on and so on. This strain is continued in the next stanza on Anne's royal portraits:

> Our Phenix Queen was portrai'd too so bright,
> Beauty alone could Beauty take so right:
> Her Dress, her Shape, her matchless Grace
> Were all observ'd as well as heav'nly Face.[21]

The manner is one of the highest and most enthusiastic praise, but it hardly fits with what Dryden is actually saying. It is no compliment to a really competent artist to tell him that he has the shape right in a portrait, that the face is recognisable and that he has made no mistakes in the portrayal of the costume. To

---

[19] *Op. cit.,* 125–6, p. 463.
[20] *Poems by Mrs Anne Killigrew,* pp. 28–9.
[21] *Ode to Anne Killigrew,* 134–7. Kinsley, p. 463.

regard this as praise is to imply that the painter is an amateur or a tyro. The irony here is hardly disguised at all:

What next she had design'd, Heaven only knows:[22]

With this stanza the modulation of the tone brings the poem to its lowest level, but the descent has been so skilful and discreet that there is no apparent incongruity with the elevation of the opening passage.

From this point Dryden begins to build up again. He cannot, without impropriety, take the great tone again at once so he modulates as it were into another key. In stanza eight the tone is, to begin with, one of tenderness and sympathy as the poet brings her before us as a person. Indeed he moves from the royal portrait to the self-portrait that provided the original of the engraving. He reflects on the cruelty of Fate and the double outrage on this charming young creature not only deprived of life but – ravaged with smallpox which destroyed her beauty first. He compares her fate with that of the Matchless Orinda. By the end of the stanza he has moved from amusement to tenderness, from tenderness to pity and from pity to enthusiasm. The poem is on its way up from earth to heaven again. It rises there by way of a stanza of what might be called personal anecdote moving into myth: a simple, moving and charming description of her brother at sea not knowing of his sister's death and seeing a new star appear amid the Pleiades. From there it crashes into the great terminal passage where Dr Johnson smelt an inappropriate jest. It is, I think, not merely a joke, but it is certainly touched with the irony that runs through the whole poem. The irony is not merely in the image of the rattling bones filling the sky as they rush together but in the whole tremendous energy and speed of the Last Day. It is just as much in the picture of the Sacred Poets bounding from their tombs like a host of jack-in-the-boxes. And although it is comic, it is impressive and beautiful, because it has the energy and vigour of one of the great baroque pictures with the Saints soaring like heavenly rockets into the sky and the spectators portrayed in dramatic movement and a sweep of limbs and draperies that may be theatrical but is successfully and impressively theatrical. It is successful and impressive here

---

[22] *Op. cit.*, 146, p. 464.

because Dryden has *not* simply turned the Last Day into a gallop –
he has suggested the enormous energy of Nature released and
triumphant in its last hour – and in the same way, the picture of
the sacred poets rocketing from their graves, though comical is
not ridiculous, because Dryden makes it natural to the "inborn
vigour on the wing" which is the nature of poetry itself, the
energy which is eternal delight. Nor is it exaggerated that Anne
Killigrew should lead them into heaven. Dryden is not being at
all ironical here. He is returning to the theme of innocence: "And
a little child shall lead them."

The most important thing about the ode is usually missed: its
superb modulation of tone. Johnson missed this perhaps – perhaps not: "All the stanzas indeed are not equal. An imperial
crown cannot be one continued diamond; the gems must be held
together by some less valuable matter." But he was aware of the
other supreme quality that makes him call it an imperial crown:
its triumphant energy – he seems to have been so conquered by
this "inborn vigour on the wing" that he does not treat the ode
with the ruthless logic and common sense which it will no more
bear than will "Lycidas":

> Passion runs not after remote allusions and obscure
> opinions . . . Where there is leisure for fiction there is little
> grief . . . In this poem there is no nature, for there is no
> truth; there is no art, for there is nothing new . . . with these
> trifling fictions are mingled the most awful and sacred truths
> . . . He who thus grieves will excite no sympathy; he who
> thus praises will confer no honour. . . .[23]

All these strictures might be applied to Dryden's ode, and sometimes with more justice than to "Lycidas". In both cases there
would be *some* justice at least – "Lycidas" has some incongruities,
some "fictions" which are hard to reconcile with the ostensible
subject and the chosen form. Dryden's ode challenges taste,
affronts propriety and common sense, and trembles on the edge of
travesty throughout – one slip in the superb management and it
would be merely ridiculous; the slightest falling off of the vigour
and power and it would be simply theatrical and rhetorical. And
the question arises: why, if we grant all the strictures that Johnson

[23] *Lives of the English Poets*, pp. 112–13.

did make in the one case and could have made in the other, why is each still a marvellous poem? In each case it is the pure and exquisite feeling for the language triumphing over and justifying the mannerisms. Milton has chosen an effete pastoral style and made it lucid and vital, Dryden has chosen a rhetorical and baroque style and by the plainness and energy of his diction has made it vigorous and lambent. By the seriousness of his theme, the celebration of poetry, he has redeemed and transfigured the triviality of its subject. So far Tillyard is right. He is wrong in supposing the trivial matter is mere padding and not an integral part of a theme that embraces the whole range of the art from the merest beginners to the supreme masters.

Jay Arnold Levine

JOHN DRYDEN'S EPISTLE TO JOHN DRIDEN[1]

In view of the speculations that Dryden's religious and political shifts have long elicited, it might be tempting to approach "To my Honour'd Kinsman, John Driden, of Chesterton" (1700) as documentary evidence of the poet's position during a crucial period, for such documents are rare in the years following 1688, and this epistle is certainly the most substantial of them. Although a biographical or historical study is not the final concern of the present reading, which will attempt to elucidate the rhetorical and poetical organisation of the epistle, some attention to the contexts of the poem is a necessary prelude to an interpretation of a work described by its author as "my Own Opinion, of what an English man in Parliament ought to be . . . a Memorial of my own Principles to all Posterity".[2]

I

Sober announcements of his troubles – age, ill health, neglect, and poverty – pervade Dryden's private and public statements

---

[1] [Reprinted from *The Journal of English and Germanic Philology*, Vol. LXII (1964) pp. 450–74.]

[2] *The Letters of John Dryden*, ed. Charles Ward. Durham, N. C. (1942) p. 120 (to Charles Montagu). For Dryden's high opinion of his poem, see pp. 123–4 and 135. Although modern critics have tended to agree with the poet's estimation of the epistle, they have allowed it no more than genial and casual praise. See, *e.g.*, Mark Van Doren, *John Dryden*, 3rd edn., New York (1946) p. 120, and D. Nicol Smith, *John Dryden*, Cambridge (1950) p. 87. For the "rare exceptions to Dryden's supposed abstentation from political allusions in the last eleven years of his life", see John R. Moore, "Political Allusions in Dryden's Later Plays", *P.M.L.A.*, LXXIII (1958) p. 36.

after the Glorious Revolution. His personal decline was matched by (and, in the case of his poverty, attributable to) his public misfortune. The former court favourite has been deprived of his official honours, duties, and emoluments, and forced into silent forbearance under a hostile regime: "If they will consider me as a Man, who have done my best to improve the Language, & Especially the Poetry, & will be content with my acquiescence under the present Government, & forbearing satire on it, that I can promise, because I can perform it; but I can neither take Oaths, nor forsake my Religion."[3] Dryden protested his forbearance too much; although he did eschew open or prolonged attacks upon William and his government, flashes of satire did indeed have room wherever he wrote.[4] The testimony of a contemporary – one ridiculed in the "Honour'd Kinsman", moreover – affirms that the covert sallies in Dryden's Dedication of the *Aeneis* were not ignored: "Tho we own Mr D. may be a Republican now, it's but agreeable to his Character; from the Beginning he was an ἀλλοπροσαλλος, and I doubt not but he'ell continue so to the end of the chapter."[5]

This imputation of republicanism to the Tory poet is not so absurd as it might seem, for the political situation of the late 1690s found the extreme Right joining the far Left in a concerted assault upon William and his ministry:

> 'Tis urg'd in behalf of the Party, that they have renounc'd their former Tory-Principles, even so far as to run to the other Extreme, and that instead of submitting all things to Royal Will and Pleasure, they are now for depressing the Prerogative, and exalting the Power of Commons . . . All suddain and unaccountable Changes, ought to be suspected; and when Men do things so very contrary to their Nature,

---

[3] *Letters*, p. 123.

[4] The largest concentration of Dryden's satiric thrusts occurs in his Dedication to the *Aeneis*, where he uses Roman politics as an allegorical screen for comments upon William's reign. In the eyes of his enemies, Dryden's silence on the death of Queen Mary was as damning as a vociferous satire would have been (see Preface to *An Ode Occasion'd by the Death of the Queen* [London, 1695] and *Urania's Temple: or a Satyr upon the Silent-Poets* [London, 1695]).

[5] Luke Milbourne, *Notes on Dryden's Virgil*, London (1698) p. 8.

Temper, and Principles, (as a Tory's acting like a Common-
wealths Man is) 'tis more probable that they dissemble.[6]

Tory revisionism cannot be so easily ascribed to political chi-
canery, since it resulted from a complex political situation in
which theory and expediency clashed; for the immediate purpose
of the present essay, the paradox is pertinent only insofar as it
warns us against attaching catchall party labels to John Dryden
or to his cousin when we find them echoing sentiments which
were actually common to a number of otherwise widely divergent
factions. Opposition to *William* did not necessarily imply
republicanism, any more than hostility towards *kingship* denoted
Jacobitism.

Even more caution is vital in any consideration touching the
practical politics of Parliament. Recent historical studies have
taught us that the easy distinction between Whig and Tory which
we often assume to have been the fixed polarity of English politics
from the time of the Restoration, did not truly come into being
until late in the eighteenth century. In the last years of the
seventeenth century, members of Commons responded to a variety
of special interests, without always committing themselves to the
rudimentary prototypes of the British party system.[7] Before
attempting to pinpoint John Driden's political affiliation, and its
possible relevance in the epistle addressed to him, we must
briefly recall the specific issues that determined an M.P.'s allegiance
in the late 1690s – issues with a direct bearing upon Dryden's
epistolary discourse.

The major debate between 1697 and 1700 may be traced to the
questions that arose once the paramount problem of the Nine
Years War had been settled by the Peace of Ryswick. William
had launched that war in order to secure his succession, block the

---

[6] [Sir Richard Blackmore?], *A Short Defence of the Last Parliament, Answer'd
Article by Article*, London (1702) p. 20. *Cf.* "Cursory Remarks upon some
late Disloyal Proceedings", in *Somers Tracts*, xi, pp. 155, 178–9.

[7] "They were 'Patriots' or 'Churchmen' before they were Whigs or Tories.
How then were they distinguished? By their reaction to certain important
events – such as . . . deciding between disbanding and the retention of a large
army in 1699" (David Ogg, *England in the Reigns of James II and William III*
[Oxford, 1955] p. 129). *Cf.* Robert Walcott, *English Politics in the Early
Eighteenth Century*, Cambridge, Mass. (1956) p. 91.

ambitions of Louis xiv, and protect Dutch interests on the Continent. Popular at first, the war (also known as the "war to the last guinea"[8]) demanded such extreme financial measures – nothing less than the establishment of the Bank of England and the National Debt, in addition to heavy taxation – that it soon wearied all factions and left William at the nadir of his popularity in England. The peace treaty accomplished little more than the forced recognition of William (withdrawn in 1701, when Louis proclaimed "James III" king of England) and a restoration of the *status quo*, but it was quickly taken by an unfriendly Parliament as the signal for a "return to normalcy", thereby forestalling William's preparations for the then-impending War of the Spanish Succession. Against William's vigorous objections, and even to his humiliation, the standing army and his own personal guards were drastically reduced in order to relieve the country's financial burden.

In the acrimonious debate over the standing army, the economic strain was but one complaint against the scheme; some Englishmen, worried about a threat to their liberties from the presence of foreign (Dutch) troops, advocated native militias as England's best protection, from both a military and a political standpoint. Another important feature of this argument was its insistence upon the development of a strong naval force as the mainline of defence and also as an instrument of English commerce.[9] Direct references to all the arguments advanced by William's opposition are to be found in the "Honour'd Kinsman".

John Driden's reactions to these issues can be discovered in some instances, but only guessed in others, since the reliable data concerning his political position is as meagre as information about the man himself.[10] Huntingdon, the county represented by Driden, was a stronghold of the Montagu family, supporters of the Whig junto to which their kinsman, Charles Montagu, belonged. Driden, however, could have had the support of a rival Tory faction led by Lady Sandwich. He was elected to the

[8] John Dalrymple, *Memoirs of Great Britain and Ireland*, London (1790) III, Pt. iii, pp. 82–3.

[9] See, *e.g.*, "Min Heer T. Van C's Answer to Min Heer H. Van L's Letter ... representing the true Interests of Holland", in *Somers Tracts*, x, p. 316, and *A Discourse concerning Militias and Standing Armies*, London (1697) p. 27.

[10] Between 1 Oct. 1698 and 11 Apr. 1700, cousin Driden is mentioned eight times in the poet's correspondence (pp. 101, 112, 123–4, 129, 131, 134–5). We

parliaments of 1690, 1698, and 1700, all of which tended to oppose William and the ministry. Driden's presence in those bodies does not allow a deduction of his allegiance, but the possibility that contests in Huntingdon followed national trends is further strengthened by his absence from the Parliament of 1695, which was loyal to the court.[11] In his correspondence, Dryden aligns his cousin with the "Country Party" (another ambiguous label) and notes his opposition to the standing army, but he elsewhere mentions Driden's unswerving loyalty to William.[12] From such bare hints, perhaps the closest estimate we can infer of Driden's political character is that, like many of his class, he opposed the Whig ministry, but unlike numerous discontented country squires, he did not drift into Jacobitism.[13] That he may have been affiliated with Harley's "Patriot" faction, is suggested

[11] For a brief account of local politics in Driden's county during this period, see the *Victoria History of the County of Huntingdon*, eds. W. Page and G. Proby, London (1926–38) III, p. 34. Driden is listed in *Cobbett's Parliamentary History of England*, London, (1809) V, pp. 544, 1186, 1229. On the composition of the Parliaments of the 1690s, see Ogg, pp. 358, 397, 444. Unaccountably, Driden is not mentioned in Walcott's *English Politics*. Driden's name appears on only one division-list, and that in 1704, as an M.P. opposed to the High Church position on Occasional Conformity ("A List of those Members . . . who are not Number'd among the Tackers nor Sneakers" in *A Collection of White and Black Lists* [London, 1715]). For a discussion of that list, see Robert Walcott, "Division-Lists in the House of Commons, 1689–1715", *Bulletin of Historical Research*, XIV (1936) pp. 28–9.

[12] In the letter to Montagu: "My cousin Driden saw them [the verses] in the Country; & the greatest Exception He made to them, was a Satire against the Dutch valour, in the late Warr. He desir'd me to omit it, (to use his Own words) out of the respect He had to his Soveraign. I obeyed his Commands; & left onely the praises, which I think are due to the gallantry of my own Countrymen" (p. 120). For the confusion in respect to "Country" as a political designation, see Ogg, pp. 478–9, and Keith Feiling, *History of the Tory Party, 1640–1714*, Oxford (1924) pp. 287–8.

[13] For a fine summary of the condition and attitudes of the country squire at that time, see J. H. Plumb, *Sir Robert Walpole: The Making of a Statesman*, London (1956) pp. 14–22.

know that he was born in 1635, remained a bachelor, and suffered poor health when Dryden knew him, but much of the additional information conveyed by Edmund Malone cannot be verified (*Critical and Miscellaneous Works of John Dryden* [London, 1800] I, pp. 322–4). On Driden's celibacy and charities, see "Dryden Family Illustrated", *Gentleman's Magazine*, LXII (1792) p. 225.

by Dryden's uncharacteristically eulogistic use of that epithet in the "Honour'd Kinsman".[14]

The political stance assumed within the "Honour'd Kinsman" – which may or may not have been Dryden's "real" position – indicates that cousin Driden's moderation and loyalty to William may have tempered Dryden's hostility (at least for the occasion of the poem), so that the poet pursues a doggedly nonpartisan course in the attempt to raise the level of his discourse to that of factionless national interest. Dryden's presentation of the poem to Charles Montagu, a former enemy and then (1700) a minister of the junto, may help support a reading of the poem as a peace-offering, albeit a concession fully in accord with Dryden's insistence upon preserving his "conscience and honour."[15] The epistle is not a fawning overture to the Whig regime – however much Dryden might have used it to assure the Establishment that he was not tainted by subversion – but a frank statement of the poet's loyal opposition and disinterested concern for the national welfare. Therefore, the "John Driden" bodied forth

[14] *Cf.* Dryden's earlier disdain for the epithet in *Absalom & Achitophel*, 965–8, and *Amphitryon* (in *Dramatic Works*, ed. M. Summers [London, 1932] VI, p. 156). For the programme of Robert Harley's "New Country Party" (which "drove everywhere a hot campaign against courtiers, taxes, placemen, and standing armies" – the same platform accepted in the "Honour'd Kinsman"), see Feiling, p. 329.

[15] At the time of the epistle, Montagu was one of William's most efficient and loyal ministers, responsible for financing the Nine Years War and charged with supporting in Commons the King's unpopular desire for a standing army. In 1687 Montagu had collaborated with Prior on the famous attack against Dryden, *The Hind and the Panther Transvers'd*, and he continued his assault three years later in the "Epistle to Dorset". Montagu was nevertheless among the hundred subscribers to Dryden's Virgil, but the famous Maecenas apparently never offered any more substantial patronage until Dryden's death, when he offered to pay the funeral expenses. That final tribute to his old enemy led to Montagu's being accepted as Dryden's benefactor, for which he was alternately damned (Tom Brown, *A Description of Mr D –n's Funeral* [London, 1700] p. 4) and praised (*Luctus Britannici* [London, 1700] p. 52). Perhaps the most accurate estimate of the relationship is contained in a bookseller's dedication to Montagu: "You have been pleased already to shew your respect to his Memory, notwithstanding He had that unhappiness of Conduct, when alive, to give you cause to disclaim the Protection of Him" (*Nine Muses* [London, 1700]). If Dryden, "when alive", used the "Honour'd Kinsman" to obtain Montagu's protection, he must have failed.

I

by the poem is neither Whig nor Tory, Court nor Country,[16] but a personification of Albion itself. The literary tradition of the "Honour'd Kinsman", to which we now turn, confirms this postulation, and aids us in considering such related matters as the seeming bifurcation of the epistle (which moves from John Driden in his country seat to a consideration of the country at large); Dryden's conversion of an apparent panegyric into a truly deliberative address; the relationship between speaker and addressee; and the use of poetical, as distinct from rhetorical, formulations.

2

The Horatian quality of the "Honour'd Kinsman" has been frequently noted, but it has never been mentioned that Dryden's particular model was the Second Epode, which he had translated almost literally in 1685. Practically all the topics treated more extensively in the epistle can be educed from the epode: the contentiousness of law, the marital situation, the riches of the land, the hunt, and the wholesomeness of country life. But several of the Horatian *données* are completely reversed by Dryden: his cousin is commended for his bachelorhood, and not for being happily married; Driden is a wealthy squire and not a poor farmer; and instead of removing himself entirely from civic affairs, cousin Driden leaves his "lov'd Retreat" in order to fulfill the duties of an M.P. Of course, it could be held that such alterations merely display Dryden's literal adherence to the actualities of John Driden's situation, but whatever the source of the poem's data, it is the fashioning of those unavoidable details into the larger pattern of the epistle which should properly engage our attention.

Another significant departure from Dryden's distant model, one which may illuminate the importance of the modifications already described, is the entire omission of the epode's conclusion, which shows the praises of rustic happiness to have been the interior monologue of a hypocritical usurer. This cancellation –

<hr/>

[16] "To my Honour'd Kinsman, John Driden, of Chesterton", 128. The text used for Dryden's prose and nondramatic work is *Poems*, ed. James Kinsley, Oxford (1958).

which Dryden surely would have expected his audience to notice – contributes to the intention and the design of the epistle, for Dryden is pointedly contrasting his *real* country squire with the pastoral daydream of the Horatian financier. The poem persists in disclaiming the possibility of any idyllic, prelapsarian, Golden Age; rather, it attempts to work out the problems of a world in which sin and death are very much with us. Poverty is no blessing in such a world; retirement cannot be complete; and marriage, like other social and political entanglements, does indeed have its pains. The weight of mortality perhaps never becomes fully oppressive in the epistle – some relief is offered – but it continually presses upon the consciousness.

In accounting for the traditional aspects of the poem, it would be a mistake to leap from Horace to Dryden, for between the Second Epode and the "Honour'd Kinsman" intervened a body of retirement poems which endowed the *beatus ille* theme with distinctive political and philosophical implications in the English seventeenth century, as Maren-Sofie Røstvig's recent studies have shown.[17] If Dryden does part from his remote primary source in the ways mentioned, he reveals at the same time an affinity with the retirement poets of his own century. In addition to such ubiquitous topics as the praise of temperance over corrupt luxury and the desire for escape from political turmoil, a recurring motif in that body of poetry is the identification of the "Happy Man" with Adam before the Fall: "*Lord of my self*, accountable to none,/ Like the first man in Paradise, alone".[18] Before taking up the significance that Dryden gave to the figure of Adam *solus*, we must take up Norris of Bemerton's suggestion that he is "Lord of my self".[19] This related *topos* appears regularly in the retirement poems: "More truly happy those! who can/ Govern the little

[17] "To the Royalist the husbandman came to represent everything that was good in the old system, and his quiet, obscure, and contented way of life became a nostalgic ideal in an age troubled by fears and insecurity" (Maren-Sofie Røstvig, *The Happy Man, I* [Oxford, 1954] p. 67).

[18] John Norris of Bemerton, "The Retirement", in *Miscellanies of the Fuller Worthies Library*, ed. A. B. Grosart, III (1872) pp. 65–6. *Cf.* John Tutchin, quoted by Røstvig, I, p. 402, ("Anchorite Adam happy still had been,/... Had not Company and Vice come rowling in"), and Marvell, "The Garden" ("Two Paradises 'twere in one/ To live in Paradise alone").

[19] *Cf.* Dryden's "Lord of Your Self" ("To my Honour'd Kinsman," 18).

Empire Man".[20]   The serenity promised by retirement poets is precisely what John Driden achieves in the rule of his own little kingdom, whether that domain be taken to mean the province of the Justice of the Peace, or his own soul;

> Just, Good, and Wise, contending Neighbours come,
> From your Award, to wait their final Doom;
> And, Foes before, return in Friendship home.
> Without their Cost, you terminate the Cause;
> And save th'Expence of long Litigious Laws:
> Where Suits are travers'd; and so little won,
> That he who conquers, is but last undone:
> Such are not your Decrees; but so design'd,
> The Sanction leaves a lasting Peace behind;
> Like your own Soul, Serene; a Pattern of your Mind.
>   Promoting Concord, and composing Strife,
> Lord of your self, uncumber'd with a Wife . . .[21]

The inflated language of war and peace with which Dryden exalts the decisions of the country J.P. is not an arch or belittling technique, but points to the broader political concerns of the epistle.

The microcosmic metaphor of the retirement theme, and the internal harmony that John Driden manifests in his legislation to his own little state, turn us ultimately to Plato, who in the *Republic* proceeds to investigate the nature of justice in the individual by projecting the qualities of that virtue in the larger terms of justice in the state.[22]   Once having located it in the political macrocosm, Plato describes justice as that serene promotion of "concord" and "composing" of strife which Dryden attributes to his cousin.   Plato's movement from the public domain of justice to its equivalent in the private sphere is reversed

[20] George Stepney, in *Dryden's Miscellany*, I, p. 178. *Cf.* Charles Dryden, *op. cit.*, IV, p. 198; *Odes of Casimire*, ed. Røstvig, Augustan Reprint Society, No. 44 (Los Angeles, 1953) p. 47; William Habington, *Poems*, ed. K. Allott, Liverpool (1948) pp. 93, 140.

[21] "To my Honour'd Kinsman," 7–18.

[22] "We think of justice as a quality that may exist in a whole community as well as in an individual, and the community is the bigger of the two. Possibly, then, we may find justice there in larger proportions, easier to make out" (tr. F. M. Cornford [Oxford, 1945] p. 55).

in Aristotle's *Rhetoric*, where the orator is advised that the means of achieving happiness in the state can be considered only after the nature of happiness in the individual, in its several components, has been understood.[23] The national issues to which Aristotle recommends that such a conception of happiness is to be applied "are some five in number, to wit: ways and means, war and peace, the defence of the country, imports and exports, legislation".[24] In the Aristotelian rhetoric, then, we find not only an explanation of the epistle's progression from Driden's private happiness to his public responsibilities, but also the authority for the particular topics discussed in the course of the poem. Each of John Driden's activities in the first part of the poem has its equivalent in the policies advocated for England in the second half; the metaphor of the individual as a kind of state could not be more thoroughly exploited.

The praise of John Driden's moderation in hunting – a sport that serves a useful (and *just*) purpose but can be dangerous in excess – foreshadows the moderation in war that Dryden urges upon his cousin and the nation at large:

> Ev'n then, industrious of the Common Good:
> And often have you brought the wily Fox
> To suffer for the Firstlings of the Flocks;
> Chas'd ev'n amid the Folds; and made to bleed,
> Like Felons, where they did the murd'rous Deed.
> This fiery Game, your active Youth maintain'd;
> Not yet, by Years extinguish'd, though restrain'd . . .[25]

> Enough for *Europe* has our *Albion* fought:
> Let us enjoy the Peace our Blood has bought. . . .
> In Wars renew'd, uncertain of Success,
> Sure of a Share, as Umpires of the Peace.[26]

Similarly, the prudence displayed by John Driden in avoiding the strife of marriage in order to *stand* alone, anticipates Dryden's recommendation for England's defence, in which he repeats the

---

[23] "Men, individually and in common, nearly all have some aim, in the attainment of which they choose or avoid certain things. This aim, briefly stated, is happiness and its component parts" (Loeb edn., p. 47 [1360b]).
[24] Aristotle, 1359b.   [25] "To my Honour'd Kinsman", 53–9.
[26] *Op. cit.*, 158–70.

necessity of *standing* alone and relying upon the nation's own resources: "How cou'd He stand, when put to double Pain,/ He must a Weaker than himself sustain!";[27] "Safe in our selves, while on our selves we stand,/ The Sea is ours, and that defends the Land".[28] John Driden's domestic economy, which is aimed solely at benefiting his own "*Israel*-Host" – "For God, who gave the Riches, gave the Heart/ To sanctifie the Whole, by giving Part"[29] – points to the later proposals for an economic and mercantile policy which will bolster England's ("*Canaans*") position:

> Nor gratifie whate'er the Great desire,
> Nor grudging give, what Publick Needs require.
> Part must be left, a Fund when Foes invade;
> And Part employ'd to roll the Watry Trade. . . .[30]

The topic of Driden's performance as a J.P.[31] adumbrates the later discussion of the nature of national legislation, for Aristotle advises that "it is on the laws that the safety of the State is based. Wherefore the orator must know how many forms of government there are; what is expedient for each; and the natural causes of its downfall, whether they are peculiar to the particular form of government or opposed to it".[32] Dryden's commentary upon the peculiar balance of the British system, and the threats to its equilibrium, meets the Aristotelian criteria:

> A Patriot, both the King and Country serves;
> Prerogative, and Privilege preserves:
> Of Each, our Laws the certain Limit show;
> One must not ebb, nor t'other overflow.[33]

Taxation, the fifth Aristotelian topic, is not so amenable to microcosmic representation as the other subjects are; for that reason, it emerges towards the close of the poem as both a personal matter (involving Driden's ancestor) and a national issue.[34]

With respect to the areas of his discourse, and to their arrangement in a bipartite scheme which passes from the "country" as a rural retreat to the "country" as a nation, Dryden has incor-

---

[27] *Op. cit.*, 27–8.   [28] *Op. cit.*, 146–7.   [29] *Op. cit.*, 38–9.
[30] *Op. cit.*, 129–32.   [31] *Op. cit.*, 8–16.   [32] Aristotle, 1360a.
[33] "To my Honour'd Kinsman", 171–4.
[34] *Op. cit.*, 184–94.

porated Aristotle's rhetorical programme. Besides this fundamental enactment of those basic procedures, Dryden has also observed the simplicity prescribed by Aristotle for the *dispositio* of a deliberative oration: "at the most the parts are four in number – exordium, statement, proof, epilogue".[35] The "Honour'd Kinsman" divides by such a principle: exordium,[36] statement,[37] proof,[38] and epilogue.[39] Moreover, what may seem to be a panegyric upon a country cousin, with "digressions more or less sardonic"[40] upon greater affairs, is actually a deliberative address advising a course of political action (or inaction), in which the proof is based upon the statement of personal virtues exemplified by John Driden; either section would be meaningless without the other. Such a reading should clarify, among other problems, the reason for the partial retirement of this particular "Happy Man"; his virtues attain their true significance only when applied to the national situation.

3

Dryden's pursuit of the analogy between the body natural and the body politic may partially explain the lengthy section on medical practice in the middle of the epistle.[41] This commentary is introduced by four lines that contain the poem's first overt reference to its political context:

> Thus Princes ease their Cares: But happier he,
> Who seeks not Pleasure thro' Necessity,
> Than such as once on slipp'ry Thrones were plac'd;
> And chasing, sigh to think themselves are chas'd.[42]

These couplets have been read as an allusion to the exiled James

[35] Aristotle, 1414b.
[36] "To my Honour'd Kinsman", 1–6.
[37] *Op. cit.,* 7–116.   [38] *Op. cit.,* 117–94.   [39] *Op. cit.,* 195–209.
[40] "It is a eulogy of country life in general and a commendation of the kinsman's own rural regimen in particular, with digressions more or less sardonic upon marriage, medicine, and the present state of Europe" (Van Doren, p. 120).
[41] "To my Honour'd Kinsman", 71–116.
[42] *Op. cit.,* 67–70.

II, which they indeed may be, but they can also be interpreted as an oblique reference to the reigning William, a famous hunter and (conjointly) a valetudinarian.[43] The hunt in which William engaged through necessity was not only the sporting exercise believed vital to his health, but also the war that he undertook in order to support his claim to the throne after he had "chas'd" James from it.[44] Furthermore, the throne on which William had been placed was indeed slippery, having in three reigns sent one king to the block and another across the Channel. The chase in which William – so used to playing the hunter himself – became the prey, may refer to the Assassination Plot of 1695, which sought to trap the king as he returned from his weekly hunt. But it is the present tense of the second couplet that appears to confirm William as at least an alternative subject; both he and James *were* placed on the throne, but the "chasing" is still in progress, and William, not James, is currently occupying the seat. William may play the hunter in the field, in politics, and in war, but he himself is being pursued by Death.

Standing as it does between an allusion to an ailing king upon a precarious throne, and the major political argument of the epistle, the extended satire upon the shortcomings of the avaricious physicians may have its origin in the concept of the body politic. The political literature of the 1690s dwelt incessantly upon the possibilities offered by that analogy, with special emphasis upon the medical role played by ministers and members of Parliament: "Our Trimmer believeth, that by the advantage of our Situation, there can hardly be any such sudden Disease come upon us, but that the King may have time enough to consult with his Physicians

[43] "That which gave the most melancholy prospect, was the ill state of the king's health, whose stay so long at St James's without exercise, or hunting, which was so used by him that it was become necessary [*cf.* Dryden, "To my Honour'd Kinsman," 68], had brought him under a weakness, as was likely to have brought very ill effects" (Gilbert Burnet, *History of his Own Time* [London, 1838] p. 525).

[44] The comparison between the hunt and warfare was, of course, a commonplace drawn from the larger analogy of the two bodies: "No Body can be healthful without Exercise, neither Body Natural nor Body Politick; and certainly to a Kingdom or Estate, a just and honourable War is the true Exercise" (Bacon, quoted in *Select Letters from Fog's Weekly Journal* [London, 1732] I, p. 167).

in Parliament.":[45] Dryden was himself often drawn to the comparison: "For who wou'd give Physick to the Great when he is uncall'd? – to do his Patient no good, and indanger himself for his Prescriptions?"[46] But Dryden *is* offering physic to the great in the "Honour'd Kinsman". The other prescribers whom he attacks or chides in this section of the poem are either murderous and avaricious or, at best, simply doing the least amount of harm with their limited knowledge.[47] The location of the medical discourse, between the private and the public sectors of the epistle, suggests its transitional function. If there is an implied equation of the medical practitioners and their political counterparts in Parliament or the king's council, then the overt discussion of national policy that directly follows the medical commentary may be viewed as John Dryden's own prescription for his ailing country.

Although its political implications seem likely, the medical section also fulfills another – and perhaps more crucial – purpose. In a poem charged with references and allusions to man's dismissal from Paradise, the section serves as both a *memento mori* and a warning against the kind of intemperance and sinful aspiration which drove Adam from the "bless'd Abode". The "Honour'd Kinsman" continually insists upon the recognition of man's mere mortality as an effective check to overweening ambition in all modes of behaviour and thought:

> When once the *Persian* King was put to Flight,
> The weary *Macedons* refus'd to fight;
> Themselves their own Mortality confess'd;
> And left the Son of *Jove*, to quarrel for the rest.[48]

---

[45] Marquess of Halifax, "Character of a Trimmer", in *Complete Works*, ed Walter Ralegh, Oxford (1912) p. 55. *Cf. A Short History of the Last Parliament,* London (1699) p. 15 ("physicians of state"); *Discourse concerning Militias. . . ,* p. 26 ("It belongs to that Wise Council to apply suitable Remedies"); Charles Davenant, *Discourses on the Public Revenues,* London (1698) pp. 82–3 (" Some Statesmen . . . will not minister the Physick"); "Cursory Remarks. . . ," in *Somers Tracts,* xi, pp. 181–2 ("these state empiricks . . . the only physicians that can cure all the distempers in the public administration"); "A French conquest neither desirable nor practicable", in *Somers Tracts,* x, pp. 475–6 ("state-quacks").

[46] Postscript to the *Aeneis,* iii, 1424.

[47] "To my Honour'd Kinsman", 81–3.   [48] *Op. cit.,* 160–3.

Men, whether warriors or physicians, are powerless in the face
of the essential fact of human mortality:

> Pity the gen'rous Kind their Cares bestow
> To search forbidden Truths; (a Sin to know:)
> To which, if Humane Science cou'd attain,
> The Doom of Death, pronounc'd by God, were vain. . . .
> God never made his Work, for Man to mend.[49]

Since death and suffering are the marks of the human condition,
the pursuit of medical knowledge may be regarded as the surest
indication of man's persisting pride. In fact, the physician's
search after forbidden knowledge is a recapitulation of Adam's
sin in Paradise: "The Tree of Knowledge, once in *Eden* plac'd,/
Was easie found, but was forbid the Taste".[50] Because our
"Grandsire" walked *with* his wife,[51] thus losing eternal life and
gaining no more than partial knowledge, only the physical and
spiritual temperance exemplified by John Driden can succeed in
softening the effects of mortality for Adam's descendants. When
Adam beseeches Raphael (in Dryden's "tagging" of Milton's
verses) if there could be no "smooth descent" or "painless way"
to the inevitable fate of man, the angel replies: "Some few, by
temp'rance taught, approaching slow,/ To distant fate, by easy
journeys, go."[52] With respect to this virtue, as well as to others,
John Driden (who "enjoy'd his Youth, and now enjoys his Age")
approaches as closely as a latter-day man could to the condition
of Adam before the Fall – that is, Adam *solus*.

The identification of a temperate, immovable Driden with the
Eve-less Adam, as the poem's particular emblem of the little
kingdom of man, offers Dryden opportunities for fusing classical
and Christian *topoi* in the epistle – although one of his Christian
motifs may be oddly heterodox. The peculiar motionlessness of
Adam that Dryden finds so laudable and enviable a condition,
recalls a dictum of scholastic theology:

> To describe Adam's condition between his creation *in
> naturaliter* and the infusion of grace, the scholastics used
> the formula *Stare poterat, pedes movere non poterat*, which meant

---

[49] *Op. cit.,* 75–95.   [50] *Op. cit.,* 96–7.   [51] *Op. cit.,* 98.
[52] *State of Innocence,* in *Dramatic Works,* III, p. 460.

that the first man could prevent himself from falling away by the natural power of his will, but that he was powerless to advance any closer to God.[53]

For the believer, then, such a neutral state could by no means be considered desirable, since it precluded movement towards God as well as movement from Him. In the particular circumstances of his epistle, however, Dryden establishes motionlessness – whether of Driden-Adam or of England – as precisely the *desideratum*, the only means left of recapturing some of man's prelapsarian nature. Bishop Burnet's *Sacred Theory of the Earth*, a critical document in the period of the "Honour'd Kinsman", relates the loss of physical stability and human longevity[54] to the shift in the earth's axis after the Fall:

> taking a perpetual Equinox, and fixing the Heavens, you fix the Life of Man too; which was not then in such rapid flux as it is now, but seem'd to stand still as the Sun did once without Declension. There is no question but every thing upon the Earth, and especially the Animate World, would be much more permanent, if the general Course of Nature was more steady and uniform; a Stability in the Heavens makes a Stability in all Things below; and that Change and Contrariety of Qualities that we have in these Regions, is the Fountain of Corruption and suffers nothing to be long in quiet. . . .[55]

In a purely political context, Dryden had advocated the attempt to restore such stability upon the occasion of his first literary work after William's accession: "How much happier is he . . . who centring on himself, remains immovable, and smiles at the madness of the dance about him. He possesses the midst, which is the portion of safety and content: He will not be higher, because he needs it not."[56] How greatly that later attitude differs

---

[53] John Freccero, "Dante's Firm Foot and the Journey without a Guide", *Harvard Theological Review*, LII (1959) p. 267. St Augustine seems to have originated this formulation (*op. cit.*, n. 64).

[54] *Cf.* Dryden, 90–1.

[55] *Sacred Theory*, 6th edn., London (1726) I, p. 273. *Cf.* Adam's vision of immortality in *State of Innocence*: "Eternity stands permanent, and fixt,/ And wheels no longer on the Poles of time" (*Dramatic Works*, III, p. 461).

[56] Dedication to *Don Sebastian*.

from that of the *poète engagé* of the 1680s, who had scorned such withdrawal: "We Trimmers are for holding all things even:/ Yes – just like him that hung 'twixt Hell and Heaven".[57] In 1700, Dryden finds the Trimmer (in the person of Adam) eminently commendable. It might be noted, moreover, that the language of trimming, particularly as it had been used by Halifax, occurs within the "Honour'd Kinsman" (where, of course, it also suits the nautical imagery proper to an argument in support of a strong navy): "Well-born, and Wealthy; wanting no Support,/ You steer betwixt the Country and the Court".[58] Although we cannot insist emphatically upon the conscious intention of the metaphysical or theological ramifications of Dryden's Adam, the overriding desire throughout the epistle for a *stable* political stance cannot be denied.

Heir to a fallen world, John Driden has nevertheless found the "paradise within" (or "Serene Pattern" of his own mind) which allows him to restore prelapsarian stability.[59] But inasmuch as we have insisted upon Dryden's refusal to leave his cousin cloistered within himself, or in his safe rural retreat, we must see what remains of an "outward Eden". Within the poem, specific references to Eden lay special emphasis upon its famous waters:

> Betwixt the Prince and Parliament we stand;
> The Barriers of the State on either Hand:
> May neither overflow, for then they drown the Land.
> When both are full, they feed our bless'd Abode;
> Like those, that water'd once, the Paradise of God.[60]

The seeming contrast in the last couplet between the "Paradise of God" and "our bless'd Abode", actually points to an identity, with a difference only in degree: the *island* Albion is a kind of Eden.

The exact location and typography of Eden was a matter of speculation for centuries. Of the numerous theories postulated,

[57] Epilogue to *The Duke of Guise*.

[58] "To my Honour'd Kinsman", 127–8.

[59] Dryden concludes his *State of Innocence* with the same image (which occurs considerably earlier in the Miltonic original) – "For outward Eden, lost find Paradise within" – and Charles Dryden's epistle to his father ends: "And for an Eden lost, gain'd Paradise of Mind" (*Dryden's Miscellany*, IV, p. 200).

[60] "To my Honour'd Kinsman", 175–9; *Cf.* 25–6.

a common one derived from Josephus: "Now this Garden was watered by a River that invironed it round about, and divided it self into four Channels or Rivers." Sir Walter Ralegh's apparently exhaustive summary of opinion eventually decides that Eden was on an island in the river Tigris.[61] The insular theory of Paradise was certainly congenial to Englishmen:

> This other Eden, demi-Paradise,
> This fortress built by Nature for herself
> Against infection and the hand of war.

Since this latter Eden exists in a corrupt world, such hymns invariably emphasised the practical aspects of the country's isolation:

> All-haile (deer ALBION) EUROP'S Pearl of Price,
> The World's rich Garden, Earths rare Paradise. . . .
> FENC'T FROM THE WORLD
> (as better-worth then That). . . .[62]

Dryden himself issued a similar proclamation in 1684: "Our land's an Eden, and the main's our fence,/ While we preserve our state of innocence."[63] And in the pamphlet war over William's standing army, an advocate of the desirability and superiority of a naval force turns to the same comparison: "Whereas England, being a country (as was said of the tree of paradise) good for food, pleasant to the eyes, and to be desired, hath been possessed by five several nations, and coveted by many more. . . ."[64] Dryden's own argument against the *standing* army in the "Honour'd Kinsman" is ironically conveyed through his application of the verb in three crucial passages, the first dealing with Adam in Eden –

> How cou'd He stand, when put to double Pain,
> He must a Weaker than himself sustain!
> Each might have stood perhaps; but each alone;
> Two Wrestlers help to pull each other down.[65]

---

[61] Josephus, *Works*, tr. Arnauld d'Andilly, London (1701) p. 28; Ralegh, *History of the World*, i, iii, p. 10. Milton grants a similar location to Paradise *after* the Fall (*P.L.*, xi, 829 *ff.*).
[62] Du Bartas, *Deuine Weekes*, tr. Josuah Sylvester, London (n.d.) pp. 355–6.
[63] Prologue to the *Unhappy Favourite*.
[64] "England's Path to Wealth and Honour", in *Somers Tracts*, xi, pp. 371–3.
[65] "To my Honour'd Kinsman", 27–30.

– the next two dealing explicitly with Albion's situation:

Safe in our selves, while on our selves we stand,
The Sea is ours, and that defends the Land.[66]

Betwixt the Prince and Parliament we stand;
The Barriers of the State on either Hand.[67]

Albion must emulate the motionless Adam-Driden, and cease struggling *for* and *with* Europe, just as "he" has scorned wrestling with Eve; England must withdraw into the security of its demi-Paradise just as Driden retires to his country estate, where the inner harmony of his soul expresses itself in the just administration of county affairs. In the case of the country at large, the same kind of inner harmony is achieved only by maintaining the correct poise between Prince and Parliament; with those forces in their proper order, England can enjoy the quiet and isolated liberty provided by the natural barriers of the sea. The serene pattern of Driden's mind thus becomes an emblem of a harmonious Albion in which justice is realised by "establishing the elements concerned in their natural relations of control and subordination".[68] When the elements of the state – Prince and Parliament – are off balance, Albion is threatened by the flood (or invasion) which overcomes the nation's natural barriers.

This danger of drowning the land may also refer to the original Flood, which was the occasion for the distribution of mankind's nations (or as the Bible puts it, "the *isles* of the Gentiles").[69] Paradise itself was believed to have been the embarkation point for the second dispersal of the race.[70] Just as "Man and Woman,

---

[66] *Op. cit.*, 146–7.   [67] *Op. cit.*, 175–6.   [68] *Republic*, IV, 444.

[69] Genesis 10:5. Simon Patrick explains that for "isles" we are to understand "nations" (*Commentary upon the Historical Books of the Old Testament*, 5th edn. [London, 1738] I, p. 46). For the popular seventeenth-century theory that the British Isles had been severed from Europe by the Flood, see D. C. Allen, *The Legend of Noah*, Urbana, Ill., (1963) pp. 95, 191.

[70] "By knowing this place [Eden], we shall the better judge of the beginning of nations, and of the world's inhabitation: for near unto this did the sons of Noah also disperse themselves after the flood, into all the other remote countries from whence all the streams [*cf.* Dryden, "To my Honour'd Kinsman", 26] and branches of mankind have followed and been deduced" (Ralegh, I, iii, p. 4).

though in one they grow,/Yet, first or last, return again to Two"[71] so in accordance with the after-effects of the Fall, the nations of the world must remain apart. Dryden's deliberative advice, therefore, is that Albion remain motionless and fenced from the Continent, thereby securing in *national* terms the proximity to the prelapsarian state that John Driden has achieved. Man *is* an island, and so indeed is England; the separateness of the human or political condition – both deriving from Original Sin – is not to be contravened without accelerating the fate that temperance and prudence can at least postpone.

The importance attached to the waters of Paradise in a poem that ultimately owes its basic analogical pattern to Platonic and Aristotelian conceptions of the relationship between the individual and the society, impels us to consider a means by which the classical and Christian sources may be further entwined within the epistle. One of the principal exegetical inheritances from the Platonist Philo (through Ambrose and Augustine) was the allegorical interpretation of the four rivers of Paradise as the cardinal virtues.[72] Of the four, moreover, justice subsumes the rest, since it appears "when the three parts of the soul corresponding to the other virtues are in harmony".[73] In another document crucial to the transmission of the pagan virtues to Christianity, Macrobius insists upon the ability of men in the civic orders of life to attain the blessedness which the virtues confer upon men of contemplation.[74] The "paradise within" possessed by John Driden, a man who shares a contemplative and an active existence, is irrigated by the rivers of the four virtues. The first presented to us, appropriately, is his justice,[75] which indicates the harmonious disposition

---

[71] "To my Honour'd Kinsman", 23–4.

[72] "These rivers are four in number, prudence, self-mastery, courage, justice" (Philo, Loeb edn., 1, 189). For the christianising of the virtues, see, *e.g.*, Charles S. Singleton, *Dante Studies 2: Journey to Beatrice*, Cambridge, Mass. (1958) pp. 168–76.

[73] Philo, 1, 195.

[74] "By these virtues the good man is first made lord of himself and then ruler of the state . . . political virtues do make men blessed . . . some men become blessed by the exercise of virtue at leisure and others by virtues exercised in active careers" (*Commentary on the Dream of Scipio*, tr. and ed. W. H. Stahl [New York, 1952] pp. 120–4).

[75] "To my Honour'd Kinsman", 7–16.

of the remaining three. His prudence is specifically demonstrated by his shunning of the "married state";[76] his temperance is notably displayed in the moderate regimen of his exercise[77] and in his freedom from the medical trade which "Excess began, and Sloth sustains";[78] and his courage is seen in his independence as an M.P.[79] and in the fortitude of his stubborn ancestor,[80] which, according to Aristotle or any other rhetorician, would be ample grounds for praise of Driden himself.

These personal virtues of John Driden are all carried into Dryden's proposals for the nation's well-being. Prudence and temperance govern the recommendations for England's economy and national defence,[81] and, as Dryden observed in his letter to Montagu, the courage of his countrymen is duly lauded.[82] As justice begins the poem, so it concludes it in Dryden's explanation of the harmony and peace to be achieved through adherence to the balanced nature of the English constitution,[83] in which passage he returns to the aquatic paradisal imagery. It cannot be fortuitous that a poet or orator should make implicit references to the cardinal virtues, but the particular care with which Dryden relates the virtues to the individual and to the state has special authority in the rules of deliberative oratory: "Advantage in political deliberation has two aspects: Security and Honour . . . The Honourable is divided into the Right and the Praiseworthy. The Right is that which is done in accord with Virtue and Duty. Subheads under the Right are Wisdom, Justice, Courage, and Temperance."[84]

4

In addition to the paradisal imagery, another Biblical and exegetical *topos* appears in Dryden's allusions to a figure who also embodies the qualities praised in Driden-Adam-Albion:

Two Wrestlers help to pull each other down. . . .
Heav'n, who foresaw the Will, the Means has wrought,
And to the Second Son, a Blessing brought:

[76] *Op. cit.*, 31–5. [77] *Op. cit.*, 50–61.
[78] *Op. cit.*, 74. [79] *Op. cit.*, 127–8.
[80] *Op. cit.*, 188–94. [81] *Op. cit.*, 129–49.
[82] *Op. cit.*, 150–3. [83] *Op. cit.*, 171–9.
[84] *Ad Herennium*, Loeb edn., III, ii, 3.

The First-begotten had his Father's share;
But you, like *Jacob*, are *Rebecca's* Heir. . . .
So free to Many, to Relations most,
You feed with Manna your own *Israel*-Host.[85]

Jacob, of course, wrestled with an angel who blessed him and called him "Israel", from which title the Chosen People derived its name. Moreover, in a stance and setting similar to Dryden's image of Adam, Jacob had stood *alone* on the other side of the river before his encounter with the angel.[86] The wrestling bout proved Jacob's strength to meet his estranged brother on the following day – not, however, in order to defeat him by force of arms, but to offer *peace*.[87] It was for this capacity to compose strife, both internally and externally, that Christian commentators invariably commended Jacob. St Ambrose's homily, significantly entitled *De Jacob et Vita Beata*, describes Jacob's peacefulness in terms eminently suitable to Dryden's Adam-Albion, with respect both to the motionlessness and to the water imagery.[88] In a somewhat less traditional interpretation, Prudentius views the wrestling-match, and the consequent laming of Jacob, as a means of quite literally preventing him from "moving" into sin – of avoiding, that is, Adam's "fall".[89]

The full relevance of Jacob's reputation as the solitary, immovable man of peace who had conquered his passions and who gave

[85] "To my Honour'd Kinsman", 30–49.
[86] Gen. 32:23–5.
[87] Gen. 33:3.
[88] "Denique petiturus a fratre concordium dormiuit in castris. perfecta uirtus habet tranquillitatem et stabilitatem quietis; ideo dominus donum eius perfectioribus reseruauit dicens; pacem meam relinquo uobis, pacem meam do uobis. perfectorum est enim non facile mundanis moueri, non turbari metu, non exagitari suspicione, non terrore concuti, non dolore uexari, sed quasi in litore tutissimo aduersum insurgentes fluctus saecularium procellarum mentem immobilem fida statione placidare" (*Sancti Ambrosii Opera*, Corpus Scriptorum Ecclesiasticorum Latinorum, Vol. xxxii, Pt. ii [Vienna, 1897], ed. C. Schenkl, p. 48). Cornelius a Lapide cites and summarises Ambrose prominently in his commentary on Gen.32:21. After the direct reference to Jacob, Dryden stresses the "blessedness" symbolised by him, in addressing his cousin: "And ever be bless'd, who lives to bless" (45). The entire epistle of course, is a variation on the *beatus ille* theme ("How Bless'd is He").
[89] Loeb edn., i, 17–19.

K

his name to his nation,[90] emerges most meaningfully when he is contrasted with his brother, Esau. The Lord had told Rebecca: "Two nations are in thy womb, and two manner of people shall be separated from thy bowels; and the one people shall be stronger than the other people; and the older shall serve the younger".[91] The difference in the "manner" of the two peoples refers to their divergent ways of life, for Jacob was a "Husbandman and Planter. For this . . . seems to have been *Adam's* chief Employment, both before and after the Fall", and Esau was a hunter, who lost his blessing while engaged in the chase, and who embraced the arts of war as Jacob did those of peace: "His Father told him that he should excel in Hunting, in force of Body, in Arms, and other such exercises."[92]

The implicit contrast between Jacob, the Husbandman who feeds his nation the manna of peace, and Esau, the hunter-warrior, directs us to the numerous and pervasive images of the chase which support Dryden's advocacy of peace in the "Honour'd Kinsman". The language of venery – in precisely both senses of the word – first appears in the account of marital discord: ". . . better shun the Bait, than struggle in the Snare".[93] The account of John Driden's hunt, a microcosmic representation of war, concludes with an emphatic emblem of the hunt as a symbol of life itself, in which the supposed hunter, Man, is himself pursued:

> The Hare, in Pastures or in Plains is found,
> Emblem of Humane Life, who runs the Round;
> And, after all his wand'ring Ways are done,
> His Circle fills, and ends where he begun,
> Just as the Setting meets the Rising Sun.[94]

As the emblem would suggest, the poem's versions of the love-hunt and the war-hunt are supplemented (or subsumed) by the personification of Death himself as a hunter.[95] Dryden thus offers three versions of the hunt, in which Man, seen from the proper

[90] Note Dryden's references to his cousin's "Israel-Host" and to England as "Canaan", the land promised Jacob's family.

[91] Gen. 25:23.

[92] Patrick, I, 23. "[Hunting] was look'd upon in all Ages, as the rudiment of Warfare" (I, 48).

[93] "To my Honour'd Kinsman", 33.

[94] *Op. cit.,* 62–6.   [95] *Op. cit.,* 78–80.

perspective, is truly the pursued rather than the pursuer. In love, the chasing male becomes himself *ensnared*, recalling Eve's admission to Adam in *Paradise Lost*: ". . . thee ordain'd/ A help, became thy snare".[96] In war, Europe may pull down Albion just as Eve did Adam. With respect to the war motif, it is noteworthy that one of Dryden's most obsessive images in the later poems, including the "Honour'd Kinsman", is that of Hannibal, the hunter-warrior who himself became the hunted and lost all he had gained by seeking too much and wandering too far (just as Esau lost his blessing by hunting far from home).[97] The warning is echoed throughout the epistle by instances of excessive aspiration generally, and immoderate warfare in particular.[98] In topical political terms, such warnings seem directed against bellicose William, whose relentless pursuit of war, according to his critics,[99] endangers the balanced security and liberty of England.

We must now return to Dryden's climatic "Emblem of Humane Life". In my earlier reading of lines 67–70, I proposed an interpretation directed against William (the "Rising Sun"), but we can now consider a possible thrust against James (the "Setting Sun") as well. The image of the lubricious hare,[1] which shifts mankind

[96] xi, 164–5. For similar uses of "snare" in *P.L., cf.* iv, 6–8; x, 872–3 and 895–8; xii, 30–2 (on hunting and war).

[97] "Thus *Hannibal*, with Foreign Laurels won,/ To *Carthage* was recall'd, too late to keep his own" (165–6). *Cf.* the Dedication of the *Aeneis*: "I must now come closer to my present business: and not think of making more invasive Wars abroad, when like *Hannibal*, I am call'd back to the defence of my own country" (iii, 1011). See also the epistles to Congreve (ii, 853) and Granville (iii, 1433).

[98] *Cf.* 10–13, 54–57, 155–7, 160–3.

[99] The reference to Alexander's arrogance (160–3) may be directed against William, who was compared to that conqueror by both his apologists and his detractors ("Remarks upon the Present Confederacy", in *Somers Tracts*, x, 507). William's claim to the throne "by conquest" also led to parallels with Alexander ("A Short and True Relation of Intrigues", in *Somers Tracts*, xi, 101). In 180–3 of the "Honour'd Kinsman", the "sole Dictator" who "sway'd" when the Gauls came, could be William the Conqueror, as well as Caesar, if we read "Normans" for "Gauls" (on the widespread – and derogatory – association of the two Williams, see E. R. Wasserman, *The Subtler Language* [Baltimore, 1959] pp. 113–19).

[1] "In Venus's venery, the soft hunt is the pursuit of *fugaces*, of those timid animals that never turn and stand – the hare, the cony, the fox, and the deer, but especially the hare. . . . It is not unusual for artists to show Venus accom-

from the position of the hunter to that of the hunted, fittingly represents the sin of Adam (ensnared in the love-hunt), which had been avoided by Jacob and John Driden. Such an image of carnal folly also suits James II, who, in addition to his attachments to the ordinary hunt (especially, like William, in his declining years), was notorious for his devotion to the other venery (unlike William); James, in fact, explained his fall from the "slipp'ry Throne" as a judgment for his having "offended God by his love of women".[2] The language with which Driden describes James's pursuit of "Pleasure" has distinctly erotic overtones. The Prince "sighs" in the manner of a lover, and the final rhyme may incorporate a pun upon "chas'd" = "chaste", referring to James's alleged concern for piety even in face of his promiscuity. James is thus the hunted hare in all respects – pursued by women, by William, and by his imminent death.

If *both* William and James may be regarded as the "Princes" discussed in the passage, the circularity of the hare's path can be explained in terms of the poem's context. In the pessimistic announcements of his last years, Dryden frequently relates his sense of personal decline to the meaningless repetition of history, in which *plus ça change, plus c'est la même chose*:

> Why am I grown Old, in seeking so barren a Reward as Fame? The same Parts and Application which have made me a Poet, might have rais'd me to any Honours of the Gown, which are often given to Men of as little Learning and less Honesty than my self. No Government has ever been, *or ever can be*, wherein Time-servers and Blockheads will not be uppermost. *The Persons are only chang'd*, but the same juglings

---

[2] Ogg, p. 220. For James's hunting, see Burnet, p. 696; for his indiscriminate promiscuity, see F. C. Turner, *James II*, London (1948) p. 61.

---

panied by the hare; its unbelievable fecundity, for it was said to conceive while it was gestating, made it a symbolic companion for the generative mother. . . . The lubricity of the hare was also long the subject of human comment" (D. C. Allen, "On *Venus and Adonis*," in *Elizabethan and Jacobean Studies Presented to F. P. Wilson* [Oxford, 1959] pp. 109–10). See also Claude K. Abraham, "Myth and Symbol: The Rabbit in Medieval France", *S.P.*, LX (1963) pp. 589–97, especially for his suggestion that "an animal which had been known for its fertility . . . became the perfect symbol of a specific part of the female anatomy, and thence of the woman as a whole".

in State, the same Hypocrisie in Religion, the same Self-Interest and Mis-management, will remain for ever. Blood and Mony will be lavish'd in all Ages, only for the Preferment of new Faces, with old Consciences.[3]

The dreary circularity of history also furnishes the dominant tone of the *Secular Masque*, published the same year as the "Honour'd Kinsman". In that valediction, the hunting image again characterises the folly of the passing century. Diana's hunt in that masque, with its famous "Beast in View", is not a *tertium quid*, different from the hunts of Mars and Venus, but rather the major image that subsumes the other two. Instead of worrying about the precise allegorical identities of Diana, Mars, and Venus, we should view the love-hunt and the war-hunt personified by Venus and Mars as subdivisions of the fruitless chase that epitomises the entire century, including the reigns of James and William, who are thus as jointly dismissed in the *Secular Masque* as they are in the hare emblem of the "Honour'd Kinsman".

The attitude of near-exhaustion in the "Honour'd Kinsman" cannot brook weighing the possible differences between reigns – all is of a piece, each age will run the same round. Relief is to be attained only through temperate retirement into oneself on the personal level, and through withdrawal into the sceptred isle on the political plane – through leading the life of Jacob, rather than that of Esau. The new age which such a dual retreat may bring into being cannot be entirely golden, but it will secure the greatest peace obtainable in a fallen world.

5

We have discounted the partisanship (in any narrow political sense) of the "Honour'd Kinsman", but beyond topical and hortatory considerations, the epistle may indeed be regarded as a *reductio* of "cosmic toryism". Whether or not Dryden was fully aware of the theological implications of his nostalgic desire for Adam's state of motionlessness and solitude, the moral and metaphysical ramifications of that image provide a foundation for his immediate advocacy of personal and political neutrality. What

[3] Dedication of *Examen Poeticum* (ii, 790). (Italics mine.)

seems at first glance an activist's correction of Horatian retirement, because of John Driden's willing movement from his rural
retreat to the hectic legislature, actually becomes an even more
sweeping recommentation of "retirement" for the country as a
whole. Political trimming, if we may so call it, is but a particular
manifestation of Dryden's longing for universal stasis and passivity.

Exactly those last-named qualities are captured within the
movement – or its absence – and language of the verse itself:

> How Bless'd is He, who leads a Country Life,
> Unvex'd with anxious Cares, and void of Strife!
> Who studying Peace, and shunning Civil Rage,
> Enjoy'd his Youth, and now enjoys his Age:
> All who deserve his Love, he makes his own;
> And, to be lov'd himself, needs only to be known.[4]

The couplets of the "Honour'd Kinsman" are unique among
Dryden's *late* verses for the exactitude and constancy of their
antithetical and parallel constructions; a heavy caesura invariably
falls after the second or third foot. In the rhythm of each line,
then, the descent in the second hemistich checks the rising
tendency in the first, so that movement virtually ceases in a final
resolution at the end of the line, as well as at the end of the couplet.
The metrical pattern thereby corresponds to, and reinforces, the
epistle's argument against rash aspiration and uncontrolled or
excessive movement.

The language and grammar of the opening lines also contribute
to the static quality of the verse. The virtues of the "Happy Man"
are characterised almost entirely in negative terms connoting
withdrawal from activity: "unvex'd", "void", and "shunning".
The last word is especially crucial, in view of its repetition in key
passages of the poem.[5] John Driden's customary status in the
epistle is that of object rather than subject, for a sense of passivity
accompanies his tendency to withdraw rather than act: "And, to be
lov'd himself, needs only to be known". John Driden is indeed
not so much an active agent in the course of the poem, as he is the

---

[4] "To my Honour'd Kinsman", 1–6.
[5] *Op. cit.,* 33–34, 119–22.

object of the poem's true subject, John Dryden, the poet who makes his kinsman (and thus himself) known to the reader.

Classical rhetoric presents a threefold task to the orator: he must prepare his arguments convincingly; he must secure the good will of his audience; and, to accomplish both these objectives effectively, he must appear to be of worthy character.[6] John Driden is the fictive audience of the epistle, and he is the subject as well, both in his individual capacity and as the personification of Albion. Where then is the speaker? In order to establish his own presence in the poem, John Dryden has pursued a course facilitated, if not suggested, by the name he holds in common with his kinsman – he forces an identity between himself and his audience-subject so that all three components of an oration become one in the "Honour'd Kinsman".[7]

At the outset of the address, the "audience" is made to surrender its good will by the usual means of the panegyric. But the characterisation of John Driden as "Just, Good, and Wise" is not an enumeration of those cardinal virtues for which he is to be praised; the qualities suggest, rather, the appearance that the orator must assume – virtue (justice, as we have seen, is the organising principle of all the elements of virtue), good will, and good sense. These attributes of John Driden are then transferred, through the body of the poem, to John Dryden. The implementation of this shift can be traced through the changing forms of address. The dual role of John Driden as both subject and audience is enforced by the movement from the third person in the exordium to the second person at the beginning of the statement.[8] In the middle of the proof, however, Dryden glides easily into the first person plural, since he is discussing England's affairs.[9] And in the

---

[6] "For the orator to produce conviction three qualities are necessary; for, independently of demonstrations, the things which induce belief are . . . good sense, virtue, and goodwill" (Aristotle, 1378a).

[7] I am indebted at this point to the lead provided by Elder Olson's reading of Pope's *Epistle to Arbuthnot* in "Rhetoric and the Appreciation of Pope", *M.P.*, xxxvii (1939) pp. 13–35. See also Lillian Feder, "John Dryden's Use of Classical Rhetoric", *P.M.L.A.*, lxix (1954) pp. 1258–78. For a survey of the rhetorical tradition of the verse epistle, see my article "The Status of the Verse Epistle before Pope", *S.P.*, lix (1962) pp. 658–84.

[8] To my Honour'd Kinsman", 8.

[9] *Op. cit.*, 140 ff.

conclusion, the promise of the epistle's title is fulfilled when Dryden presents his character of the Patriot ancestor whom he shares with John Driden, and, appropriately, moves into the first person singular.[10] Insofar as the epistle is a panegyric, it praises the poet as well as his kinsman – more so, perhaps, since the poet actually performs to a greater extent than his ostensible subject acts.[11] Had Dryden presented a political poem of the 1690s as a direct expression of his own, he would have found it difficult to secure the oratorical *captatio benevolentiae* before a hostile audience ("liable to be misconstrued in all I write"); by using his unassailable kinsman as apparent audience and subject, he succeeds in delaying the reaction of the *public* audience until it has accepted his ethical proof unawares. The praises that are justly heaped upon the modest John Driden pass unobtrusively to the other John Dryden, and validate the argument of the epistle.

It is appropriate that the poem end elegically, for Dryden has insisted throughout the epistle upon a sense of individual decline, a distrust of vitality, and a resignation to the vanity of human history:

> For ev'n when Death dissolves our Humane Frame,
> The Soul returns to Heav'n, from whence it came;
> Earth keeps the Body, Verse preserves the Fame.[12]

All three subjects of the poem – John Driden, England, and John Dryden – have been reconciled to an almost moribund state. The possibility that Dryden wrote, in effect, his own epitaph in the final triplet was recognised by the contemporary who placed it upon the title page of *Luctus Britannici; or Tears of the British Muses for the Death of John Dryden*.

[10] *Op. cit.*, 195–206.

[11] Dryden's assertion in lines 203–4 notwithstanding. The fused identity of the members of the same house is suggested, moreover, by their sharing similar stations and conditions in life – both country squires (for an attack on "Squire Dryden", see Hugh MacDonald, *John Dryden: A Bibliography* [Oxford, 1939] p. 188), and both ailing old men. The ancestor must be Erasmus Dryden, a forebearer of both Driden and Dryden, and not Sir Robert Beville (as some editors have suggested), whom only Driden could claim (see Malone, 1, 23).

[12] "To my Honour'd Kinsman", 207–9. This traditional tag for a funeral elegy had been used by Dryden a few years earlier in his *Eleonora*. *Cf.* the conclusion of Donne's First *Anniversary* (mentioned by Dryden in his preface to *Eleonora*) and of Surrey's "Third Tribute to Wyatt".

T. W. Harrison

DRYDEN'S *AENEID*

When Virgil's *Aeneid* emerged from centuries of allegorical interpretation, which still informs the first translation of the epic into
anything like English, Gavin Douglas's *Eneados* (1513), it was sub-
jected to more and more political specialisation. The hidden
general truths and sentences become specific moral and political
lessons for seventeenth-century England, especially for the years of
the Civil War, the Protectorate, and the Restoration. This sharp-
ening of focus can be quite clearly demonstrated in two separate
translations of the *Aeneid* produced by the indefatigable John
Ogilby (1600–76); the first in 1649 and the second in 1654. The
two versions are distinctly different, and the second shows a great
deal of rewriting with an eye on the events leading to the execu-
tion of Charles I in 1649. The second is a far more explicitly
"Royalist" version than the first. One revision concerns a passage
in Book VII where Juno has gone to seek the help of the bellige-
rent Fury Allecto to sever the truce between the Trojans and the
Latins. Juno generalises on Allecto's chaotic powers:

> tu potes unanimos armare in proelia fratres
> atque odiis versare domos, tu verbera tectis
> funereasque inferre faces, tibi nomina mille,
> mille nocendi artes. fecundum concute pectus,
> disice compositam pacem, sere crimina belli;
> arma velit poscatque simul rapiatque iuventus.[1]

Allecto's subversive powers are *generally* invoked. She can cause
war, albeit civil, and destroy houses. It is thus generally interpreted by John Vicars in his translation of 1632:

[1] *Aeneid*, VII, 335–40.

143

Thou canst belovedest brethren force to fight
And overturn whole families by spight,
And cast from house to house combustious flames,
Assume a thousand shapes, false, feigned names:
And thou a thousand cheating tricks canst use:
Then pump thy plenteous breast, break off abuse.
Their peace compacted, sowe thick seeds of warres,
Their youths do look, like, long for Martiall jarres.[2]

The effects of war are upon homes; the flames destroy houses.
Ogilby's own version of 1649 is similar enough to Vicars:

Thou loving brothers canst provoke to War,
Houses destroy with hate, both sword and flames
Bring to their roofs; thou hast a thousand names,
As many nocent arts; then quickly shake
Thy pregnant breasts, and peace confirmed, break;
Lay grounds for cruel war, make with thy charms
Their wilde youth rage, require, and take up arms.[3]

Apart from the superfluous "wilde" this translation, like that of
Vicars seventeen years earlier, retains the simple *domos, tectis,* and
iuventus of Virgil. But the folio version, only five years afterwards,
sumptuously illustrated by Vaclav Hollar and others, presents a
more specific, and to the period, highly relevant picture:

Unanimous Brothers thou canst arm to fight,
And *settled Courts* destroy with deadly spight:
Storm *Palaces* with Steel, and Pitchy Flames,
Thou hast a thousand wicked Arts: and Names,
Thy Bosom disembogue, with Mischief full,
And Articles concluding Peace annull.
Then raise a War, and with bewitching Charms
Make *the mad People* rage to take up Arms.[4]

The implications of the changes are obvious; war has become

[2] John Vicars, *The XII Aeneids of Virgil, the most renowned Laureat-Prince of
Latine Poets: Translated into English decasyllables,* London (1632) p. 201.
[3] John Ogilby, *The Works of Publius Virgilius Maro,* London (1649). *The
Seventh Book,* p. 12.
[4] John Ogilby, *The Works of Publius Virgilius Maro. Translated and adorn'd
with Sculpture, and Illustrated with Annotations,* London (1654).

revolution. Virgil is no longer talking about the general destructiveness of war, civil or otherwise, but of rebellion against Monarchy. When the same John Ogilby came to produce his account of Charles II's triumphal procession to his coronation, he quotes this passage in the Latin and in his version of 1654 and comments "we cannot take a better view of Sedition and Discord".[5] When one recalls the claim of John Dryden that he wrote "for lawful established government against anarchy, innovation, and sedition",[6] it comes as a matter of course that his Allecto too has the power ". . . to ruin Realmes, o'return a State".[7]

2

The Restoration of 1660 brought with it a great profusion of explicit Roman and Virgilian parallels. The use of illustration and quotation from the history of Augustan Rome and from Virgil's *Aeneid* confirms the contemporary significance of the poem, and it is this significance, stratified by the neo-classical theories of the epic, which helped to shape Dryden's great translation.

At the Restoration, and for the actual coronation of King Charles II, John Ogilby was appointed "to conduct the poetical part thereof, consisting of speeches, emblems, mottoes, inscriptions, & c".[8] Triumphal arches in Roman style were erected for the occasion; on the first in Leadenhall Street, near Lime Street End, along with depictions of the mounted King driving many-headed usurpation into the jaws of Hell, were Virgilian tags under a trophy of disembodied heads:

AUSI IMMANE NEFAS AUSOQUE POTITI

and

DISCITE JUSTITIAM MONITI

[5] John Ogilby, *The Entertainment of his Most Excellent Majestie Charles II, In His Passage through the City of London to His Coronation*, London (1662), p. 15. This is an expanded and lavishly illustrated edition of *The Relation of His Majesties Entertainment Passing through the City of London, to his Coronation: With a Description of the Triumphal Arches, and Solemnity*, London (1661).

[6] *The Vindication of the Duke of Guise* (1683–4). *The Works of John Dryden*, ed. Sir Walter Scott. 18 Vols, London (1808) VII, p. 164. *cf. Works*, VII, pp. 156–7.

[7] *Virgil's Aeneis*, VII, 467.

[8] *Calendar of State Papers*, Domestic Series. Charles II (1660–1) p. 553.

These very same mottoes are similarly extracted as texts for the times by John Boys in his translation of *Aeneid* Book VI, in 1661. He italicises his translation of these words and adds a marginal note to

All have bin
As happy in success, as bold in sin.

saying, "such were, for a time, the late Traitors".[9]

The parallels between Charles II and Augustus, "the best of Heathen Monarchs",[10] are everywhere in use in the poems and panegyrics of 1660, and since Augustus was considered the model for Aeneas in the *Aeneid*, the parallels include Aeneas too. Thomas Higgins is just one typical example:

The most Renowned Kings this fate have had,
To mount the Throne after tempestuous times,
And their own Vertues more conspicuous made,
By the reflections of preceding Crimes.
When Rome was ruin'd with intestine hate,
Augustus took the rudder of the State.[11]

Having associated Charles and Augustus he extends the identification to Aeneas:

Thus great Aeneas when his Troy was lost,
And nought but ruine left of all that State,
Wander'd at Land, and on the Floods was tost,
And hurried up and down the World by Fate,
Before he could to promis'd Alba come,
Alba the Mother of Victorious Rome.

So great a work it was to found that State,
Which to the conquer'd World was Lawes to give,
So must you suffer e're you would be Great,
For Fortune always does with Nature strive.[12]

---

[9] John Boys, *Aeneas His Descent into Hell: As it is inimitably described by the Prince of Poets in the Sixth of his Aeneis*, London (1661) p. 23.
[10] *Op. cit.,* p. 46.
[11] Thomas Higgins, *A Panegyrick to the King*, London (1660) p. 5.
[12] *Op. cit.,* p. 10.

Rachel Jevon puts similar parallels into Latin hexameters:

At pius AENEAS noster vult ferre Penates;
Deferret cultus nec saevit tempore fati
Antiquos Patrum, jus ut repararet Avorum
Pectoribus populi PRINCEPS regnavit ubique,
Devictis pietate sua, quae fortior armis.[13]

Dryden's own contribution to the fanfares, *Astraea Redux*, as his American editors point out, has the phrase "toss'd by Fate"[14] "almost inevitably recalling Virgil's *'fato profugus'*.[15] Just as Aeneas was the prototype of Augustus . . . so Augustus becomes . . . the prototype of Charles."[16]

Oh Happy Age! Oh times like those alone
By Fate reserv'd for Great *Augustus* Throne.[17]

The epic aspirations of the age, frustrated like Dryden's and Milton's on Arthur or the Black Prince, must have burst into new life and many poets must have felt as John Boys did:

Had I, *Great Monarch, Maro's* divine spirit
Or did the Prince of Poets wit inherit,
You should be my *Aeneas*, and what He
His *Heroe* gave, to you ascrib'd should be.[18]

That only the incredible John Ogilby had energy for this need not surprise us. He tells us in an autobiographical preface to his folio description of Africa, dedicated to Charles II as "a second Augustus",[19] that in his translation of the *Iliad* he "had a double Design, not merely to bring over so Antient and Famous an

---

[13] Rachel Jevon, *Carmen ΘΡΙΑΜΒΕΥΤΙΚΟΝ Regiae Majestati Caroli II Principium et Christianorum Optimi in Exoptatissimam eius Restaurationem.* London (1660) p. 2. Cf. Arthur Brett, *The Restoration. Or, A Poem on the Return of the Most Mighty and ever Glorious Prince, Charles the II. To His Kingdoms,* London (1660) pp. 15–16.

[14] *Astraea Redux,* 51.   [15] *Aeneid,* I, 2.

[16] *The Works of John Dryden,* eds. E. N. Hooker and H. T. Swedenberg, Jr. Vol. I. (*Poems 1649–1680*), University of California Press (1956) p. 215.

[17] *Astraea Redux, A Poem on the Happy Restoration and Return of His Sacred Majesty Charles the Second,* London (1660) 320–1. *The Poems of John Dryden,* ed. James Kinsley. 4 vols., Oxford (1958) Vol. I, p. 24.

[18] John Boys, p. 229.

[19] John Ogilby, *The Preface to Africa* etc., London (1670) sig., C1., *verso.*

Author, but to enable my self the better to carry on an *Epick Poem*
of my Own Composure".[20] His epic in twelve books was called
CAROLIES, "from our miracle of Hero's, Charles the First, being
the best Pattern of true Prudence, Valor, and Christian Piety'.[21]'
This effort perished, along with Ogilby's whole estate and most of
London, in the Great Fire of 1666. Dryden never wrote his own
epic, and towards the end of his life he must have decided that the
best pattern of piety and valour he could grant the dignity of
English heroic verse was Virgil's. The perfection he chose to
invest Aeneas with is not in Virgil, but the two poets meet fairly
equally in those static tableaux of piety and valour, which stand
as admonishments and examples to the age.

3

W. Warde Fowler tells us that "the *development* of the character of
Aeneas under stress of perils, moral and material, was much more
obvious to the Roman than it is to us".[22] It is at least evident from
the arguments of commentators like Heinze and Warde Fowler
that the wavering uncertainty of Aeneas is a key point in the
narrative. But for Dryden "Virgil designed to form a perfect
prince",[23] "a pattern of perfection".[24] The perfection of a prince,
as in Dryden's other heroic *exempla*, depended chiefly on piety,
"that essential virtue on which the rest depend".[25] The actions of
the hero are intended as vehicles by which an ideal virtue is made
manifest. Manners must be "constant and equal"[26] and "maintained throughout the whole design".[27] Committed as Dryden
was to this unusually orthodox theory of the epic he must inevitably claim that "when once Virgil had given the name of pious to
Aeneas, he was bound to show him such, in all his words and
actions, through the whole poem".[28] The action or design of the
heroic poem is, in theory, to reveal an ideal virtue embodied in its
hero. There can be no room for struggle. Aeneas cannot win

[20] *Ibid.*   [21] *Ibid.*, sig., C2., *recto.*
[22] W. Warde Fowler, *The Religious Experience of the Roman People,* London
(1911) p. 410.
[23] *The Dedication of the Aeneis* (1697), *Essays of John Dryden,* ed. W. P. Ker,
2 vols. Oxford (1900) II, p. 179.
[24] *Op. cit.,* II, p. 180.   [25] *Ibid.*
[26] *Preface to Troilus and Cressida* (1679). Ker, I, p. 215.
[27] *Ibid.*   [28] *Ibid.*

through to determination, even with the help of the state gods, or through the trials of fortune. He is perfect from the beginning. War and tribulation, so far from *making* him great, serve only to manifest that ideal greatness with which he is endowed once and for all. Like the Cromwell of *Heroique Stanza's*:

> His *Grandeur* he deriv'd from Heaven alone
> For he was great e're Fortune made him so;
> And Warr's like mists that rise against the Sunne
> Made him but greater seem, not greater grow.[29]

As Dryden refines on the imperfect, faltering Aeneas, so he heightens his historical material for his heroic portraits of Charles II and Cromwell. The hero for Dryden, though, it should be clear, not for Virgil, was some sort of invisible lay figure, whose qualities can only be made visible by the actions with which he is ordained. An ideal piety is only apparent when clothed in frequent pious actions.

Significantly for Dryden the end of the wanderings of Aeneas is associated – not as for Gavin Douglas or Mapheus Vegiu with the assumption or apotheosis of the saintly Aeneas or the human soul – but with "Sov'raign Sway"[30] and the rewards of this ideal piety with a "promised Throne".[31] Evander exhorts Aeneas in Dryden:

> Where Fate and smiling Fortune shew the Way,
> Pursue the ready Path to Sov'raign Sway[32]

> tu, cuius et annis
> et generi fata indulgent, quem numina poscunt,
> ingredere, o Teucrum atque Italum fortissime ductor.[33]

And Anchises in the Underworld:

> And doubt we yet thro' Dangers to pursue
> The Paths of Honour, and a Crown in view?[34]

> et dubitamus adhuc virtutem extendere factis
> aut metus Ausonia prohibet consistere terra?[35]

Here *metus*, fear, disappears as it does in many other places, since it does not accord with the perfect prince, and *terra firma* melts into

[29] 21–4.　　　[30] VIII, 677.　　　[31] I, 343.　　　[32] VIII, 676–7.
[33] VIII, 511–13.　　[34] VI, 1101–2.　　[35] VI, 806–7.

the abstract ways of piety to monarchy. For Dryden, as for John
Boys in 1661, the purpose of Aeneas like that of Charles II was to
"lay the foundations of a never-declining Monarchy",[36] or in
Dryden's interpolated line in the opening resumé of the poem, to
settle "sure Succession in his Line".[37] Faction of all kinds,
anarchy, innovation, sedition, democracy, are inimical to the
hero's chief virtue, piety, which harnesses all the other virtues to
defend the numerous established objects of its devotion. The
virtue of Dryden's Aeneas is that which recreates and preserves
the established order against all those sources of panic in what
Bernard Schilling has aptly called the conservative myth.[38]

4

The most obvious example of Dryden's heightening of Virgil's
Aeneas is in his consistent substitution of an heroic title for the
simple name Aeneas or even a Latin pronoun. Aeneas is called
gratuitously "the Heroe"[39] "the Trojan Heroe",[40] "the Prince',[41]
"the Godlike Hero,[42] and "the Godlike Man".[43] Aeneas is the
hero, whose chief virtue, piety, "excludes all ill qualities and comprehends valour itself, with all other qualities which are good".[44]
The characteristic virtues of the heroic Cromwell, *sans* warts, and
Charles II were piety and valour, and the "manners" of Aeneas
may be summed up under the same headings. Dryden's explanation of why Virgil chose piety as the chief characteristic, in pre-
ference to valour, centres upon the exclusion of any weak or
vicious element contrary to the idea of the perfect prince:

> A man may be very valiant, and yet impious and vicious. But
> the same cannot be said of piety, which excludes all ill
> qualities, and comprehends even valour itself, with all other
> qualities which are good.[45]

[36] John Boys, *Aeneas His Errors, or His Voyage from Troy into Italy, An Essay
Upon the Third Book of Virgil's Aeneis*, London (1661) p. 57.

[37] I, 8.

[38] Bernard N. Schilling, *Dryden & the Conservative Myth: A Reading of Absalom and Achitophel*, New Haven & London (Yale University Press) 1961.

[39] I, 1000, *Aeneid*, I, 715; x, 217, *Aeneid*, x, 147; xii, 636, *Aeneid*, xii, 430.

[40] x, 799, *Aeneid*, x, 569; xi, 105, *Aeneid*, xi, 73.   [41] xi, 51, *Aeneid*, xi, 36.

[42] v, 1012, *Aeneid*, v, 774.   [43] xi, 19. *Aeneid*, xi, 12.

[44] *Dedication of the Aeneis*. Ker, ii, p. 180.   [45] *Op. cit.*, ii, p. 180.

Piety then could exclude the kind of detrimental attribute that he felt to be offensive in, say, Fletcher's hero Valentinian, and include almost everything else, even, as we shall see, the crucial virtue, valour.

Dryden understood well the comprehensive nature of Roman *pietas*, knowing "that the word in Latin is more full than it can possibly be expressed in any modern language; for there it comprehends not only devotion to the gods, but filial love, and tender affection of all sorts". In *Threnodia Augustalis* (1685) he uses the word almost archly aware of the range it could borrow from the Latin:

> Th' extreamest ways they first ordain,
> Prescribing such intollerable pain,
> As none but *Caesar* cou'd sustain:
> Undaunted *Caesar* underwent
> The malice of their Art, nor bent
> Beneath what e'r their *pious* rigour cou'd invent.[46]

Fully aware of all the implications of Roman *pietas*, as he imagined it perfectly and consistently embodied in Aeneas, Dryden is well-equipped to discover all the necessary repeated acts of piety he needs to establish the ideal and raise the admiration of the reader. Whenever he discovers such acts he labels them explicitly. Virgil's own use of *pius* is as comparatively sparing and effectively economical as his use of the patronymic *Anchisiades*, but Dryden must make explicit not only by epithet but by a re-alignment of complete actions.

> Advancing to the Front, the Heroe stands,
> And stretching out to Heav'n his Pious Hands;
> Attests the Gods, asserts his Innocence,
> Upbraids with breach of Faith th' *Ausonian* Prince:
> Declares the Royal Honour doubly stain'd,
> And twice the Rites of holy Peace profan'd.[47]

> ipse inter primos dextram sub moenia tendit
> Aeneas, magnaque incusat voce Latinum
> testaturque deos interum se ad proelia cogi,
> bis iam Italos hostis, haec altera foedera rumpi.[48]

---

[46] 173–8. v. also 36; 71; 304; 386; and *To Her Grace the Duchess of Ormond* (1700) 165.

[47] XII, 849–54. [48] XII, 579–82.

It is not merely the addition of the gratuitous *pious*[49] which makes Dryden's lines centre on the piety of Aeneas in a way which Virgil's do not. Not only does Aeneas raise "Pious Hands" to heaven, he asserts his innocence and contrasts it with the implied impiety of "breach of Faith" and the profanation of "*holy* Peace". It is a good example of the way Dryden's couplets serve to do for the poem's hero what he declared as essential in an essay prefixed to a version of the Latin poem, *De Arte Graphica* by the French painter Charles Alphonse du Fresnoy, and written at the time when work on his *Aeneid* was still in progress:

> . . . the hero of the piece must be advanced foremost to the view of the reader . . . he must outshine the rest of all the characters; he must appear the prince of them, like the sun in the Copernican system, encompassed with the less noble planets: because the hero is the centre of the main action; all the lines from the circumference tend to him alone: he is the chief object of . . . admiration in the epic poem.[50]

Mostly Dryden makes more explicit, by epithet and realignment, some demonstration of piety implicit in his original, but he does violence to Virgil when he allows Aeneas himself to commend his own piety. There is enough contention about the famous "sum pius Aeneas"[51] and that is the only time Aeneas uses the epithet himself, and we moderns prefer it to be heavily ironic. Dryden has no such scruples, little delicacy and much less reticence.

5

On the question of his hero's valour Dryden is even more inventive. There were critics in Dryden's time who censured Virgil's Aeneas "for want of courage".[52] Dryden is inevitably forced on the defensive but, once committed to his theory, he does all he can to protect his perfect prince. Between them the detractors of Aeneas make him "little more than a St Swithin hero, always raining"[53] or contend that there never was "such a weeping,

---

[49] 850.
[50] *A Parallel of Poetry and Painting* (1695). *Ker.* II, pp. 142–3.
[51] *Aeneid*, I, 378.   [52] *Dedication*, Ker, II, p. 181.   [53] *Op. cit.,* II, p. 184.

blubbring, sighing, groaning, nay bawling Hero in all History".[54] The hero's tears, which would recommend him to the eighteenth century as a man of feeling of antiquity,[55] represent to his seventeenth-century critics an unmanly reaction to adversity. What they brand as unmanliness Dryden turns to positive account and makes them manifestations of the hero's chief virtue, piety. To the French critics Perrault and St Evremond, Dryden replies that "the tears of Aeneas were always on a laudable occasion. Thus he weeps out of compassion and tenderness of nature, when in the temple of Carthage he beholds the pictures of his friends, who sacrificed their lives in the defence of their country. He deplores the lamentable end of his pilot Palinurus, the untimely death of young Pallas, his confederate and the rest, which I omit."[56] The real bone of contention is the storm scene of Book I:

One of those censors is bold enough to argue him of cowardice, when in the beginning of the First Book, he not only weeps, but trembles, at an approaching storm . . . But to this I have answered formerly that his fear was *not for himself, but for his people*. And what can give a sovereign a better commendation, or recommend a hero more to the affection of the reader? They were threatened with a tempest, and he wept; he was promised Italy, and he prayed for the accomplishment of that promise. All this in the beginning of a storm; *therefore he showed the more early piety*, and the quicker sense of compassion.[57]

Dryden's doublethink, not peculiar to him alone, and forced upon him by an unusually rigid application of neoclassical codes to the moral of the epic, directs passages of the translation where the valour of its hero may be brought into question by those less disposed than Dryden to see Aeneas as the "perfect prince". In his translation of the passage discussed above, Dryden qualifies the fear of Aeneas as much as is necessary to show that it was "not for himself but for his people".

[54] *Verdicts of the Learned concerning Virgil's and Homer's Heroic Poems,* London (1697) p. 12.

[55] v. T. W. Harrison, "English Virgil: The *Aeneid* in the Eighteenth Century", *Philologica Pragensia*, Vol. 10. Nos. 1–2 (1967).

[56] Ker, II, p. 184.   [57] *Ibid.* (My italics.)

Struck with *unusual* Fright, the *Trojan Chief*
With lifted Hands and Eyes invokes Relief.[58]

extemplo Aenaea solvuntur frigore membra;
ingemit et duplicis tendens ad sidera palmas
talia voce refert.[59]

Luke Milbourne, one of the most vituperative critics of Dryden's
translation, is also committed to the same theories of heroic poetry,
and has in his own version of the First Book in 1688:

Aeneas, trembling with Paternal fear,
With deep drawn sighs, his Pious Hands did rear,
To angry Heaven, and thus his woes exprest.[60]

Dryden marks the fear as "unusual", and it is felt not by Aeneas,
as in Virgil, but by a far more heroic "Trojan Chief". Fear felt in
this capacity as leader or prince is "not for himself, but for his
people", in Milbourne's phrase, paternal, or, in other words,
pious. And thus when Aeneas has finished his terrified out-
pourings, the *"talia iactanti"*[61] of Virgil becomes in Dryden:

Thus while the Pious Prince his Fate bewails.[62]

Having extricated his hero from his most difficult predicament,
Dryden makes certain on almost every occasion that there shall be
no doubt of his hero's lack of fear. At the beginning of *Aeneid* V
the Trojans, having left Carthage, run into another storm. In
Virgil's text Palinurus gives orders to the crew, and he himself
turns the sail aslant the wind. Dryden makes what is simply reported in Virgil dramatic, and, in so doing, draws a contrast
between the crew and Aeneas, the leader "who must outshine the
rest".

The Pilot, Palinurus, cry'd aloud,
What Gusts of Weather from that gath'ring Cloud
My thoughts presage, e're yet the Tempest roars,
Stand to your Tackle, Mates, and stretch your Oars;

---

[58] I, 135–6.   [59] I, 92–4.
[60] Luke Milbourne, *The First Book of Virgil's Aeneis. Made English,* London
(1688) p. 6.
[61] *Aeneid*, I, 102.   [62] I, 146.

Contract the swelling Sails, and luff to Wind:
The *frighted* Crew perform the Task assign'd.
Then to his *fearless* Chief, not Heav'n, said he,
Tho Jove himself shou'd promise Italy,
Can stem the Torrent of this raging Sea.[63]

ipse gubernator puppi Palinurus ab alta:
'heu quianam tanti cinxerunt aethera nimbi?
quidve, pater Neptune, paras?' sic deinde locutus
colligere arma iubet validisque incumbere remis,
obliquatque sinus in ventum ac talia fatur:
'magnanime Aenea, non, si mihi Iuppiter auctor
spondeat, hoc sperem Italiam contingere caelo.'[64]

Dryden's direct speech for Virgil's reported speech, and his making Palinurus order the "frighted" crew to do what he is reported in Virgil to have done himself (*obliquatque sinus in ventum*), help once again to realign the passage in such a way as to make the "fearless Chief" conspicuous by contrast. The examples cited are simply two of many, which help to highlight the "perfect prince" and rescue him from his imperfections. Such "artifice" Dryden recommends to Fletcher; it is, indeed, characteristic of Dryden's heroic poetry as a whole:

> . . . for though Fletcher has taken his picture *truly, and shown him as he was,* an effeminate voluptuous man, yet he has forgotten he was an emperor, and has given him none of those royal marks which *ought* to appear in a lawful successor to the throne. If it be inquired, what Fletcher should have done on this occasion; ought he not to have represented Valentinian as he was; – Bossu shall answer this question for me, by an instance of the like nature: Mauritius, the Greek emperor, was a prince far surpassing Valentinian, for he was endued with many kingly virtues; he was religious, merciful, and valiant, but withal he was noted of extreme covetousness, a vice which is contrary to the character of a hero, or a prince: therefore says the critic, that emperor was no fit person to be represented in a tragedy, unless his good qualities were only

[63] v, 18–26. (My italics.)
[64] v, 12–18.

to be shown, and his covetousness (which sullied them all)
were slurred over by the artifice of the poet.[65]

Fletcher, like Lucan, "followed too much the truth of history".[66]
It is the role of history to give a bare representation of Valentinian
or Mauritius, or Charles, Cromwell or Aeneas, "as they were"
warts and all, but poetry should give kings those royal marks that
should appear; it should represent kings as they *ought* to be.
Poetry "must be ethical",[67] but it must be something more than
ethical, for Dryden considered "that even the instructions of
morality were not so wholly the business of the poet, as that the
precepts and examples of piety were to be omitted".[68] Dryden's
use of Le Bossu, "the best of modern critics", to censure Fletcher,
confirms the rigid Aristotelian rules which applied to the *Aeneid*
distort the original, but distort it so consistently as to make at least
a surrogate epic for the seventeenth century.

6

In Dryden's paraphrase of the Latin hymn *Veni Creator Spiritus* the
lines

infirma nostri corporis
virtute firmans perpeti

become a typical piece of seventeenth century and Drydenian
psychology:

Our Frailties help, our Vice controul;
Submit the Senses to the Soul;
And when Rebellious they are grown,
Then lay thy hand, and hold 'em down.[69]

The pattern of control, a sun in a Copernican system, exists in
Universe, state and man. Passions of any kind are detrimental to
virtue in general and to piety in particular, because piety involves
unselfish devotion; the self, the passions must be conquered and

---

[65] *Preface to Troilus and Cressida* (1679). Ker, I, pp. 218–9.
[66] *An Essay of Heroic Plays* (1672). Ker, I, p. 152.
[67] *Defence of an Essay of Dramatic Poesy* (1668). Ker, I, p. 121.
[68] *Preface to Tyrannic Love* (1670). *Works*, III, p. 349.
[69] Kinsley, II, p. 843, 22–25.

controlled by reason and, in the case of the hero, by an ideal nature divinely bestowed, so that love of parents, children, country, gods, and institutions may be consolidated by discipline and action. Rage is unreasonable, and yet this passion is often the mainspring of that heroic virtue, valour, as we see in Virgil's Mezentius and Turnus. It is as subersive to perfect virtue as any other of those passions which "rule" or "reign" when the soul is in disorder. Courage as the conquest and control of fear is plainly preferable to courage as unthinking wrath. Dryden's hero proceeds almost meticulously with conscious purpose and not through fear, rage, or desperation, or any of the more usual goads to military courage.

> Spurr'd by my Courage, by my Country fir'd;
> With Sense of Honour, and Revenge inspir'd.[70]

> furor, iraque mentem
> praecipitat, pulchrumque mori succurrit in armis.[71]

Virgil's Aeneas is spurred, quite simply, by rage, and, as Warde Fowler[72] points out, we are reminded of the mad fury of Mezentius and Turnus. This is a defect in the perfect prince and it is "slurred over" by Dryden's artifice. If at times the fact of rage is unavoidable, Dryden allows it to be displayed only long enough for it to be demonstrably subdued. Like Alphonso in *Love Triumphant*, Aeneas controls the passion almost as soon as it is born:

> And did you not, my lord, observe Alphonso,
> How, though at first he could not rule his passion, –
> Not at the very first, for that's impossible
> To hasty blood, like his, and yours, my lord, –
> Yet in the second moment, he repented,
> As soon as thought had leisure to be born?[73]

In Dryden's *Sixth Book* Aeneas is terrified by apparitions and yet bravely prepared to assail them with his sword:

> The Chief unsheath'd his shining Steel, prepar'd,
> *Tho'* seiz'd with sudden Fear, to force the Guard.
> Off'ring his brandish'd Weapon at their Face;
> Had not the Sibyl stop'd his *eager* Pace,

[70] II, 427–8. [71] II, 316–17.
[72] Warde Fowler, p. 413. [73] *Works*, VIII. p. 355.

And told him what those empty Fantomes were;
Forms without Bodies, and impassive Air.[74]

corripit hic subita trepidus formidine ferrum
Aeneas strictamque aciem venientibus offert.
et ni docta comes tenuis sine corpore vitas
admoneat volitare cava sub imagine formae,
inruat et frustra ferro diverberet umbras.[75]

The Latin, *subita trepidus formidine*, is clearly more causal than
concessive, but Dryden's simple conjunction *Tho'* is sufficient to
effect the whole realignment of the sense. Even that anger
provoked by a violated treaty, and so perhaps justifiable in the
name of anxious piety, Dryden must make unmistakably righteous
and imply a conscious and permissible slackening of restraint.

Forc'd by this hostile Act, and fir'd with spight,
That flying *Turnus* still declin'd the Fight;
The Prince, whose Piety had long repell'd
His inborn ardour, now invades the Field:
Invokes the Pow'rs of violated Peace,
Their Rites, and injur'd Altars to redress:
Then, to his Rage abandoning the Rein,
With Blood and slaughter'd Bodies fills the Plain.[76]

tum vero adsurgunt irae, insidiisque subactus,
diversos ubi sensit currumque referri,
multa Iovem et laesi testatus foederis aras
iam tandem invadit medios et Marte secundo
terribilis saevam nullo discrimine caedem
suscitat, irarumque omnis effundit habenas.[77]

Dryden's interpolation, "whose Piety had long repell'd His inborn
ardour", at once tells us that normally Aeneas is in control of his
passions and that he is no craven when occasion calls. The
arrangement of "violated Peace" and "injur'd Altars", followed
by the braking colon, and the resumption with *Then* confirm that
the passions are consciously released as religious and righteous
indignation, another guise, in fact, of the usually much calmer

[74] VI, 404–8.   [75] VI, 290–4.
[76] XII, 717–24.   [77] XII, 494–9.

piety. Piety is almost here synonymous with control, and when we have in Latin a description of the *departure* of fear, *postquam pavor ossa reliquit*,[78] Dryden has an effective effort at control:

Now, when my Soul had shaken off her Fears,[79]

The *Aeneid* ends for Dryden, almost inevitably, on a final act of piety, at a point where Virgil leaves us in no doubt that Aeneas is beside himself with rage:

hoc dicens ferrum adverso sub pectore condit fervidus.[80]

The adjective, *fervidus*, in the run-over position, and also at the end of a sentence, is as emphatic as it could possibly be, and ends the poem on what is, to more recent readers, a typically Virgilian ambiguity, a dubious triumph and the shade of Turnus grudgingly leaving the earth. Anchises had advised, *parcere subiectis*,[81] but Aeneas succumbs to bitter revenge; yet Dryden includes in his catalogue of pious actions "his grief for Pallas, and his revenge taken on his murderer, whom otherwise, by his natural compassion, he had forgiven".[82]

7

A sun surrounded by lesser planets, which reflect its light and lead the mind to contemplate the source, describes the hero in the *Aeneid* as Dryden saw it, a hero ringed by minor examples of piety to recall the virtue when Aeneas is off-stage. But there are many characters, neither pious nor even virtuous, who also serve indirectly to recall the hero. Dryden would have agreed with that anthology of learned opinion on the heroic poem, published in the same year as his *Aeneid*, when it says that "the characters of vertues and vices must be carefully drawn".[83] And it was on these lines that Dryden had other criticisms to make of Fletcher, complaining that one did not know whether his characters resembled vice or virtue. If characters do not resemble virtue, they must

[78] III, 57.
[79] III, 82.
[80] XII, 950–1.
[81] VI, 853.
[82] *Dedication*, Ker, II, p. 177.
[83] *Verdicts of the Learned* . . . etc. p. 9.

resemble vice, and they "are remembered with a brand of infamy; and are set as sea marks for those who behold them to avoid".[84] They will "set off" the character of Aeneas by contrast, as in *Tyrannic Love*, "the part of Maximin . . . was designed . . . to set off the character of St Catharine'..[85] And so we find in the *Aeneid*, in direct contrast to the hero and other lesser examples of piety, characters, even princes, as "sea-marks", often at the expense of that which has, since the eighteenth century, come to be regarded as essentially Virgilian, that note of profound sympathy for all the sufferings of men, whether the instruments or the victims of fate. Dryden labels these examples as explicitly as he labelled his examples of piety, and he often castigates where Virgil pities.

One such example is, of course, Turnus, the rival of Aeneas for the hand of Lavinia. Our earliest example of Dryden's remoulding of a Latin passage to throw his hero's piety into sharp relief, showed Aeneas stretching out his "Pious Hands" and asserting "his Innocence". When Turnus has a very similar grievance over broken promises against Latinus, Dryden's emphasis is quite different:

> *Ambitious* Turnus in the Press appears,
> And, aggravating Crimes, augments their Fears:
> *Proclaims his Private Injuries aloud,*
> A solemn Promise made, and disavow'd;
> A foreign Son is sought, and a mix'd Mungril Brood.[86]

It is impossible to find the words italicised in Virgil's Latin,

> Turnus adest medioque in crimine caedis et igni
> terrorem ingeminat: Teucros in regna vocari,
> stirpem admisceri Phrygiam, se limine pelli.[87]

Turnus, one would think, has a legitimate grievance, but the one, in Dryden's additions, is "Pious" and "Attests the Gods, asserts his Innocence" and the other is "Ambitious" and "proclaims his Private Injuries aloud". The two portraits are interdependent in the epic scheme Dryden has opted for. The vice of Turnus is ambition, and "Ambition", along with "Faction", "Zeal",

---

[84] *Preface to Tyrannic Love* (1670). *Works*, III, p. 351.
[85] *Op. cit., Works*, III, p. 350.
[86] VII, 795–9.   [87] VII, 577–9.

"Democracy",[88] "Tyrrany", and "Arbitrary Sway", is one of those threats to stability that were the bugbears of many besides Dryden in the late seventeenth century. Dryden includes Turnus among the other princes who seek the hand of Lavinia, less out of love than out of ambition to extend their dominion:

> Fir'd with her Love, and with Ambition led,
> The neighb'ring Princes court her nuptial Bed.
> Among the crowd, but far above the rest,
> Young *Turnus* to the Beauteous Maid address'd.[89]

Again there is no evidence of ambition in the original:

> multi illam magno e Latio totaque petebant
> Ausonia; petit ante alios pulcherrimus omnis
> Turnus . . .[90]

Dryden even grudges Turnus his beauty, which disappears in the vague, "far above the rest". The two rivals in another typical Dryden expansion are contesting "their Titles to the State",[91] and although Turnus inspires more sympathy with Virgil himself and with Victorian editors like T. E. Page, Dryden consistently makes it incontestably clear where he expects his readers' allegiances to lie.

8

Perhaps no character better exemplifies the way in which Dryden places his characters than Latinus, who serves both as an example of piety and then as a "sea-mark"; first of stability, then of disorder. The first passage occurs immediately after those where Turnus "proclaims his Private Injuries".[92] Chaos is fomented in Latium by Amata, who has been maddened at the instigation of the implacable Juno by Allecto who has the power "to ruin Realmes and o'return a State". Dryden, with real confidence, builds up a scene of disorder, which leads into an image of stability centred in the old, but for the moment, resolute King Latinus, making explicit or expanding, in the lines I have italicised,

[88] *e.g.* v. *Albion and Albanius* (1685). *Works*, VII, p. 236; p. 238.
[89] VII, 80–3.   [90] VII, 55–6.
[91] XII, 1033.   [92] VII, 797.

anything that serves to underline the theme of order which runs through his whole translation:

> Then they, whose Mothers, frantick with their Fear,
> In Woods and Wilds the Flags of *Bacchus* bear,
> And lead his Dances *with dishevell'd hair*,
> Increase the Clamour, and the War demand,
> (Such was *Amata's* Interest in the Land)
> *Against the Public Sanctions of the Peace*,
> Against all Omens of their ill Success;
> With Fates averse, *the Rout in Arms resort*,
> *To Force their Monarch, and insult the Court.*
> But like a Rock unmov'd, a Rock that braves
> The rageing Tempest and the rising Waves,
> *Prop'd on himself he stands*: His solid sides
> Wash off the Sea-weeds, and the sounding Tides:
> *So stood the Pious Prince unmov'd: and long*
> *Sustain'd the madness of the noisie Throng.*[93]

> tum quorum attonitae Baccho nemora avia matres
> insultant thiasis (neque enim leve nomen Amatae)
> undique collecti coeunt Martemque fatigant.
> ilicet infandum cuncti contra omina bellum,
> contra fata deum perverso numine poscunt.
> certatim regis circumstant tecta Latini;
> ille velut pelagi rupes immota resistit,
> ut pelagi rupes magno veniente fragore,
> quae sese multis circum latrantibus undis
> mole tenet; scopuli nequiquam et spumea circum
> saxa fremunt laterique inlisa refunditur alga.[94]

The disorder is characteristcally worked up even to the additional detail of dishevelled hair, and Dryden lifts the verb *insultant*[95] used by Virgil of the Bacchanals and employs it to describe the mob bursting in upon the king, whereas in Virgil they simply *surround* the palace. The imagery of tempest and storm to represent the factious element of society is one Dryden himself frequently uses in his own poems, for example, in *Astraea Redux*:

[93] VII, 800–14.　　　　[94] VII, 580–90.
[95] VII, 581.

The Rabble even now such Freedom did enjoy,
As winds at Sea that use it to destroy.[96]

The phrase "Prop'd on himself he stands", used of Latinus, inevitably calls to mind the words of Cleomenes:

My mind on its own centre stands unmoved
And stable as the fabric of the world,
Propt on itself.[97]

The lines which characterise Latinus as a "Pious Prince" are, typically, Dryden's own. But Latinus does not withstand the mob for very long. He cannot control the people, and fails in his duty as a monarch:

The helpless King is hurry'd in the Throng,
And what e're Tide prevails, is born along.[98]

This in Virgil is simply:

ipsumque trahunt in moenia regem.[99]

The heroic couplet inevitably forces Dryden to expand the original, but the content of his expansions is consistently related to his interpretation of Virgil's epic. Finally the Trojans advance on Latium and the end is near. Amata hangs herself, but not before she has confessed not only her guilt, as in the original, but also its cause:

She calls her self the Cause of all this Ill,
And owns the dire Effects of her *ungovern'd Will*.[1]

se causam clamat crimenque caputque malorum.[2]

The stability of the state is ruined by both an "ungovern'd Will" and "ambition" and those that exhibit these defects act as contrasts to the stabilising piety of the hero. Apart from the more complex "sea-marks" Dryden is ever ready with labels of condemnation, for example, for Allecto's "impious Will",[3] Phaedra's "impious

---

Love"[4] and Achedmolus's "impious Lust".[5] The ghosts of Pasi-
phae and Phaedra are "a foul, incestuous pair",[6] and Aeneas is
made to call Helen "the Strumpet".[7] It is not Virgil's way to
condemn so openly; his restraint is central to the finest parts of his
poetry, and Dryden's condemnations do real violence to Virgil's
pity. Virgil's pervasive human sympathy, which during the
Romantic period was understood as a vague disquiet, and even
with Chateaubriand as "Ossian dans Virgile",[8] attaches itself not
to this camp or that, but to whoever suffers as a man an unjust,
untimely or cruel fate, Trojan or Latin. Virgil does not discrimi-
nate so severely as Dryden, when he uses such epithets as *infelix*
or *miserandus*. Dryden dispenses with the pity and substitutes
castigation.

One such unfortunate victim of Dryden's coarseness is Cydon,
who is both *infelix* and *miserandus*. He is keeping close to the
youth he loves and as a consequence is nearly killed. Virgil
implies in *nova gaudia*[9] that Cydon's passions were habitual and
short-lived, but the adjectives of compassion exclude the kind of
condemnation that Dryden introduces into his translation of the
passage. Virgil's lines *address* Cydon directly, in a way that
Dryden's would never do:

> tu quoque, flaventem prima lanugine malas
> dum sequeris Clytium infelix, nova gaudia, Cydon,
> Dardania stratus dextra, securus amorum
> qui iuvenum tibi semper erant, miserande iaceres,
> ni fratrum stipata cohors foret obvia, Phorci
> progenies, septem numero, septenaque tela
> coniciunt;[10]

To come to Dryden after this is barely tolerable. He weighs in
with any epithet but those of pity and leaves nothing unsaid, in a
manner typically heavy-handed whenever he had occasion to deal
with love or sex:

---

[4] VII, 1052.   [5] X, 544.
[6] VI, 605.   [7] II, 783.
[8] *Essai sur la Littérature Angloise* (1801). v. *Oeuvres Complètes*, Paris 1830–1,
20 vols. Vol. 16, p. 25.
[9] X, 325.   [10] X, 324–30.

Then wretched *Cydon* had receiv'd his Doom,
Who courted *Clytius* in his beardless Bloom,
And sought with lust obscene polluted Joys:
The Trojan Sword had cur'd his love of Boys,
Had not his sev'n bold Brethren stop'd the Course
Of the fierce Champion, with united Force,[11]

Virgil's sympathy is nowhere. These are not minor blemishes but do narrow down the scope of Virgil's own moral concern, and indicate how ham-fisted Dryden can be away from his political and ethical preoccupations, and how, sometimes as a direct consequence of those very preoccupations, he tramples crudely on a sensitivity which is captured well in the less rhetorical Middle Scots of Gavin Douglas, whose concern with medieval "reuth" provides an answering response. Virgil's sympathy is never more apparent than when he deals with the civilian victims of war. The haunting line and a half, whether we take the half-line as an "effective hemistich"[12] or not, in Book II showing the women and children straggling among the heaped spoils is just one example:

> huc undique Troia gaza
> incensis erepta adytis, mensaeque deorum
> crateresque auro solidi, captivaque vestis
> congeritur. pueri et pavidae longo ordine matres
> stant circum.[13]

Similarly in Book V when Aeneas commends those Trojans who feel they can no longer endure the wandering, to the good care of Acestes, Virgil is full of pity, and achieves the kind of "pathetic" scene which would appeal to the later eighteenth century:

> complexi inter se noctemque diemque morantur.
> ipsae iam matres, ipsi, quibus aspera quondam
> visa maris facies et non tolerabile numen,
> ire volunt omnemque fugae perferre laborem.
> quos bonus Aeneas dictis solatur amicis
> et consanguineo lacrimans commendat Acestae.[14]

---

[11] x, 449–54.

[12] v. John Sparrow, *Half-Lines and Repetitions in Virgil*, Oxford (1931) pp. 38–9.

[13] ii, 763–7.   [14] v, 767–71.

Dryden's Aeneas is, of course, characteristically dry-eyed, and the passage is used to contrast the resolution of the leader with the timid reluctance of those who are left behind. His passage does typical violence to Virgil:

> Now loud Laments along the Shores resound,
> Of parting Friends in close Embraces bound.
> *The trembling Women, the degenerate Train,*
> Who shun'd the frightful dangers of the Main;
> Ev'n those desire to sail, and take their share
> Of the rough Passage, and the promis'd War.
> Whom Good *Aeneas* chears; and recommends
> To their new *Master's* Care, his *fearful* Friends.[15]

No tears for his comrades from this Aeneas. "Matres", mothers, become "the trembling Women, the degenerate Train". The hero is advanced, but at what expense! A few lines earlier, when the choice was offered to those who wished it to stay behind and not sail on for Italy, Dryden has:

> They list with Women each degenerate Name,
> Who dare not hazard life, for future Fame.
> These they cashier; the brave remaining few,
> Oars, Banks, and Cables half consum'd renew.[16]

There is no question of despised, effeminate men contracting out of destiny, in Virgil. Again it is simply "matres" and "populum volentum",[17] the people who wanted to stay. As Sidgwick notes in his comment on the line, Virgil "does not condemn them". With Dryden's condemnation they may make a better contrast to the "brave, remaining few", but Virgil's tenderness is crudely overriden. It is hard not to agree with Tillyard when he says that Dryden's "coarse energy and tendency to distort did constant violence to Virgil's subtle, pathetic, or mystical genius".[18] The "sublime" and the "pathetic" were salvaged from Virgil after the destruction of the neoclassical "rules" for the epic in the eighteenth century.

Dryden's Virgil is public, political, and moral. The two poets come together best in those tableaux of control, and piety, in

---

[15] v, 1001–8.   [16] v, 980–3.   [17] v. 750.
[18] *The English Epic and its Background*, London (1954) p. 480.

situations, like that of Latinus, where dangerous, subversive passions are at work. One pre-eminent example is that first simile in the *Aeneid*:

> ac veluti magno in populo cum saepe coorta est
> seditio saevitque animis ignobile vulgus;
> iamque faces et saxa volant, furor arma ministrat;
> tum, pietate gravem ac meritis si forte virum quem
> conspexere, silent arrectisque auribus astant;
> ille regit dictis animos et pectora mulcet.[19]

Dryden is here on familiar ground, the celebration of government, political and psychological:

> As when in Tumults rise th' ignoble Crowd,
> Mad are their Motions, and their Tongues are loud;
> And Stones and Brands in ratling Vollies fly,
> And all the Rustick Arms that Fury can supply:
> If then some grave and Pious Man appear,
> They hush their Noise, and lend a list'ning Ear;
> He sooths with sober Words their angry Mood,
> And quenches their innate desire of Blood.[20]

The additional "innate", which Joseph Trapp condemns as being "too gross and horrid for Virgil's Meaning",[21] is almost Hobbesian, and as significant as anything of the fears of the seventeenth century, and its conservative celebration of order, the order of monarchy, as Dryden found it exemplified in his over-pious Aeneas:

> Our Temperate Isle will no extremes sustain,
> Of pop'lar Sway, or Arbitrary Reign:
> But slides between them both into the best;
> Secure in Freedom, in a Monarch blest.[22]

---

[19] I, 148–53.   [20] I, 213–20.

[21] Joseph Trapp, *The Aeneis of Virgil Translated into Blank Verse*, 2 vols. London (1718–20). Preface, vol. I, p. li.

[22] *The Medall. A Satyre Against Sedition* (1682) pp. 248–51.

M

III. THE PROSE AND CRITICISM

Bonamy Dobrée

DRYDEN'S PROSE

When writing about Dryden's prose, one cannot – nor would one wish to – avoid quoting Dr Johnson's encomium, if only as a challenge to try to add something, to be, if not more explicit, at least illustrative:

> Criticism, either didactic or defensive, occupies almost all his prose, except those pages which he has devoted to his patrons; but none of his prefaces were ever thought tedious. They have not the formality of a settled style, in which the first half of the sentence betrays the other. The clauses are never balanced, nor the periods modelled: every word seems to drop by chance, though it falls into its proper place. Nothing is cold or languid; the whole is airy, animated and vigorous; what is little is gay; what is great is splendid.[1]

One may remember also what Landor makes Southey say in his *Imaginary Conversation* with Porson: they were talking of his poetry, but what they say is equally applicable to his prose:

> Dryden possesses a much richer store of thoughts [than Cowper], expatiates upon more topics, has more vigor, vivacity, and animation. He is always shrewd and penetrating, explicit and perspicuous, concise where conciseness is desirable, and copious where copiousness can yield delight.[2]

Praise cannot go further than those two statements. We might

[1] Samuel Johnson. *Lives of the Poets*, ed. Peter Cunningham, London (John Murray) 1854, Vol. I. p. 345.
[2] Walter Savage Landor, *Imaginary Conversations*. London (J. M. Dent & Co.) 1859.

add, however that, as we know, "he found the language brick and left it marble" though it might be better to say that he found it an untended forest and left it an ordered park. But Pater, in his essay on "Style" is not so enthusiastic:

> . . . his sense of prosaic excellence affected his verse rather than his prose [Pater did not think highly of Dryden's verse] which is, not only fervid, richly figured, poetic as we say, but vitiated all unconsciously, by many a scanning line. Setting up correctness, that humble merit of prose, as the central literary excellence, he is really a less correct writer than he may seem, with an imperfect mastery of the relative pronoun.[3]

Somewhat pedantic criticism (Eliot called it "cheap journalism"); many of us are guilty of confusing "that" and "which"; and why the occasional scanning line should vitiate a prose passage is not clear. Does "And wild enormities of ancient magnanimity" "vitiate" that superb passage in *Urn Burial*? Or many others one can think of especially, perhaps, in Landor with: "of which the echo is not faint at last"; or De Quincey with: "and when the sun has gone down to his rest"; even with Pater himself, when he writes "the perishing gray bones of a poor man's grave". Dryden's "scanning" lines do not obtrude, and he was aware of the danger, referring as he does in the "Epistle Dedicatory" of *The Rival Ladies*: to Shakespeare being the first who, to shun the pains of continual rhyming, invented

> that kind of writing which we call blank verse, but the French, more properly, *prose mesurée*; into which the English tongue so naturally slides, that, in writing prose, it is hardly to be avoided.[4]

Dr Johnson's division into the didactic or defensive does not provide much guidance as to the variation in his prose; in both, however, we can see the effect of what Dryden thought about language, and can begin with what he said in the Preface to *Annus Mirabilis* (1666) – a very general statement:

---

[3] Walter Pater, *Appreciations with an Essay on Style*. London (Macmillan) 1911.

[4] W. P. Ker, *Essays of John Dryden*, 2 vols. Oxford (Clarendon Press) 1926, I, p. 6.

. . . the first happiness of a poet's imagination is properly invention, or finding of the thought; the second is fancy, or the variation, deriving, or moulding, of that thought, as the judgment represents it proper to the subject; the third is elocution, or the art of clothing and adorning the thought, so found and varied, in apt, significant, and sounding words.[5]

Again and again we get the crucial phrase "significant and sounding"; it echoes through his pages.

In the earlier Epistle Dedicatory to Lord Orrery of *The Rival Ladies* he is full of suggestions, and it is at the beginning of that piece that, strangely enough for him, he describes the process of creation in almost romantic terms:

My Lord,
This worthless present was designed you, long before it was a play; when it was only a confused mass of thoughts, tumbling over one another in the dark; when the fancy was yet in its first work, moving the sleeping images of things towards the light, there to be distinguished, and then either chosen or rejected by the judgment.[6]

His concern with language is already evident here; and in a passage forestalling Swift he says:

I have endeavoured to write English, as near as I could distinguish it from the tongue of pedants, and that of affected travellers. Only I am sorry, that (speaking so noble a language as we do) we have not a more certain measure of it, as they have in France, where they have an Academy erected for that purpose, and endowed with large privileges by the present king. I wish we might at length leave to borrow words [we would say "stop borrowing" words] from other nations, which is now a wantonness in us, not a necessity; but so long as some affect to speak them, there will not want others, who will have the boldness to write them.[7]

The "affected travellers", presumably, were the courtiers of Charles II who had returned from France, and he makes fun of this "affectation" in the superb scene of *Marriage A-la-Mode*, where

[5] *Op. cit.,* I, p. 15.   [6] *Op. cit.,* I, p. 1.   [7] *Op. cit.,* I, p. 5.

Philotis teaches Melantha an engaging string of French words, beginning with *sottises* and ending *en ridicule*. But Dryden was not rigid in his views – he was great enough to change his mind – and to quote from the *Dedication of the Æneis*, he says:

> 'Tis true, that, when I find an English word significant and sounding, I neither borrow from the Latin, nor any other language; but when I want at home, I must seek abroad.
> If sounding words are not of our growth and manufacture, who shall hinder me to import them from a foreign country? I carry not out the treasure of the nation, which is never to return; but what I bring from Italy I spend in England; here it remains and here it circulates; for, if the coin be good, it will pass from one hand to another. I trade both with the living and the dead, for the enrichment of our native language.[8]

The choice he found unfortunately limited; there are not enough words to vary the utterance as much as one might wish for;

> Words are not so easily coined as money; and yet we see that the credit not only of banks but of exchequers cracks, when little comes in, and much goes out. Virgil called upon me in every line for some new word: and I paid so long, that I was almost bankrupt; so that the latter end must be more burdensome than the beginning or the middle; and, consequently, the Twelfth Æneid cost me double the time of the First and Second. What had become of me, if Virgil had taxed me with another book? I had certainly been reduced to pay the public in hammered money, for want of milled; that is in the same old words which I had used before: and the receivers must have been forced to have taken any thing, where there was so little to be had.[9]

How far he ever got to coining words we may find in the *Annus Mirabilis* preface where he explains to Sir Robert Howard:

> Upon your first perusal of this poem, you have taken notice of some words, which I have innovated (if it be too bold for me to say refined) upon his [Virgil's] Latin; which, as I offer not

---

[8] *Op. cit.*, II, p. 234.   [9] *Op. cit.*, II, p. 232.

to introduce into English prose, so I hope they are neither improper, nor altogether unelegant in verse . . . if a Roman poet might have liberty to coin a word, supposing only that it was derived from the Greek, was put into a Latin termination, and that he used this liberty but seldom, and with modesty; how much more justly may I challenge that privilege to do so with the same prerequisites, from the best and most judicious of Latin writers?[10]

He has much the same sensible attitude as regards old words. In *A Discourse concerning the Original and Progress of Satire* (1693) he says "in my opinion obsolete words may be laudably revived, when they are more sounding, or more significant, than those in practice"; and as a final utterance, in the *Preface to the Fables* (1700):

> When an ancient word for its sound and significancy deserves to be revived, I have that reasonable veneration for antiquity to restore it. All beyond this is supersitition. Words are not like landmarks, so sacred as never to be removed; customs are changed, and even statutes are silently repealed, when the reason ceases for which they were enacted.[11]

He himself almost invariably employs words in common use: but occasionally a comparatively rare one appears, such as "protatick", where he is using a cant term for persons entering at the beginning of a play. Exactness, of course, was a prime consideration with him; though words must be "sounding"; the sound, to use Pope's phrase, must be an echo to the sense. There is an interesting passage in the *Preface to the Fables* setting a limit to the sheer use of sound:

> Mr Hobbes . . . tells us, that the first beauty of an epic poem consists in diction; that is, in the choice of words, and harmony of numbers. Now the words are the colouring of the work, which, in the order of nature, is last to be considered. The design, the disposition, the manners, and the thoughts, are all before it: where any of those are wanting or imperfect, so much wants or is imperfect in the imitation of human life, which is the very definition of a poem. Words,

[10] *Op. cit.,* I, pp. 17–18   [11] *Op. cit.,* II, pp. 266–7.

indeed, like glaring colours, are the first beauties that arise and strike the sight; but if the draught be false or lame, the figures ill disposed, the manners obscure or inconsistent, or the thoughts unnatural, then the finest colours are but daubing, and the piece is a beautiful monster at best.[12]

It must be noted, however, that though in his remarks about writing it is nearly always poetry or the drama that he is referring to, much nevertheless is applicable to prose.

The originality of his own prose lies in its colloquialism. He said in his *Defence of the Epilogue* that "the last and greatest advantage of our writing, which proceeds from *conversation*. . . .", and though once more he was referring to plays, he was evidently himself making use of this advantage, in the writing of prose. So with him there are few traces of the purple of Donne or Browne, or of the elaborations that characterise Greene and Lodge. Others, certainly, had been simple and direct, as had Bacon: but there is always a considerable formality about their writing, as in Earle's *Microcosmography*. Dryden seems to talk rather than to write, and he talks, not *at* you but *with* you. He may have got a hint from the somewhat stilted semi-dialogue work of Deloney in his *The Gentle Craft*, but he discovered and explored the manner suitable to his genius in *An Essay of Dramatic Poesy*. It is not, perhaps, a good dialogue compared with later ones, say Landor's, since the talkers sometimes discourse too lengthily, and the voice throughout is that of Neander, that is to say, of Dryden himself. This to be sure is worth listening to, though it is not so varied and picturesque as it often is, as in the earlier Dedicatory Epistle of *The Rival Ladies*. He is arguing in favour of rhyme:

> But the excellence and dignity of it were never fully known till Mr Waller taught it; he first made writing easily an art; first showed us to conclude the sense most commonly in distichs, which, in the verse of those before him, runs on for so many lines together, that the reader is out of breath to overtake it. . . .
>
> But that benefit which I consider most in it, because I have not seldom found it, is, that it bounds and circumscribes the fancy. For imagination in a poet is a faculty so wild and

[12] *Op. cit.,* II, pp. 252–3.

lawless, that like an high-ranging spaniel, it must have clogs tied to it, lest it outrun the judgment.[13]

Given the reaction of the times from poetry such as Donne's, that is a sound observation. Yet it echoes what Earle had said a good many years before: "Is a man too quick for himself: one whose actions put a leg still before his judgment, and outrun it."

It will already have been noticed how beautifully firm Dryden's conclusions always are: that is the only point where one can say that his style is at all "settled"; and even then it is characteristically different on various occasions. But it is time to look at more examples of his critical utterances, both didactic and defensive, though it is hard to distinguish between the two, since when he is didactic he is defending his own practice, or at least what he hoped to accomplish.

We may take him in *An Essay of Dramatic Poesy* where he is discussing a poet whom he leaves un-named. Crites (Howard) is speaking:

> He is one of those who, having had some advantage of education and converse, knows better than the other [poet discussed] what a poet should be, but puts it into practice more unluckily than any man; his style and matter are everywhere alike: he is the most calm, peaceable writer you ever read: he never disquiets your passions with the least concernment, but still leaves you in as even a temper as he found you; he is a very Leveller in poetry: he creeps along with ten little words in every line, and helps out his numbers with *For to* and *Unto*, and all the pretty expletives he can find, till he drags them to the end of another line; while the sense is left tired half way behind it: he doubly starves all his verses, first for want of thought, and then of expression; his poetry neither has wit in it, nor seems to have it; like him in Martial:
>
> *Pauper videri* Cinna *vult, et est pauper.*
>
> He affects plainness, to cover his want of imagination: when he writes the serious way, the highest flight of his fancy is some miserable antithesis, or seeming contradiction; and in the comic he is still reaching at some thin conceit, the ghost of

[13] *Op. cit.,* I, pp. 7–8.

a jest, and that too flies before him, never to be caught; these
swallows which we see before us on the Thames are the just
resemblance of his wit; you may observe how near the water
they stoop, how many proffers they make to dip, and yet how
seldom they touch it; and when they do, 'tis but the surface:
they skim over it but to catch a gnat, and then mount into the
air and leave it.[14]

It is a devastating condemnation, beautifully done in varied
imagery, one phrase of it evidently sticking in Pope's memory
when he wrote:

> While *Expletives* their feeble Aid *do* join;
> And ten low Words oft creep in one dull line.[15]

In 1693, in the *Satire* essay, he spoke of the "ill-sounding
monosyllables of which our barbarous language [not here, we
note, so noble a language] affords . . . a wild plenty:" but in 1697,
in the *Dedication of Æneis*, he tempered his judgment, though with
great caution; and after complaining that our verses are "clogged
with consonants, which are the dead weight of our mother
tongue", and of which monosyllables are inevitably largely composed, he goes on:

> 'Tis possible, I confess, though it rarely happens, that a
> verse of monosyllables may sound harmoniously; and some
> examples of it I have seen. My first line of the *Æneis* is not
> harsh—
> Arms, and the Man I sing, who forc'd by Fate, &c.
> But a much better instance may be given from the last
> line of Manilius, made English by our learned and judicious
> Mr Creech –
> Nor could the World have borne so fierce a Flame –
> where the many liquid consonants are placed so artfully,
> that they give a pleasing sound to the words, though they are
> all of one syllable.[16]

Where prose is concerned the question does not obtrude, and

---

[14] *Op. cit.*, I, pp. 31–2.
[15] Alexander Pope, "Essay on Criticism", 346–7, *Poems of Alexander Pope*,
Vol. I, eds. E. Audra and A. Williams, London (Methuen) 1961, p. 278.
[16] Ker, II, p. 226.

Dryden is not afraid to use monosyllables as he will. In the *Satire* essay he can write an almost uninterrupted sequence of no less than fourteen: "Thus far, my Lord, you see it has gone very hard with Persius: I think he. . . ." A clear enough illustration.

That essay provides an extraordinary variety of rhythms and pressures. From being analytical about satire, he can become eloquent about Stoicism:

> The philosophy in which Persius was educated, and which he professes through his whole book, is the Stoic; the most noble, the most generous, most beneficial [we note again the triple emphasis] to human kind, among all the sects, who have given us the rules of ethics, thereby to form a severe virtue in the soul; to raise in us an undaunted courage against the assaults of fortune; to esteem as nothing the things that are without us, because they are not in our power; not to value riches, beauty, honours, fame, or health, any further than as conveniences, and so many helps to living as we ought, and doing good in our generation. . . . Passions, interests, ambition, and all their bloody consequences of discord and of war, are banished from this doctrine. Here is nothing proposed but the quiet and tranquillity of the mind; virtue lodged at home, and afterwards diffused in her general effects, to the improvement and good of human kind.[17]

Dryden, we see, is not always concise. The above passage is somewhat repetitious; and though throughout his work he rubs in what he means, it is usually by some delightful image, metaphor or simile.

Congreve held that Dryden was "an improving writer to the last", so it might be enlightening to see whether this is as true of his prose as it is of his plays and verse, which were what Congreve was referring to. We can take a passage from his early work, the opening of *An Essay of Dramatic Poesy* (1668):

> It was that memorable day, in the first summer of the late war, when our navy engaged the Dutch; a day wherein the two most mighty and best appointed fleets which any age had ever seen, disputed the command of the greater part of the

---

[17] *Op. cit.*, II, pp. 75–6

globe, the commerce of nations, and the riches of the universe.[18]

It would be difficult to find any fault there – except, possibly, the intrusion of the word "ever": it is clear, with good firm endings to the sentences: but there is nothing striking or individual about it. It has, as is so frequent in English writing, the triple formation: "the greater part of the globe, the commerce of angels . . . the riches of the universe." Now let us look at the opening of the *Dedication of the Aeneis* (1697):

> A Heroic Poem, truly such, is undoubtedly the greatest work which the soul of man is capable to perform. The design of it is to form the mind of man to heroic virtue by example; 'tis conveyed in verse, that it may delight while it instructs. The action of it is always one, entire, and great.[19]

That is very much easier, and at the same time more compact; the triple ending is more effective because it is more terse. We might declare that in prose also Dryden was an improving writer to the last.

For the moment let us turn to the passages we might call auto-biographical. They are, as one would assume, later work, and the first notable one we come across is in the Satire *Discourse*, where he explains how it is that he has written little personal satire, a remarkable piece of abnegation in a man who could write *Absalom and Achitophel*. He has been speaking of forgiveness:

> the forgiveness which we beg is the pardoning of others the offences which they have done to us; for which reason I have many times avoided the commission of that fault, even when I have been notoriously provoked. Let not this, my Lord, pass for vanity in me; for it is truth. More libels have been written against me, than almost any man now living; and had I reason on my side, to have defended my own innocence. . . . I speak of my morals, which have been sufficiently aspersed: that only sort of reputation ought to be dear to every honest man, and is to me. But let the world witness for me, that I have been often wanting to myself in that particular; I

---

[18] *Op. cit.,* I, p. 28.   [19] *Op. cit.,* II, p. 154.

have seldom answered any scurrilous lampoon, when it was
in my power to have exposed my enemies: and being naturally
vindicative, have suffered in silence, and possessed my soul in
quiet.[20]

This occurs in that portion where he is speaking of Horace,
Persius, and Juvenal, claiming that they truly performed the
cleansing function of satire.

> but how few lampooners are there now living, who are
> capable of this duty! When they come in my way, 'tis im-
> possible sometimes to avoid reading them. But, good God!
> how remote they are, in common justice, from the choice of
> such persons as are the proper subject of satire! And how
> little wit they bring for the support of their injustice! . . .
> No decency is considered, no fulsomeness omitted; no
> venom is wanting, as far as dulness can supply it.[21]

After that beautiful shaft, he adds a little in the same vein about the
bunglers in satire, ending with some of his rich figuring:

> To conclude: they are like the fruits of the earth in this un-
> natural season; the corn which held up its head is spoiled
> with rankness; but the greater part of the harvest is laid
> along, and little of good income and wholesome nourishment
> is received into the barns.[22]

It is all beautifully conversational, as always; he is talking to, not
at, the addressee of the essay, Lord Dorset, and he throws the
whole thing off as a digression which a just indignation has forced
from him. "Now I have removed this rubbish, I will return to the
comparison of Juvenal and Horace." In the course of this we get
one of his epigrammatic phrases, at once summing up and explain-
ing: "The meat of Horace is more nourishing; but the cookery of
Juvenal more exquisite."

He was, however, stirred to retort when Jeremy Collier attacked
him in his decried but by no means despicable *A Short View of the
Immorality and Profaneness of the Stage.* Here in the *Preface to the
Fables* Dryden is not conversational, but dignified, even a little
aloof:

---

[20] *Op. cit.,* II, p. 80.   [21] *Op. cit.,* II, p. 81.   [22] *Op. cit.,* II, p. 81.

I shall say the less of Mr Collier, because in many things he has taxed me justly; and I have pleaded guilty to all thoughts and expressions of mine, which can be truly argued of obscenity, profaneness, or immorality, and retract them. [Why all this fuss? After all, everybody in the lay world makes his occasional smutty joke.] If he be my enemy, let him triumph; [a contemptuous shrug of the shoulders] if he be my friend, as I have given him no personal occasion to be otherwise, he will be glad of my repentance. It becomes me not to draw my pen in the defence of a bad cause, when I have so often drawn it in a good one. Yet it were not difficult to prove, that in many places he has perverted my meaning by his glosses, and interpreted my words into blasphemy and bawdry, of which they were not guilty. Besides that, he is too much given to horse-play in his raillery, and comes to battle like a dictator of the plough. I will not say, *The Zeal of God's House has eaten him up*; but I am sure it has devoured some part of his good manners and civility.[23]

He has warded off the blow, and now he hits back, not harshly, but, rather, administering a gentle, and most efficacious, tap with the gloves on:

It might also be doubted, whether it were altogether zeal which prompted him to this rough manner of proceeding; perhaps it became not one of his function to rake into the rubbish of ancient and modern plays; a divine might have employed his pains to better purpose, than in the nastiness of Plautus and Aristophanes, whose examples, as they excuse not me, so it might possibly be supposed, that he read them not without some pleasure.[24]

He goes on to show that Collier is really being rather ridiculous, pointing out that Fletcher's *The Custom of the Country* contains more bawdry than any written by himself or his contemporaries, but which he can remember as often having been acted. "Are the times so much reformed now, than they were five-and-twenty years ago? If they are, I congratulate the amendment of our morals." As to others who have attacked him, notably Milbourne and Blackmore, whom he refers to only by single initials, "they

[23] *Op. cit.*, ii, p. 272.   [24] *Op. cit.*, ii, pp. 272–3.

are such scoundrels, that they deserve not the least notice to be taken of them". The whole thing is gracefully done, if not altogether with the tone, at all events the structure of the conversational ease of which he was master; nor, in this last of his writings, is there any falling off in vigour.

It was in the "Postscript to the Reader" of the Dedication of the *Æneis* that he stated his abandonment of satire. The piece opens with a paragraph made moving not only by its subject-matter, but by the quality of the prose, its musical variation, with phrases not exactly balanced, though the periods are modelled:

> What Virgil wrote in the vigour of his age, in plenty and at ease, I have undertaken to translate in my declining years; struggling with wants, oppressed with sickness, curbed in my genius, liable to be misconstrued in all I write; and my judges, if they are not very equitable, already prejudiced against me, by the lying character which has been given them of my morals. Yet steady to my principles, and not dispirited with my affliction, I have, by the blessing of God on my endeavours, overcome all difficulties, and, in some measure, acquitted myself of the debt which I owed the public when I undertook this work.[25]

He goes on to justify, very mildly, what he has accomplished in his own writing, and he speaks of those who "relying on the beauty of their thoughts have judged ornament of words, and sweetness of sound, unnecessary". Here he supplies his readers with two images:

> Others have no ear for verse, nor choice of words, nor distinction of thoughts: but mingle farthings with their gold, to make up the sum. Here is a field of satire opened to me: but, since the Revolution, I have wholly renounced that talent. For who would give physic to the great, when he is uncalled? – to do his patient no good, and endanger himself for his prescription? Neither am I ignorant, but I may justly be condemned for many of those faults of which I have too liberally arraigned others.[26]

[25] *Op. cit.*, II, pp. 240–1.
[26] *Op. cit.*, II, pp. 241–2.

N

He is tremendously varied – in pace, metaphor, and vowel sound. And he can, without any sense of jarring, drop from what is great and splendid to what is little and gay, or at any rate from what is seriously expressed to something rather ridiculous. Here, for example, from *An Essay of Dramatic Poesy*:

> The end of tragedies or serious plays, says Aristotle, is to beget admiration, compassion, or concernment; but are not mirth and passion things incompatible? And is it not evident that the poet must of necessity destroy the former by intermingling of the latter? That is, he must ruin the sole end and object of his tragedy, to introduce somewhat that is forced in, and is not of the body of it. Would you not think that physician mad, who, having prescribed a purge, should immediately order you to take restringents upon it?[27]

So Lisideius [Sedley], but Neander [Dryden], taking a different view, expresses himself with a great range of metaphor:

> As for their [the French] new way of mingling mirth with serious plot, I do not, with Lisideius, condemn the thing, though I cannot approve their manner of doing it. He tells us, we cannot so speedily recollect ourselves after a scene of great passion and concernment, as to pass to another of mirth and humour, and to enjoy it with any relish: but why should we imagine the soul of man more heavy than his senses? Does not the eye pass from an unpleasant object to a pleasant in a much shorter time than is required to this? And does not the unpleasantness of the first commend the beauty of the latter? The old rule of logic might have convinced him, that contraries, when placed near, set off each other. A continued gravity keeps the spirit too much bent; we must refresh it sometimes, as we bait in a journey, that we may go on with greater ease. A scene of mirth, mixed with tragedy, has the same effect upon us which our music has betwixt the acts; and that we find a relief to us from the best plots and language of the stage, if the discourses have been long.[28]

[27] *Op. cit.,* I, p. 58.
[28] *Op. cit.,* I, pp. 69–70.

Also he is fond of using a series of metaphors for saying the same thing. Eugenius [Buckhurst], speaking of clenches and catachresis, says:

> Wit is best conveyed to us in the most easy language; and is most to be admired when a great thought comes dressed in words so commonly received, that it is best understood by the meanest apprehensions, as the best meat is the most easily digested: but we cannot read a verse of Cleveland's without making a face at it, as if every word were a pill to swallow: he gives us many times a hard nut to break our teeth, without a kernel for our pains. [We are put in mind of Cleveland's "Come keen *Iambicks* with your Badgers feet/And Badger-like, bite till your teeth do meet."] So there is this difference betwixt his *Satires* and doctor Donne's; the one gives us deep thoughts in common language . . . the other gives as common thoughts in abstruse words.[29]

He likes, too, to round off a point with a firm utterance, as in the Preface to *Annus Mirabilis*:

> The composition of all poems is, or ought to be, of wit; and wit in the poet, or *Wit writing*, (if you will give me leave to use a school-distinction), is no other than the faculty of imagination in the writer, which, like a nimble spaniel, beats over and ranges through the field of memory, till it springs the quarry it hunted after; or, without metaphor, which searches over all the memory for the species or ideas of those things which it designs to represent. *Wit written* is that which is well defined, the happy result of thought, or product of imagination. But to proceed from wit, in the general notion of it, to the proper wit of an Heroic or Historical Poem, I judge it chiefly to consist in the delightful imagining of persons, actions, passions, or things. 'Tis not the jerk or sting of an epigram, nor the seeming contradiction of a poor antithesis (the delight of an ill-judging audience in the play of rhyme), nor the jingle of a more poor paronomasia. . . .[30]

Here, we see, he is trying to make the language definite, endeavouring to do without metaphor. He falls, however, to the

[29] *Op. cit.,* I, p. 52.   [30] *Op. cit.,* I, pp. 14–15.

lure of his favourite spaniel, and we may be reminded that Dryden, after all, liked to spend a deal of time in the country, following its pursuits, especially fishing. But all the time he is labouring to make the language not only definite but irreproacheable, as we can tell from the many corrections, or minor alterations he makes in successive editions of his writing. It is odd that he should resort to a word like "paronomasia", when "play upon words", or "pun", would have suited him as well, or better still, a favourite word in his day, "clench".

A man who writes as much as Dryden did is bound to repeat a phrase at intervals, even in a different context; thus in the Dedication of *Examen Poeticum* he tells us that "the corruption of a poet is the generation of a critic"; an error – since in common with himself the best poets are often the best critics. In the *Defence*, where he is being bantering rather than satirical with Howard, he varies the phrase:

> *Well he is now fettered in business of a more unpleasant nature:* the Muses have lost him, but the Commonwealth gains by it; the corruption of a poet is the generation of a statesman.[31]

Knowing Dryden's opinion of politicians, the banter almost becomes satire.

Dryden had a remarkable, and happy capacity, for interposing what is little and gay in what is great and splendid. One can pick up the gay phrases, by way of epigram or aphorism, in almost all his work. Speaking of Ben Jonson's borrowings, for instance, he states that "He invades authors like a monarch". A play, as we have been told again and again, is an imitation of Nature: but "we know we are to be deceived, and we desire to be so". Discussing verse in plays he declares "Thus Prose, though the rightful prince, yet is by common consent deposed, as too weak for the government of serious plays." Both of these are from the *Defence*. These general statements may be a little extended, as in the *Essay*: "Homer describes his heroes as men of great appetites, lovers of beef broiled upon the coals, and good fellows; contrary to the practice of the French Romances, whose heroes neither eat, nor drink, nor sleep, for love." There is, of course, considerable humour in what he writes but it is rather as an undercurrent than a

[31] *Op. cit.,* I, p. 119.

direct attempt to raise a laugh; he demands, rather, a smile, as when at the beginning of the *Essay*, Crites (Howard) "could scarce have wished the victory at the price he knew he must pay for it, in being subject to the reading and hearing of so many ill verses as he was sure would be made upon it". And later he notes that: "I have observed that in all our tragedies, the audience cannot forbear laughing when the actors are to die; it is the most comic part of the whole play." In the *Rival Ladies* epistle, he compares the appreciation of poetry to digestion; in the Dedication of *Examen Poeticum* he refers to "those ungodly man-killers, whom we poets, when we flatter them, call heroes".

But there are no boundaries to be set to what he can do in this medium, which he found as natural to him as poetry. As he says in the moving *Preface to the Fables*:

> By the mercy of God, I am already come within twenty years of [eighty-eight], a cripple in my limbs, but what decays are in my mind, the reader must determine. I think myself as vigorous as ever in the faculties of my soul, excepting only my memory, which is not impaired to any great degree; and if I lose not more of it, I have no great reason to complain. What judgment I had, increases rather that diminishes; and thoughts, such as they are, come crowding in so fast upon me, that my only difficulty is to choose or to reject, to run them into verse, or to give them the other harmony of prose: I have so long studied and practised both, that they are grown into a habit, and become familiar to me.[32]

"The other harmony", the phrase is revealing, as is "the long study", implying that he gave the same labour to prose as to verse, was as eager to find suitable rhythms, and "apt, significant, and sounding words", in the one as in the other. But he was never altogether satisfied, correcting and re-correcting in successive editions, as recorded in W. P. Ker's selected *Essays of John Dryden*, the text which has been used here, where the spelling and so on is "normalised", wherever possible, but retaining forms where the sound would be altered, such as "thrid" where we would say, and write, "thread". For instance, he changes "one that" and "one which" into "one who", which might have reassured Pater; he

[32] *Op. cit.*, II, p. 249.

changes "writ" to "written"; he avoids prepositions at the end of a sentence, a common fault with Shakespeare, he judges; he tries not to write "it" in reference to what he is talking about, and in the *Essay* changes "go through with it" to "go through the work". Near the same reference he writes "they suffer you not to behold him" instead of "you behold him not". Later we find him changing "to the most mean ones, those which," to read "to those which are most mean, and which;" the *Essay* is full of such changes, though his subsequent writings seem free of them, perhaps because he went through them more carefully than he had the *Essay*, which had been written in the country, where he had fled to avoid "the violence of the plague".

It will be conceded – or so it may be hoped – that the praises bestowed upon Dryden's writing quoted at the beginning of this essay are well justified. One can, of course, demur here and there; is he always as concise as he might be where conciseness is desirable? And does his copiousness always yield delight? We have seen that he is prone to a proliferation of metaphors, yet that is part of the delight, one of the reasons why we never find any of his prefaces tedious. Reading him today, we may be slightly held up by differences in common usage, one of which has already been noted, saying, for instance, "I must remember you . . ." where we would say, "I must remind you . . ." He writes, "this hinders not that there may be . . ." rather than "this does not hinder there being . . ." Sometimes we find a word now disused, such as "compellation" for "appelation"; or the obsolete word "opiniatre" for "holding fast to one's opinions" (we would probably say "obstinate"); and the older form "interessed" for "interested". We might not know what he means by "an olio of a play", the word oleo – so more correctly spelt – meaning hotch-potch. But it is all so beautifully balanced, so well paragraphed, the endings of sentences so firm, and above all so unmistakably clear, that one can only sum it all up in a quotation as inescapable as those which prelude these remarks, and whole-heartedly agree with Matthew Arnold's saying: "Here at last we have the true English prose, a prose such as we would all gladly use if only we knew how."

William Frost

DRYDEN'S THEORY
AND PRACTICE OF SATIRE

Published in 1693, Dryden's translations of Juvenal and Persius were prefaced by an essay on satire, the translator's "Discourse concerning the Original and Progress of Satire", which occupies slightly more than one-third of the volume and which, like the better-known "Essay of Dramatic Poesy" and "Preface to the Fables" constitutes one of Dryden's finest and most sustained literary discussions. It has not been much appreciated in modern times. In 1942 Mary Claire Randolph, in her excellent study of "Formal Verse Satire" in *Philological Quarterly*, called Dryden's Discourse "the most generally neglected and inadequately edited major critical essay in our literature",[1] and as recently as 1965 Alvin Kernan in his lively book *The Plot of Satire* exemplifies this neglect once more by practically dismissing the Discourse as "fragmentary, poorly organized, frequently ambiguous, and conventional in the extreme".[2] Worse still, in their provocative and intelligent short history of literary criticism Wimsatt and Brooks, two of the best analysts living, deal with the Discourse by quoting from it only a single passage, the one about there being a "vast difference between the slovenly Butchering of a Man, and the fineness of a stroak that separates the Head from the Body, and leaves it standing in its place. A man may be capable, as *Jack Ketches's* Wife said of his Servant, of a plain piece of Work, a bare Hanging; but to make a Malefactor die sweetly, was only belonging

---

[1] Mary Claire Randolph, "Formal Verse Satire", *Philological Quarterly*, Vol. 21 (1942) pp. 368–84, p. 380.

[2] Alvin Kernan, *The Plot of Satire*. New Haven, Conn. (Yale Univ. Press) 1965, p. 6.

to her Husband".[3] A splendidly quotable passage, to be sure, but one which might just as well have come out of an essay on invective or on the lampoon as out of a Discourse on Satire. It hardly epitomises the view of satire implied and developed in Dryden's Discourse, nor does it at all embody Dryden's chief contribution to discussion of satire in England.

Briefly, the literary circumstances of the Discourse are these: Satire specifically imitating Roman satire began appearing in England in the 1590s, not long before the date of *Hamlet*. There had been a few straws in the wind earlier, and Wyatt himself in the first half of the sixteenth century had written poems imitating Alemanni, a modern Italian imitator of the Roman satirists: but essentially this kind of poetry in English begins at the end of the century preceding Dryden's. Joseph Hall is very nearly right in proclaiming his own title as innovator – "Follow me who list, and be the second English satirist". The group writing what they called satires in the 1590s included Marston, Lodge, Donne, and others less well remembered; after a brief outburst of their efforts, the government stepped in and outlawed the genre. A few more verse satires were nevertheless published during the next twenty years, and Hall himself came to the further attention of the reading public by entering the theological lists against Milton in the pamphlet war of the 1640s, by which time Hall was a bishop, soon to be deprived of his office by the Commonwealth government: but no events worth remembering in the history of English satire took place till the Restoration. The last third of the seventeenth century saw the great success of Samuel Butler's anti-Puritan narrative burlesque poem *Hudibras* as well as the careers of John Oldham and of Dryden himself; by 1693, when he writes the Discourse, all of Dryden's best-known original poems have appeared.

What Dryden leaves out of the Discourse on Satire is, in a way, as important as what he puts in. Not only does he ignore innovator Hall completely, but almost the only English satirist he mentions earlier than his own age is Donne, whom he mentions only to criticise rather adversely. Furthermore he says almost nothing about the entire background out of which, in standard

[3] William K. Wimsatt Jr. and Cleanth Brooks, *A Short History of Literary Criticism*. New York (Knopf) 1957, p. 207.

studies like Alden's *Rise of Formal Verse Satire in England* or Peter's *Complaint and Satire in Early English Literature*, the satire of the 1590s is sometimes seen as having arisen: I mean the so-called native tradition, which includes among predecessor satirists Chaucer, Langland, Barclay, Skelton, and a host of others in the Middle Ages and early Renaissance. Satire for Dryden, it is evident, consists of the work of Horace, Juvenal, and Persius, plus Boileau's, to some extent Donne's, and that of the nobleman to whom Dryden dedicates the Discourse, Dorset. Dryden does mention himself, Spenser, and Samuel Butler, but only rather incidentally. It may be as much his omissions as his inclusions that have led his essay to be neglected or to be termed "conventional" or "fragmentary".

Furthermore, from the point of view of modern discussions of satire, Dryden's account at first glance seems to leave out nearly everything worth attending to. Theoretical discussion of satire in the last decade has included the influential work of Northrop Frye in his *Anatomy of Criticism* (1957), work which had been preceded by Frye's essay on satire in the *Toronto Quarterly* for 1944–5;[4] and three noteworthy books specifically on satire: Robert Elliott's *Power of Satire* (1960), and Alvin Kernan's *The Cankered Muse* (1959) and *The Plot of Satire* (1965). Elliott takes satire from its earliest known beginnings in Irish or Arabic magic formulae or the lampoons of Archilochus in the Greece of the seventh century B.C., down to two satirists of the first half of the twentieth century, the novelist and painter Wyndham Lewis and the South African poet Roy Campbell. En route he gives extended analyses of two plays (*Timon of Athens* and Moliere's *Misanthrope*) plus one piece of prose fiction (*Gulliver's Travels*), and also devotes a chapter to Roman verse satire. More theoretical in aim and more limited in scope, Kernan's first book, *The Cankered Muse*, delineates a theory of the nature of satire, describes the outburst of satire in the 1590s, and uses all this as background for an analysis of satiric elements in the English theatre of the early seventeenth century, especially in Marston's plays. Kernan's second book *The Plot of Satire*, is a series of discussions of separate satiric works: Pope's *Peri Bathous* and *Dunciad*, Gay's *Trivia*, Swift's *Mechanical Operation of the Spirit*, West's *Day of the Locust*, Jonson's *Volpone*,

[4] *Toronto Quarterly*, Vol 14 (1944-5), pp. 75-89.

and Evelyn Waugh's early novels. As for Northrop Frye, the *Magus im Norden* whose genius evidently presides over such more recent outcroppings as the Kernan and Elliott books, his approach is well typified by his 1945 essay in which doggerel Skeltonics jostle the conclusion of the *Dunciad* and a quotation from *The Duchess of Malfi* is followed by a modern American ballad "of uncertain parentage" which most of us probably recognise from our unregenerate childhoods:

And your eyes drop out and your teeth fall in,
And worms crawl over your mouth and chin, etc., etc.

To summarise, then, from the point of view of modern discussions of satire Dryden's Discourse omits almost everything modern discussers seem to find worth discussing.

What then does the Discourse include? In place of a point by point rundown of its contents, I shall mention two general matters important in the Discourse and analyse each one separately: Dryden's view of satire in relation to society and his view of satire as a thing in itself.

I

As for the first of these two topics, Dryden is interested, to begin with, in the kind of man who writes satire, the kind of ideology satire stems from or promulgates, and the kind of things it attacks or defends. It is easy to read Dryden's opening remarks to Dorset, the literary nobleman to whom the Discourse is dedicated, as mere servile flattery or as the sort of exaggerated acknowledgement that a modern fellowship holder might make in a lunatic moment to the foundation that endowed his research, but to do so would be to neglect both Dryden's wit and his use of Dorset, whom he calls almost the only satirist (except for Donne) produced in England so far, as an embodiment of certain qualities he says are essential to good satire: I knew, he says in effect, that you would be a good writer because I knew you to be a good man. Virtue implies intelligence. Beneficence and candor (candor in the sense of "generosity") come from right reason. Discussing the ancient Roman satirist Persius, whom the barrier of centuries prevents him from knowing personally, Dryden puts the major stress on

Persius's ideas, praising him for being more serious, consistent and didactic than either Horace or Juvenal, and also praising the merits of his doctrine, the celebrated stoic non-concern with things beyond our power. Persius keeps clear, Dryden says, of absurdities for which Christians have attacked stoics, and is in fact a better teacher than any controversial theologian. In contrast to Dorset or Persius, Dryden says, are a number of unnamed writers who have attacked Dryden over a period of years – writers both unnamed, and, he implies, nameless because their writings are now forgotten.

In view of his interest in satiric ideology, it is not surprising to find Dryden noting that satire in the past has had two faces – while it means only attack now, it could in ancient Rome mean also positive advocacy of praiseworthy deeds or attitudes. Dryden also comments on the specific sorts of things attacked or defended by Roman satire: how Horace, for example, stigmatises passions, vice, unnaturalness, boundless desires, confusion between truth and falsehood or appearance and reality, prejudice, and obstinacy in clinging to inherited opinions. How on the other hand Horace advocates, directly or by implication, self-confidence, agreeableness, loyalty, discretion, serviceability, good breeding, and above all, good sense.

All the foregoing tend to put satire in a beneficent light in relation to ordinary private life. Dryden also takes an interest in the individual satirist's relation to *public* life and to the climate, literary or moral, of his age. In connexion with the genre of epic, Dryden brings up his own failure to get funding for a project dealing with Edward the Black Prince as protagonist, and he elsewhere goes in some detail into the upbringing and career of Horace, a career significant because it led to the production of the first fully successful satire ever written. Dryden contrasts the situations of Horace and Juvenal, deriving Horace's urbanity and familiar style from his rapport with the leaders of his society and Juvenal's loftier, more distant stance from his lack of rapport with those of his. Rapport between satirist and society is illustrated in more recent times by the relations between Louis xiv and Boileau (Louis's taste in approving Boileau's work is so obviously good, Dryden says, that even we, Louis's enemies, can't cavil at it); or it is illustrated by Dorset himself, the dedicatee of the Discourse, who as Lord Chamberlain adjudicates the taste and morals of the stage, at the same time that his poetry shows his own qualifications to validate the good works of others. Dryden's interest in how the political and literary leaders of a society do or don't relate to each other has an obvious affinity with his interest in different periods of the past, the golden ages of Pericles, Augustus, or the Medici, when emulation stimulated creative genius, and in the good prospects for modern times, with Shakespeare (and of course Dorset!) in England and Boileau in France, even though for the most part ancient writers, especially the masters of epic, easily outgo such more recent imitators as Ariosto, Tasso, the French epic-writers, Spenser, and Milton. This comparison of ages (written during the period of the great ancient-modern quarrel across the channel) leads Dryden into a consideration of whether Graeco-Roman or Christian symbols are more appropriate for epic – or more specifically, how Christian ones might be made as useful as the Graeco-Roman were. This discussion, ostensibly a digression, parallels his remarks about the sort of ideology, stoic or Christian, most appropriate for satire.

2

So much for what the Discourse says about satire, the satirist, and society. Next, its other major topic, satire as a thing in itself. First I shall briefly summarise Dryden's views of satire's nature, origins, and subject-matter; then I shall take up certain comments he makes on the evaluation of satire and on satire as an art.

In establishing satire's identity as a distinct mode of composition Dryden separates it from three related but distinguishable modes: narrative satire like Spenser's *Mother Hubbard's Tale* or Apuleius's *Golden Ass*; the satyr play annexed to ancient Greek tragedy; and the lampoon. As for the satyr play, Dryden points out that it's obviously a different genre: an action on the stage is vastly different from a paper of verses. As for narrative satire, Dryden here includes prose dialogues like those of Varro or Lucian, and he rules out *Hudibras, Absalom and Achitophel,* and *MacFlecknoe* from the category of true satire at the same time, calling them Varronian or Menippean satires.

The satyr play and Varronian satire are evidently excluded on the grounds of form; the lampoon, on the other hand, – which Johnson later defined as "personal satire; abuse" – fails to qualify on the grounds of content. A lampoon alone (as with some of Horace's epodes) is not satire in the sense in which Dryden's Discourse uses the term; and lampoons, in addition, are potentially anti-social destructive instruments to be viewed with suspicion for the harm they might do if wielded by wittily malicious poetasters. Dryden, by the way, regards the play *The Rehearsal*, which makes fun of his kind of heroic drama, as a lampoon.

On satire's genetics and embryology, Dryden takes note of its roots in language itself (which contains terms of praise and blame), in such primitive uses of language as cursing and invective, in folk poetry and folk festivals (early precursors of Elvis Presley's spirited ditty "You Ain't Nothin' But a Hound Dog"), and in Roman vaudeville or Greek choric dances. A very large part of the Discourse, into which I shall not go here, carefully distinguishes both the Roman word *satura* and the works to which it was applied from similar-sounding Greek words and similar-seeming early Greek and Roman plays, poems, and other writings. This scholarly part of the Discourse is solidly based on Renaissance philology of the most advanced sort, primarily on Isaac Casaubon's great essay (1605) on Greek satiric poetry and Roman satire: but Dryden, whose stance towards philology tends to be rather lofty, doesn't bring it all in to qualify for a Doctor of Philosophy. He wants embryology to serve the purposes of identity. The purpose is not to amalgamate, but to sort out.

On the subject-matter of satire a significant passage runs as follows:

Heav'n be prais'd, our common Libellers are as free from the imputation of Wit, as of Morality; and therefore, what ever Mischief they have design'd, they have perform'd but little of it. Yet these ill Writers, in all justice ought themselves to be exposed: as *Persius* has given us a fair example in his First Satire; which is level'd particularly at them: And none is so fit to Correct their Faults, as he who is not only clear from any in his own Writings, but is also so just, that he will never defame the good; and is arm'd with the power of Verse, to Punish and make Examples of the bad. But of this, I shall have occasion to speak further, when I come to give the Definition and Character of true Satires.[5]

In this passage we see that lampoons are distinguished from true satires on extra-literary grounds. To distinguish the true satirist from the falsely seeming one, the reader must make a judgment of the character of the producer as well as of the product. The distinction made here is made over again in the Discourse later when Dryden first mentions that lampoons, though legitimately used by Horace before he graduated to true satire, may well be inappropriate to a Christian age: we are supposed to love our enemies. But Dryden then goes on to argue that against people so notorious as to be public nuisances lampoons may have a degree of justification even today. I doubt if he was thinking, by the way, of his own *MacFlecknoe*, which he regarded as satire, though of the Varronian subspecies. He may possibly have had in mind an epigram he is said to have sent to his publisher Tonson as a threat when he felt that Tonson was cheating him. It is arguable that to an intelligent author, publishers, advertisers, and other middlemen might occasionally seem to be classifiable as public nuisances.

So much for what the Discourse says about the nature and origins of satire. Dryden is also a critic of completed works, interested in why Milton's epic is inferior to Virgil's, or why Aristotle thought tragedy the best genre (answer: it was the best unified), or what can be said in defence of epic (it is more ancient than tragedy and instructs not just an audience, but a prince). With interests of this sort, it is natural for Dryden to devote a large part of the Discourse to comparing the satires of Horace, Persius, and Juvenal in respect to style, subject-matter, and relative success. It is also natural – or seems to me natural – for him as translator of Juvenal and Persius, as well as writer of original satiric verse, to take up questions relating to the way satires should be written, the way language in satire should be handled, the semantic and linguistic shapes most appropriate for the genre. Thus he laments the lack of a strong English critical tradition – Shakespeare (he says) got results, but only by instinct; Jonson knew Horace, but failed to propagate his expertise; the French

[5] *Discourse concerning Satire. The Poems of John Dryden*, ed. James Kinsley, Oxford (1958) Vol. II, pp. 605–6.

have critics, but not useful ones to us because their tastes are unlike ours. Elsewhere he praises Dorset's metrics by comparison to Donne's; attacks Persius for clumsy metres, ill sorted diction, lurid metaphors, and strained tropes, as well as for his obscurity, whether it arose from his too closely knit style or as a defence mechanism against Big Brother Nero. Though a better stylist than Persius, Horace can't be forgiven by Dryden for having used puns; in fact if we compare writers for their finesse, Dryden believes that Juvenal has improved on Horace as much as Virgil did on Homer. In another respect, however, Dryden finds Persius more praiseworthy than either of the other two Romans: each of Persius's satires is well unified – Dryden implicitly agrees with Aristotle on the importance of this aesthetic criterion. In satire, unity means unity of theme, which Juvenal, as well as Persius, often achieves.

On style, Dryden goes into detail, with ample quotations to illustrate such a nicety as the turn, or repetition of the same word in a different grammatical form. He suggests two things here, as I interpret him – first, that satire should be at least as well written as other forms of poetry, that it makes just as heavy demands on an author's fertility of resource; second, that certain kinds of literary effect are more probable, or more appropriate, in one literary species or subspecies than in another. Discussion of style leads on to metre, and Dryden touches on the English ten-syllable line as compared to the longer Latin hexameter. This topic comes up because of Dryden's sense (a very practical sense, if the book is to sell) that an audience for translations of Juvenal will expect the exhibition of an art, not merely antiquarian reconstruction or prosaic moralising. The latter commodities, from Dryden's point of view, were already available through the baldly literal translations of Roman satire ground out by Dryden's miserable translating predecessors, Holiday and Stapylton.

This concludes my selective summary of some of the contents of Dryden's Discourse on Satire. I now want to attempt a definition of what Dryden wrote the discourse about. What he was writing about was something so obvious both to him and to his readers that it would never have occurred to him, except in the most general terms, to *give* a definition. But it is *not* obvious today, and one reason why the essay is neglected and misread is our own lack of contact with the thing Dryden is talking about, or rather our failure to make certain connexions in literary history, even among matters we may theoretically know quite well.

3

In the winter of 1966–7 the Oxford Union exhibited for a short time a painting of a crucifixion in which the crucified figure was a Negro and two of the Roman soldiers thrusting spears into his side were given the features of Verwoerd and Vorster, the two most recent Prime Ministers of South Africa. This painting, in terms of much modern writing about satire – that of Elliott, Frye, and Kernan, for example – would be fairly easily classifiable as a satire, and so would Chaucer's *Prioress's Tale*, in which are attacked certain wicked Jews who cut the throat of a little Gentile boy and throw him into a privy – all such are forms of satire, without very much stretching the canons of Kernan, Frye, and Elliott. But this is not satire in Dryden's sense.

Satire in Dryden's sense is first of all the verbal art practised by Horace, Persius, and Juvenal and imitated later by Boileau in France, Donne and Dorset in England, and perhaps by others; just as tragedy, when Dryden uses the term, means the theatrical art practised by Aeschylus, Sophocles, and Euripedes, imitated in Rome by Seneca, and later revived, in differing but analogous forms, by Shakespeare and others in England, and Corneille and others in France. Or just as epic, to Dryden, means first what Homer and Virgil wrote, and later what Milton, among others, consciously imitated. Each of these three arts operated in certain well understood ways, offered certain characteristic satisfactions, and made certain specific individual demands on its practitioners.

How does Dryden's art of satire – the Horace-Persius-Juvenal kind of satire – differ from a lurid story by Chaucer, or a parody of traditional music by John Cage? The best approach to an answer for this question is the learned and specific article already referred to by Mary Claire Randolph, and I will help myself to some of its contents now. A satire is a poem of a certain length, say between 60 and 660 lines – a poem as dramatic in manner as a monologue by Browning but differing from a Browning monologue in that its source of unity is a theme or an attitude, not the creation of a single portrait, however satiric such a portrait might be. Thus Pope's "Epistle to Arbuthnot" uses several portraits, expressed or implied – that of Pope himself, that of Arbuthnot (implied by his objections), that of Sporus, that of Atticus, and so on. Pope's "Epistle to Augustus" really contains only one major human figure (George the Second) sketched at any length, but much of its contents have nothing to do with this figure, since the topic is poetry and the modern state. Satire, by the way, often takes the form of a dramatic monologue or dialogue or the closely related form of a verse epistle (since some of Horace's took this latter form): but non-satiric verse epistles were also frequent, both in antiquity and in Dryden's age.

The targets of a satire are vice and folly, knaves and fools, and the satirist tries to dramatise these aspects of experience in as universal a form as he can: the folly must be folly that will be recognised as such by all intelligent readers, not simply by the members of a nation, sect, or coterie; the vice must be something that most people in most places and times would think discreditable.

As a practical matter, a continuing theme of satire has been bad writing, including bad satire; and certain recognised literary devices, such as parody, are traditional satiric weapons. Pope uses one such device, the turn, when he speaks of the insomniac creative energy of certain extremely boring poets; they are he says

Sleepless themselves to give their readers sleep.[6]

A device like the turn is to be distinguished from the cruder pun, or from the feminine rimes used by a writer like Butler. Burlesque is to satire as Victor Herbert is to Verdi – a cruder, inferior analogy to the true art. By succeeding in creating brilliancies like "Sleepless themselves to give their readers sleep" Pope established his ascendancy as a writer over the venal writers, the public nuisances – often people who would be better employed in some other profession – the poetasters whom he attacks. Devices like the turn, which call attention to themselves and thus impede the forward flow of the verse, are appropriate to satiric poetry because of their electric quality, but perhaps less so to epic, where they may seem

[6] *The Dunciad*, Book I, 94. *The Poems of Alexander Pope*, ed. John Butt, London (1963) p. 724.

o

overornamental (Dryden's remarks in the Discourse need to be supplemented by further comments on this topic in his *Dedication to the Aeneis* and *Preface to the Fables*).

Using words to communicate strongly felt attitudes, the satirist tries to use them as well as possible; he is the high-seeded tennis player, the chess grand master in verbal dexterity – he is, or he'd better stay out of satire. When Dryden in his great epitaph on Oldham wrote that if Oldham had lived, advancing age

> ... might (what Nature never gives the young)
> Have taught the numbers of thy native Tongue.
> But Satyr needs not those, and Wit will shine
> Through the harsh cadence of a rugged line —[7]

he is not to be taken literally (the writer of an obituary is not upon oath); Dryden is here paying a compliment he can hardly mean. We must read "numbers of thy native Tongue" in the sense recently explicated by George McFadden:[8] "numbers" means the "auditory imagination", "the interpenetration of a poet's vision of the world with the stock of words, phrases, and cadences, chosen in great part for their sound, which are characteristic of his way of putting that world before the reader". Used in this sense, the numbers of one's native tongue are as essential to the creation of satire as to that of any other type of poetry, and to whatever extent an author fails to command the numbers – producing harshness and obscurity – he is the lesser satirist.

Satire is written in verse because verse is the most expressive way of using language and the satirist, like the epigrammatist, aims at maximum intensity of expression:

> Swift has sailed into his rest;
> Savage indignation there
> Cannot lacerate his breast.
> Imitate him if you dare,
> World-besotted traveller; he
> Served human liberty.[9]

[7] "To the Memory of Mr Oldham", 13–16. Kinsley, Vol. 1, p. 389.

[8] In Herbert H. Petit, *Essays and Studies in Language and Literature*, (Duquesne University Press) 1964, p. 88.

[9] W. B. Yeats, "Swift's Epitaph", *Variorum Edition*, eds. P. Allt, and R. K. Alspach, New York (Macmillan) 1957, p. 493.

This cannot be said so well in prose, and not said so well, it's not the same statement. Like the epigram or the epitaph, satire uses an arsenal of compressive devices: the aphorism, the anecdote, the miniature portrait, the mini-parody, "compressed beast fables (often reduced to animal metaphors), brief sermons, sharp debates, series of vignettes, figure processions, little fictions and apologues, visions, apostrophes, and invocations to abstractions".[10] To get such variety into a unified poem great control is needed. The kind of verse to be chosen is "the numbers of one's native tongue" – that is, the verse used most widely and naturally in the period when the satire is written; in Rome, the dactylic hexameter of Virgil and Lucretius; in France, the twelve-syllable couplet of Corneille and Racine; in England, the ten-syllable couplet recently perfected by Waller and made familiar on the stage in a series of Restoration plays. The metre, the verse form, must not call attention to itself (as it does in the doggerel verse of Samuel Butler and others), but must permit modulation from the most familiar conversational tone (that of Horace) to the grandeur of the mock-heroic (as practised by Juvenal).

The satirist's work has two aspects, public and private: the successful satirist is a public figure, either praised and rewarded by the political standard bearers of his society (Maecenas, Dorset, Louis XIV) or neglected by them to society's discredit (as George II was later to neglect Pope). What the satirist says is relevant to his society; and his fate (whether there's enough money to bury him in state or not) is an implicit judgment on that society. In a good age, the satirist attacks folly, like Horace; in a bad, vice, like Juvenal. The attack on folly is harder and demands the subtler, more conversational style; the attack on vice is more spectacular and can give the greater pleasure. Samuel Johnson, a great satirist who came to public attention first by his imitation of Juvenal in the poem *London* is, apart from his satires, a penetrating critic of the quality of his own society, as every one familiar with *Rasselas*, the Rambler essays, or the review of Soame Jenyns knows.

Besides being the best writer of his time, or equal to the best (as Horace is equal to Virgil, or Boileau to Racine, in skill), the satirist

[10] I take my list partly from Miss Randolph, *op. cit.,* p. 373, slightly condensed.

is defender as well as enemy. There is an integrity he perceives to be threatened, there is a fertility he sees being eroded, and in behalf of these he writes. Or, as in *The Vanity of Human Wishes*, there is a point of view to be expressed in terms of a series of living illustrations, a dead idea to be animated as a dead metaphor revives in a life-giving writer's hands. Without this point of view, without such a defending aspect implicit in his work, the satirist is a satirist *manqué* – perhaps excellent as a partisan propagandist, as an entertainer or literary attention-getter, but not likely to be long remembered. *With* this point of view, and with the command of the tools of satire exemplified by the three Romans, by Dryden, by Pope, and by Johnson, classic satire can be produced in the meaning of the term as it is used in Dryden's Discourse on the Original Progress of Satire.

4

So much for the theory of satire. To turn to a concrete example, Juvenal's tenth satire is not "satiric" in the conventional sense of the word as it might be used to describe a modern cabaret skit or television playlet, but rather resembles Donne's famous third satire, "On Religion", in being a serious philosophic poem putting forward a positive point of view by the force of a series of vividly negative examples. It is above all a *poem*, and a characteristic Juvenalian interest in the use of language in verse comes out in the passage in which Juvenal quotes a bad line of Cicero's with the mocking comment that if Cicero had only stuck to producing bad poetry instead of composing great speeches he might have survived the dangerous political upheavals of his lifetime. This device of quoting an actual line of bad verse was later burlesqued by Byron, at the end of Canto I of *Don Juan*:

> The first four rhymes are Southey's every line:
> For God's sake, reader! take them not for mine.[11]

A splendid ending, even though broader, more egocentric, and less stinging than the Juvenalian original.

Both Dryden's translations of Juvenal's tenth and Johnson's

[11] Byron, *Don Juan*, Canto I, stanza 222. *Byron's Poems*, ed. V. de Sola Pinto, London (Dent) 1963, III, p. 61.

later adaptation of it are original English satires, Johnson's the more independent poem. Each faces a problem of obscurity, and to the extent that each *is* obscure fails somewhat as a satire. Dryden had to use footnotes to explain some of Juvenal's allusions, and also had to leave one or two of the grosser obscenities *un*explained; Johnson was attacked by Garrick for having made the *Vanity* "as hard as Greek" – "Had he gone on to imitate another satire, it would have been as hard as Hebrew", Garrick said.[12] Garrick was referring to Johnson's compression, his enormous abstractness, which to the alert reader can, however, be a source of pleasure as well as a momentary impediment.

Comparing Johnson and Dryden I should first of all stress their melody: each can readily command verbal structures capable of imparting intense auditory pleasure by complex semantic and linguistic internal echoes. Take Dryden's ending, for example:

> The Path to Peace is Virtue: What I show,
> Thy Self may freely on Thy Self bestow:
> Fortune was never worshipped by the Wise;
> But, set aloft by Fools, Usurps the Skies.[13]

The links between "Path" and "Peace"; "Thy Self" and "Thy Self"; "worshipped" and "Wise"; and "Fortune", "Fools", and "Usurps" are functional and dramatic. Similar points can be made about Johnson's

> . . . Reason frowns on War's unequal game,
> Where wasted nations raise a single name,
> And mortgag'd states their grandsires wreaths regret,
> From age to age in everlasting debt;
> Wreaths which at last the dear-bought right convey
> To rust on medals, or on stones decay.[14]

As for the differences between the two poems it is important to remember, I think, that Dryden calls Dorset (almost none of whose works had been published in 1693) the first English satirist, with the dubious exception of Donne. While poems like *Hubidras,*

[12] Boswell, *Life of Johnson*, ed. George B. Hill, revised L. F. Powell. Oxford (Clarendon Press) 1934, I, p. 194.

[13] "The Tenth Satire of Juvenal", 558–61. Kinsley, Vol. II, p. 735.

[14] *The Vanity of Human Wishes*, 185–91. *Poems*, ed. E. L. McAdam, Jr., New Haven, Conn. (Yale University Press) 1964, p. 100.

Absalom, and *MacFlecknoe* have certainly created a particular audience for satire in England, Dryden cannot count on his readers being actually familiar with any satires of the true Horace-Persius-Juvenal kind – unless, indeed, they read Latin or French. Dryden himself has not produced any such satires, and as for writers like Hall or Oldham, evidently reference to their satires would not necessarily awake a response in Dryden's readers. Dryden is, therefore, faced with the task of putting before his public an art probably unfamiliar, and his method seems to be to translate the lofty Juvenal in a rather colloquial, even Horatian style, at least by comparison to the greater formality, the greater intensity of Johnson later on. Thus in Dryden the couplet summarising the lesson to be drawn from Hannibal's fate –

> Go climb the rugged *Alps*, Ambitious Fool,
> To please the Boys, and be a Theme at School –[15]

has a jauntier, less heroic ring than its Johnsonian analogue, the justly more famous

> He left the name, at which the world grew pale,
> To point a moral, or adorn a tale.[16]

And thus some minor examples of obscenity which Dryden, a man of the Restoration angling for a Restoration clientele, translates with rather unctuous detail (I forbear to quote) – these have no analogue in Johnson closer than the line about lust dying out in old age:

> Now pall the tasteless meats, and joyless wines,
> And Luxury with sighs her slave resigns.[17]

To summarise, I should say that Dryden's poem makes fewer demands on the reader, offers more obvious entertainment value (even of a lurid character), and suits the intrinsically tragic nature of Juvenal's basic material somewhat less well than Johnson's methods do.

A reason for this difference lies in the dates of the two poems,

[15] "The Tenth Satire of Juvenal", 271–2. Kinsley, Vol. II, p. 727.
[16] *The Vanity of Human Wishes*, 221–2. McAdam, p. 102.
[17] *Op. cit.*, 265–6, p. 104.

1693 and 1749. Between these dates lies the entire career of Pope, born five years before Dryden's Discourse and dead five years before Johnson's *Vanity*. Pope in his imitations of Horace and original poems similar in method is the greatest examplar of satire as discussed in the Discourse; the greatest examplar in English, if not also (as I believe) the greatest of all time. When Dryden writes the Discourse, satire is still more or less a theoretical possibility – achieved in France and Rome, yes, but only foreshadowed as yet in England. When Johnson writes *The Vanity of Human Wishes* the full possibilities of satire have been exploited in a series of poems known and studied wherever English is spoken and English poetry read. To add to an achievement like Pope's was a challenge Dryden never had to face. Johnson faced it twice, and each time with brilliant success: but after him there were no others.

SELECT BIBLIOGRAPHY

I. BIBLIOGRAPHY AND CONCORDANCE

MACDONALD, HUGH. John Dryden: *A Bibliography of Early Editions and of Drydeniana.* Oxford (Clarendon Press) 1939.

MONK, SAMUEL HOLT. *John Dryden: A List of Critical Studies Published from 1895 to 1948.* Minneapolis (University of Minnesota Press) 1950.

MONTGOMERY, GUY, *et al. Concordance to the Poetical Works of John Dryden.* Berkeley and Los Angeles (University of California Press) 1957.

II. EDITIONS OF DRYDEN'S WORK

DAY, CYRUS LAWRENCE. *The Songs of John Dryden.* Cambridge, Mass. (Harvard University Press) 1932.

FROST, WILLIAM. *Selected Works of John Dryden.* New York and Toronto (Rinehart) 1953.

GARDNER, WILLIAM BRADFORD. *The Prologues and Epilogues of John Dryden.* New York (Columbia University Press) 1951.

HOOKER, EDWARD N., H. T. SWEDENBURG, JR. *et al. The Works of John Dryden.* Berkeley and Los Angeles (University of California Press), Vol. I, 1956 – in progress.

KER, W. P. *Essays of John Dryden*, 2 Vols. Oxford, 1900.

KINSLEY, JAMES. *The Poems of John Dryden.* 4 vols. Oxford (University Press) 1958.

NOYES, GEORGE R. *The Poetical Works of Dryden.* Boston (Houghton Mifflin) 1950.

SCOTT, SIR WALTER. *The Works of John Dryden*, 18 vols. London, 1808. Revised by George Saintsbury, London, 1882.

WATSON, GEORGE. *John Dryden: Of Dramatic Poesy and Other Critical Essays*, 2 vols. London (J. M. Dent) 1962.

III. BIOGRAPHY AND LETTERS

The Letters of John Dryden, with Letters Addressed to Him, ed. Charles E. Ward. Durham, N.C. (Duke University Press) 1942.

OSBORN, JAMES M. *John Dryden: Some Biographical Facts and Problems.* New York (Columbia University Press) 1940. Revised edition, Gainesville (University of Florida Press) 1965.

SAINTSBURY, GEORGE. *Dryden.* New York, 1881.

WARD, CHARLES E. *The Life of John Dryden.* Chapel Hill (University of North Carolina Press) 1961.

IV. OTHER BOOKS

All for Love: A Collection of Critical Essays, ed. Bruce King. Englewood Cliffs, N.J. (Prentice-Hall) 1968.

AMARASINGHE, UPALI. *Dryden and Pope in the Early Nineteenth Century.* Cambridge (University Press) 1962.

BREDVOLD, LOUIS I. *The Intellectual Milieu of John Dryden.* Ann Arbor (University of Michigan Press) 1934.

Dryden: A Collection of Critical Essays, ed. Bernard N. Schilling. Englewood Cliffs, N. J. (Prentice-Hall) 1963.

ELIOT, THOMAS STEARNS. *John Dryden: The Poet, the Dramatist, the Critic.* New York (Holiday) 1932.

FROST, WILLIAM. *Dryden and the Art of Translation.* New Haven, Conn. (Yale University Press) 1955.

HAGSTRUM, JEAN H. *The Sister Arts: The Tradition of Literary Pictorialism . . . from Dryden to Gray.* Chicago (University Press) 1958.

HARTH, PHILLIP. *Contexts of Dryden's Thought.* Chicago (University Press) 1968.

HOFFMAN, ARTHUR W. *John Dryden's Imagery.* Gainesville (University of Florida Press) 1962.

HOLLANDER, JOHN. *The Untuning of the Sky: Ideas of Music in English Poetry, 1500–1700.* Princeton, N.J. (University Press) 1961.

HOPE, A. D. *The Cave and the Spring.* Adelaide (Rigby) 1965.

JACK, IAN. *Augustan Satire . . . 1660–1750.* Oxford (University Press) 1952.

KANTOROWICZ, ERNST. *The King's Two Bodies: A Study in Medieval Political Theology.* Princeton, N.J. (University Press) 1957.

KING, BRUCE. *Dryden's Major Plays.* Edinburgh (Oliver and Boyd) 1966.

KIRSCH, ARTHUR. *Dryden's Heroic Drama.* Princeton, N.J. (University Press) 1965.

MINER, EARL. *Dryden's Poetry.* Bloomington (Indiana University Press) 1967.

NEVO, RUTH. *The Dial of Virtue: A Study of Poems on Affairs of State in the Seventeenth Century.* Princeton, N.J. (University Press) 1963.

PRIOR, MOODY E. *The Language of Tragedy*. New York (Columbia University Press) 1947.

PROUDFOOT, L. *Dryden's Æneid and its Seventeenth Century Predecessors*. Manchester (University Press) 1960.

ROPER, ALAN. *Dryden's Poetic Kingdoms*. London (Routledge and Kegan Paul) 1965.

SCHILLING, BERNARD N. *Dryden and the Conservative Myth*. New Haven, Conn. (Yale University Press) 1961.

SMITH, DAVID NICHOL. *John Dryden*. Cambridge (University Press) 1950.

VAN DOREN, MARK. *John Dryden: A Study of His Poetry*, 3 edn. New York (Holt) 1946.

VERRALL, A. W. *Lectures on Dryden*. Cambridge (University Press) 1914.

WAITH, EUGENE M. *The Herculean Hero in Marlowe, Chapman, Shakespeare and Dryden*. New York (Columbia University Press) 1962.

WALLERSTEIN, RUTH. *Studies in Seventeenth-Century Poetic*. Madison (University of Wisconsin Press) 1950.

ZEBOUNI, SELMA A. *Dryden: A Study in Heroic Characterization*. Baton Rouge (Louisiana State University Press) 1965.

V. ARTICLES

BENSON, DONALD R. "Theology and Politics in Dryden's Conversion", in *Studies in English Literature*, IV (1964) pp. 393–412.

BROWER, REUBEN A. "An Allusion to Europe: Dryden and Tradition", in *Journal of English Literary History*, XIX (1952) pp. 38–48.

———"Dryden's Poetic Diction and Virgil", in *Philological Quarterly*, XVIII (1939) pp. 211–17.

CHAMBERS, A. B. "*Absalom and Achitophel*: Christ and Satan", in *Modern Language Notes*, LXXIV (1959) pp. 592–6.

CHIASSON, ELIAS J. "Dryden's Apparent Scepticism in *Religio Laici*", in *Harvard Theological Review*, LIV (1961) pp. 207–11.

DAVIES, GODFREY. "The Conclusion of Dryden's 'Absalom and Achitophel'", in *Huntington Library Quarterly*, X (1946) pp. 69–82.

FREEDMAN, MORRIS. "Dryden's Miniature Epic", in *Journal of English and Germanic Philology*, LVII (1958) pp. 211–19.

———"Milton and Dryden on Rhyme", in *Huntington Library Quarterly*, XXIV (1961) pp. 337–44.

FUJIMURA, THOMAS H. "Dryden's *Religio Laici*: An Anglican Poem", in *Publications of the Modern Language Association*, LXXVI (1961) pp. 205–17.

HEMPHILL, GEORGE. "Dryden's Heroic Line", in *Publications of the Modern Language Association*, LXXII (1957) pp. 863–79.

HOOKER, EDWARD N. "The Purpose of Dryden's Annus Mirabilis", in *Huntington Library Quarterly*, X (1946) pp. 49–67.

HOOKER, HELENE M. "Dryden's *Georgics* and English Predecessors", in *Huntingdon Library Quarterly*, IX (1945–6) pp. 273–310.

JEFFERSON, D. W. "All, all of a piece throughout", in *Restoration Theatre*, London (Arnold) 1965, pp. 159–76.

——"Aspects of Dryden's Imagery", in *Essays in Criticism*, IV (1954) pp. 20–41.

KING, BRUCE. "'Lycidas' and 'Oldham'", in *Etudes Anglaises*, XIX (1966) pp. 60–3.

KINSLEY, JAMES. "Dryden and the Art of Praise", in *English Studies*, XXXIV (1953) pp. 57–64.

KORN, A. L. "*MacFlecknoe* and Cowley's *Davideis*", in *Huntington Library Quarterly*, XIV (1951) pp. 99–127.

LEAVIS, F. R. "'Antony and Cleopatra' and 'All for Love': A Critical Exercise", in *Scrutiny*, V (1936) pp. 158–67.

LEVINE, JAY ARNOLD. "The Status of the Verse Epistle Before Pope", in *Studies in Philology*, LIX (1962) pp. 658–84.

——"John Dryden's Epistle to John Driden", in *Journal of English and Germanic Philology*, LXIII (1964) pp. 450–74.

LEWALSKI, BARBARA KIEFER. "The Scope and Function of Biblical Allusion in *Absalom and Achitophel*", in *English Language Notes*, III (1965) pp. 29–35.

MAURER, A. E. WALLACE. "The Design of Dryden's *The Medall*", in *Papers on Language and Literature*, 2 (1966) pp. 293–304.

MINER, EARL. "The Wolf's Progress in *The Hind and the Panther*", in *Bulletin of the New York Public Library*, LXVII (1963) pp. 512–16.

OSBORN, SCOTT C. "Heroical Love in Dryden's Heroic Plays", in *Publications of the Modern Language Association*, LXXIII (1948) pp. 480–90.

ROPER, ALAN. "Dryden's *Medal* and the Divine Analogy", in *Journal of English Literary History*, XXIX (1962) pp. 386–417.

SUCKLING, N. "Dryden in Egypt: Reflections on *All for Love*", in *Durham University Journal*, N. S. XIV (1952) pp. 2–7.

SUTHERLAND, W. O. S., JR. "Dryden's Use of Popular Imagery in *The Medal*", in *University of Texas Studies in English*, XXXV (1956) pp. 123–34.

SWEDENBERG, H. T., JR. "England's Joy: *Astraea Redux* in its Setting", in *Studies in Philology*, L (1953) pp. 30–44.

WALLERSTEIN, RUTH. "Dryden and the Analysis of Shakespeare's Techniques", in *Review of English Studies*, XIX (1943) pp. 165–85.

────── "On the Death of Mrs Killigrew: The Perfecting of a Genre", in *Studies in Philology*, XLIV (1947) pp. 519–28.

────── "To Madness Near Allied: Shaftesbury and His Place in the Design and Thought of *Absalom and Achitophel*", in *Huntington Library Quarterly*, VI (1943) pp. 445–71.

WASSERMAN, EARL R. "Dryden's Epistle to Charleton", in *Journal of English and Germanic Philology*, LV (1956) pp. 201–12.

WINTERBOTTOM, JOHN A. "The Development of the Hero in Dryden's Tragedies", in *Journal of English and Germanic Philology*, LII (1953) pp. 161–73.

────── "The Place of Hobbesian Ideas in Dryden's Tragedies", in *Journal of English and Germanic Philology*, LVII (1958) pp. 665–83.

────── "Stoicism in Dryden's Tragedies", in *Journal of English and Germanic Philology*, LXI (1962) pp. 868–83.

INDEX

Absalom and Achitophel, 16–18, 31, 33, 58, 59, 65–83, 119 *note*, 180, 194, 204.
Aeneid, Dryden's translation of, 1, 143–67.
Aeneid, Virgil's, 5, 58, 61, 62, 143–67.
Aeneis, Dedication to, 115, 137 *note*, 174, 178, 180, 183, 200.
Albion and Albanius, 161.
Alexander's Feast, 21–3, 37.
All for Love, 13–15, 37–9.
Amphitryon, 119 *note*
Annus Mirabilis, 1, 4–8, 25, 31, 46, 51, 64.
Annus Mirabilis, Preface to, 5, 18, 19, 172–5, 185.
Aristotle, 57, 92, 123, 124, 125, 134, 141 *note*, 156, 196, 197.
Arnold, Matthew, 188.
Astraea Redux, 19, 25, 45, 55–64, 147, 162, 163.
Auden, W. H., 47.
Aureng-Zebe, 11–13, 29–33, 35, 37, 38.

Baker, H., 85, 93, 96.
Barrow, Isaac, 87, 90.
Blackmore, Sir Richard, 1, 116, 182.
Boys, John, 146, 147, 150.
Bredvold, L. I., 39 *note*, 84, 88 *note*, 89 *note*, 90 *note*, 93, 94, 95, 97 *note*.
Burnet, Gilbert, 126 *note*, 129, 138 *note*.
Busby, Dr, 47, 48.
Butler, Samuel, 190, 191, 199, 201, 203.
Byron, Lord, 202.

Cambridge Platonists, 85 *ff*, 89, 90.
Casaubon, Isaac, 195.
Castlemaine, To The Lady, 46.
Chancellor, To My Lord, 46.
Charles I, 23, 63, 143, 148.
Charles II, 2, 23, 45, 55, 58, 59, 61, 145, 146, 147, 149, 150.
Charleton, To Dr, 46.
Clarendon, Earl of, 46, 57.
Cleomenes, 163.
Cleveland, John, 4, 48, 185.
Collier, Jeremy, 181, 182.
Congreve, William, 10, 45, 179.
Conquest of Granada, The, 8, 9, 27–9, 34, 35.
Corneille, Pierre, 8, 198, 201.
Cotton, Charles, 49.
Cowley, Abraham, 4, 17, 21, 48.
Crabbe, George, 101.
Cudworth. Ralph, 86.

Defence of the Epilogue, 176.
Defence of an Essay of Dramatic Poesy, 156, 186.
Deists, 85, 91, 93, 97, 98.
Denham, Sir John, 5, 48.
Discourse Concerning the Original and Progress of Satire, 175, 178, 189–205.
Donne, John, 24, 35, 48, 49, 50, 52, 64, 87 *note*, 92, 94, 142 *note*, 176, 177, 185, 190, 191, 192, 197, 198, 202, 203.
Don Sebastian, 37 *note*.
Douglas, Gavin, 143, 149, 165.
Dramatic Poesy, An Essay of, 177, 179, 184, 186, 187, 188, 189.
Driden, To My Honour'd Kinsman, John, 114–42.

Dryden, Charles, 122 *note*, 130 *note*.
Dryden, Honor, 53.
Du Bartas, 131.
Du Fresnoy, Charles Alphonse, 152.

Eikon, Basilike, 63.
Eleonora, 104, 142 *note*.
Eliot, T. S., 25, 172.
Elliot, Robert, 191, 192, 198.
Essay of Heroic Plays, 156.
Examen Poeticum, Dedication of, 138-9, 186, 187.

Fables, Preface to, 175, 181, 182, 187, 189.
Fletcher, John, 8, 151, 155, 156, 159, 182.
Fowler, W. Warde, 148, 157.
Freccero, John, 128, 129.
Frye, Northrop, 191, 192, 198.

Halifax, Marquess of, 127, 130.
Hall, Joseph, 190, 204.
Hastings, Upon the Death of the Lord, 45, 47-53, 64.
Heroique Stanzas, 19, 45, 51, 53-5, 64, 149.
Hind and the Panther, The, 8, 31, 32, 35, 39-41, 93, 98, 107.
Hobbes, Thomas, 36, 167, 175.
Hoddesdon, To John, 45, 53.
Hooker, Richard, 85, 86, 88 *note*, 89, 90, 91, 94, 95, 96, 97.
Horace, 105, 120, 121, 181, 191, 193, 196, 197, 198, 199, 201, 204, 205.
Howard, To My Honored Friend, Sir Robert, 45.

Indian Emperor, The, 33, 35.
Italicus, Silius, 5.

James 1, 23.

James 11, 2, 23, 125, 126, 138, 139.
Jevon, Richard, 147.
Johnson, Samuel, 25, 46, 47, 48, 55, 79, 101, 102, 103, 104, 105, 111, 112, 171, 172, 195, 196, 201, 202, 203, 204, 205.
Jonson, Ben, 65, 186, 191.

Kernan, Alvin, 189, 191, 192, 198.
Killigrew Ode (To the Memory of Mrs Anne Killigrew), 19-21, 99-113.

Landor, Walter Savage, 171, 172.
Latitudinarians, 86 *ff*.
Laud, William, 90, 94.
Leavis, F. R., 42, 65.
Le Bossu, 156.
Love Triumphant, 157.

Majesty, To His Sacred, 46.
Marriage à la Mode, 15-16, 173, 174.
Marvell, Andrew, 5 *note*, 34, 48, 121 *note*.
MacFlecknoe, 18-19, 33, 194, 196, 204.
Medal, The, 167.
Milbourne, Luke, 154, 182.
Milton, John, 17, 19, 48, 62, 72, 112, 113, 128, 147, 190, 194, 196, 198.
Montagu, Charles, 114 *note*, 117, 118 *note*, 119 *note*, 134.

Oates, Titus, 33, 37.
Ogg, David, 116 *note*, 118 *note*.
Ogilby, John, 143, 144, 145, 147, 148.
Oldham, John, 105, 108, 190, 200, 204.
Ovid, 42, 58.

Paradise Lost, 1, 17, 62, 68, 70, 72, 82 *note*, 128, 137, 196.

Parallel of Poetry and Painting, A, 152.
Pater, Walter, 172.
Patrides, C. A., 68 *note*, 70 *note*, 71 *note*.
Perrault, Charles, 153.
Persius, 41, 179, 181, 189, 191, 192, 193, 196, 198, 204.
Philips, Katherine, 94.
Plato, 92, 122, 132.
Plutarch, 89, 90, 92.
Pope, Alexander, 2, 18, 19, 23, 42, 77, 79, 178, 191, 192, 199, 201, 202, 205.

Racine, Jean, 6, 201.
Ralegh, Sir Walter, 131, 132 *note*.
Randolph, Mary Claire, 183, 198, 201 *note*.
Rehearsal, The, 10, 195.
Religio Laici, 35, 84–98.
Rival Ladies, Epistle Dedicatory to, 172, 173, 176, 187.
Rival Queens, The, 13, 22.
Royal Society, 5, 84.

Schilling, B., 65 *note*, 150.
Scott, Sir Walter, 48, 49.
Secular Masque, The, 23, 137.
Shaftesbury, Earl of, 17, 31.
Shakespeare, William, 13, 172, 188, 194, 196.
Shadwell, Thomas, 18, 33.
Siege of Rhodes, The, 8.
Simon, Father, 93, 94.
Smith, John, 85, 86.

Spanish Friar, The, 15.
Spenser, Edmund, 2, 18, 62, 63, 64, 191, 194.
State of Innocence, The, 128, 130 *note*.
Stepney, George, 121, 122.
South, Robert, 87, 90.
Swift, Jonathan, 79, 173, 191, 200.

Threnodia Augustalis, 19, 151.
Tillyard, E. M. W., 101–2, 103, 113, 166.
Troilus and Cressida, Preface to, 148, 155, 156.
Tyrannick Love, 28, 34.
Tyrannick Love, Preface to, 156, 161.

Unhappy Favourite, Prologue to, 151.

Van Doren, Mark, 24, 45, 48, 53, 114 *note*.
Veni Creator Spiritus, 156.
Vickers, John, 143, 144.
Vindication of the Duke of Guise, 145.
Virgil, 5, 58, 59, 61, 62, 63, 69 *note*, 106, 174, 196, 198, 201.

Waller, Edmund, 5, 62 *note*, 201.
Wallerstein, Ruth, 48, 49, 50.
William III, 115, 116, 117, 118, 126, 131, 137, 138, 139.

Yeats, W. B., 47, 200.
Young, Edward, 21, 22.